OLD NEUTRIMENT

John Burkman—"Old Neutriment."

Courtesy of Mr. I. D. O'Donnell.

OLD NEUTRIMENT

By

Glendolin Damon Wagner

Introduction by Elizabeth B. Custer

*Introduction to the Bison Book Edition
by Brian W. Dippie*

University of Nebraska Press
Lincoln and London

Introduction to the Bison Book Edition copyright © 1989 by the
University of Nebraska Press
All rights reserved
Manufactured in the United States of America

First Bison Book printing: 1989
Most recent printing indicated by the first digit below:

1   2   3   4   5   6   7   8   9   10

Library of Congress Cataloging-in-Publication Data
Wagner, Glendolin Damon.
    Old neutriment / by Glendolin Damon Wagner; introduction
by Elizabeth B. Custer; introduction to the Bison Book edition by
Brian W. Dippie.
        p.   cm.
    Reprint. Originally published: Boston: R. Hill, 1934.
ISBN 0-8032-9725-4 (alk. paper)
    1. Little Big Horn, Battle of the, 1876. 2. Burkman, John.
3. Custer, George Armstrong, 1839–1876. 4. United States.
Army—Military life. 5. Soldiers—West (U.S.)—Biography.
6. Frontier and pioneer life—West (U.S.) I. Title.
E83.876.B962W34   1989
973.8'2'0924—dc19   CIP 88-31145
[B]

Reprinted from the 1934 edition published by Ruth Hill, Publisher, Boston.

The paper used in this publication meets the minimum require-
ments of American National Standard for Information Sciences—
Permanence of Paper for Printed Library Materials, ANSI
Z39.48-1984.

The addition of a new introduction has altered the numeration of
the front matter, which carried arabic numeration in the original
edition, so that this edition has no pages numbered arabic 1
through 4. No pages, however, have been deleted.

INTRODUCTION TO
THE BISON BOOK EDITION

By Brian W. Dippie

A trim, dark-haired man with regular features, a receding hairline and luxuriant whiskers, John Burkman at 5' 7" tall was the very model of a cavalryman before Hollywood planted the image in our heads of towering "Glory Guys" in blue. He was a typical trooper in other respects as well, having served in the Civil War before enlisting in the Seventh U.S. Cavalry in 1870. He missed the Seventh's early service on the southern plains, including the controversial battle of the Washita in 1868. But Burkman was in on all the storied campaigns of the 1870s—the Yellowstone Expedition of 1873, the Black Hills Expedition of 1874, the Sioux Expedition of 1876, and the Nez Perce campaign the next year. He was discharged for disability on May 17, 1879. The record noted he was a private of good character.[1]

Such a plain recitation of facts does no man justice, but it comes close in Burkman's case. The army was his life, his home; he thrived on its routine, accepting and unexceptional save for the fact that one exceptional officer became his lifelong idol—George Armstrong Custer. Custer was a force to reckon with. He had the power to attract and to repel. Certain officers were loyalists, part of his clique; others detested him. Enlisted men knew him mostly at a distance, as a stern, demanding taskmaster given to the privileges of rank, unmindful of his own humble roots on an Ohio farm, where he was born in 1839, the same year as John Burkman. Seemingly, they had little else in common. Custer had gone on to West Point and fame in the Civil War as the Boy General while Burkman, a German immigrant, apprenticed as a teamster out west before enlisting in the Fifth Missouri Volunteers. But in the Seventh Cavalry they met on ground that eroded the social distance between them when Burkman became Custer's personal orderly, or striker. In that capacity they discovered a common bond, a love for dogs and horses that bordered on obsessive. Custer was a high-strung, mercurial man, given to outbursts of temper and fits of enthusiasm; boyish and coltlike, a prankster and a teaser, he could also be unreasonable and severe. Burkman, in contrast, was stolid, unimaginative, plodding. Custer had literary pretensions, fancied the high life in the East, cavorted with actors and entrepreneurs, and was caught up in the spirit of the Gilded Age. Burkman was taciturn, unlettered; slow of speech and thought, he turned things over in his head, nursed grudges. Incapable of articulating his emotions, he nevertheless was capable of unshakable, dogged loyalty. He was born to be the general's striker.[2]

A striker, Elizabeth Custer explained, was "a military servant." Another Seventh Cavalry officer's wife was blunter: "The poor privates are perfect slaves." Mrs. Custer recast her meaning in a positive light:

The "strikers" were perfectly invaluable to us. They quietly slid about the house doing more and more for our comfort . . . and gradually made themselves so indispensable that we were at first almost helpless when away from the regiment on leave. Eliza [the maid] taught each man we had to cook, wait on table, take care of the uniforms and equipments, and keep up the fires. They anticipated our wants and apparently sprang from the seams of the floors before their names were fully called.

This was not every man's idea of soldiering for Uncle Sam. Thus assignment as an officer's striker was voluntary. "A 'striker' had to go through a deal of sarcasm from his comrades before he was permitted to settle to his place in peace," Elizabeth Custer admitted, "but after he was installed nothing rooted him out but the completion of his enlistment." And, she reasoned, there were compensations. The soldier found a home away from home, a domestic setting in which he was comfortable, a sense of belonging. "The officer and his family trusted him. And he apparently threw his whole heart into the affairs of those he served."[3]

Such was the type, John Burkman a prime specimen. A bunkie nicknamed him "Old Neutriment" because of his appetite, though the name is reminiscent of Custer's affectionate reference to Elizabeth as "Dear

BISON INTRODUCTION

Old Standby"—both dependable and always there.
Charles Windolph, a sergeant in the Seventh, recalled
Burkman as a loner who could neither read nor write.
"Most of the time he'd be with the General's two
horses or with his string of hunting dogs." As an old
man Burkman still distinctly remembered the animals
he had tended and often talked to, meals eaten and simple pleasures taken; his relations with women were
strictly of the paid variety. Apart from drinks and
cards, he shared little with his comrades. Fittingly,
then, it was Elizabeth Custer who made him a part of
Seventh Cavalry history by including him as an eccentric character in her reminiscences of life with General
Custer. Perhaps members of his own Company L
would have recalled him as well, but most of those he
served with perished with Custer on the Little Bighorn
on June 25, 1876. It was the chief tragedy of John
Burkman's life that he could not have been there with
them.[4]

Burkman often pondered that fateful day and how
he came to be left behind. "When the column was on
the move," he wrote Mrs. Custer through an aman-
uensis in 1910,

[Custer] turned to me with "Burkman, saddle up my war
horse, Vic; and you will have to remain with the pack train as
I issued orders that there were to be no led horses in the
front." [Burkman was to lead the general's other mount,
Dandy, and accompany the packtrain under Captain
Thomas M. McDougall, while his troop accompanied Cus-

ter.] The men were all in good spirits when they passed me. Then was the time I begged his nephew, Arthur Reed, to remain back with [for] me for I would rather have taken my chances in the front, but you know, I had to obey orders. I could tell you word for word, Mrs. Custer, if I were beside you. That was the last I saw of the General as they left the pack train.

A favorite plot in juvenile fiction about the battle of the Little Bighorn has a boy hero ride with Custer almost to the end, then survive by carrying his last message to Major Reno or Captain Benteen, or by accompanying the packtrain. Burkman's escape fit the plot to a "т" but for him it was all wrong. His life ended with the bullets that killed Custer, only he did not get to die. Into an embittered old age he treasured two gold pieces, one dated 1839, the year he and Custer were born; the other 1876, the year both met their different ends. Burkman outlived Custer by almost half a century—a grumpy recluse out of joint with the world, suspicious of kindness, petulant, difficult—before he finally ended his existence on November 6, 1925, and was buried near the monument marking the spot where Custer fell.[5]

This is the story Glendolin Damon Wagner tells in *Old Neutriment*, first published in 1934. It is compiled from notes taken by I. D. "Bud" O'Donnell, the one who managed to befriend Burkman after he moved to Billings, Montana, in the 1890s to be near the scenes of his campaigns and the field where Custer died. To the extent the O'Donnells provided the old striker a second family they were surrogates for the Custers. They, however, waited on him, and accepted his cantankerous behavior as the price of his company. In time trust replaced suspicion, and Burkman opened up. His story, artfully rendered by Wagner, is full of pathos and human interest.

Burkman lived and observed life in Custer's shadow. What he remembered was shaped by his intense devotion. With O'Donnell as intermediary, Burkman struck up a late-life correspondence with the general's widow. They became comrades in memory. It thrilled Elizabeth Custer to think Burkman unwavering in his loyalty as they grew old together while the general remained forever a golden-haired cavalier in the prime of life, dashing across the open prairies under a vast and cloudless sky, freed from the burden of their own advancing years. Elizabeth Custer and John Burkman had shared a favorite joke when they were young. As he helped her with her horse, he would ask: "How old be you, Miss Libby?" And always she coyly refused to say. He asked again in 1910, this time as spokesman for all the veterans who had made the pilgrimage to Monroe, Michigan, for the unveiling of an equestrian statue of Custer. "I don't think the General would want me to tell gentlemen my age, John," she replied on cue (though the first answer that popped into her head, she admitted, was "as old as I look"). One event had cleaved past from present, denying both of them a comforting transition. They were young, and then they were old. "I cannot believe that the veteran with the heavy white beard and almost closed eyes," Mrs. Custer wrote on receiving a photograph of Burkman, "is the active, slim young athlete that used to fling himself in the saddle and tear after his young general, over those Dakota fields." And when she at last revealed her secret to him in a letter—"Talking about *age*, Burkman, I find that I don't mind being eighty and more nearly as much as I feared I would"—he mused, "Wall, life goes on. To me she'll allus be jist Miss Libby, young and purty and sweet." It is this sense of time standing still in memory while racing on in life that gives *Old Neutriment* its special poignancy. Green springs recollected through a golden mist. "Oh," Mrs. Custer exclaimed, "those were merry days!"[6]

But is *Old Neutriment* history? We look to books like this for something more than objective fact. In all Custer literature only Elizabeth Custer's own reminiscences and Katherine Gibson Fougera's *With Custer's Cavalry,* a daughter's fond tribute based on her mother's memoirs, are comparable as loving re-creations, steeped in nostalgia and yearning, of a vanished time and place. They look back with regret on something lost, never to be regained. *Old Neutriment* is different because it is an enlisted man's account, and as such stands out among the books on Custer. It may

[xi]

well be that the only way we can understand what happened at the Little Bighorn is to abandon our reliance on logical analyses of strategy and responsibility and orders, the *plan* of action there, and seize instead upon the tales of ordinary troopers who fought with Reno in the valley and Benteen on the hill and recounted their personal adventures in narratives sometimes as jumbled, chaotic, full of panic and desperation and heroism, as their actual experiences. In the very telling of their stories we come close to what probably happened to Custer's men as plans, such as they were, collapsed before a catastrophic reality. "Don't know's I kin tell things in reg'lar order," Burkman conceded in narrating his experiences with the packtrain and on the hill where Reno and Benteen's men entrenched. "It's a long time to remember back and even then . . . we was bemuddled."[7]

In truth, Burkman misremembered much of what he did at the Little Bighorn, and *Old Neutriment's* mixture of opinion and observation is muddled indeed. But Burkman's remembered *response* to the disaster is utterly convincing. After trying to absorb the news of Custer's death, his first thought was of a horse: "Now I won't have to tell him that maybe Dandy's goin' to die." Refused permission to accompany the burial detail, Burkman did not even get to say goodbye. Instead, he was left with his musings as he went about his duties:

BISON INTRODUCTION

Life was goin' on same's if Custer want layin' dead over on tother ridge, only another officer was givin' orders now. And whilst I worked funny thoughts went runnin' through my head, same's, 'Wonder what'll become of the hounds now?' Or, 'Wonder can I make Bleuch and Tuck understand?

"Whilst I chopped up a saddle I thought of Phil Sheridan [a horse] buried on the Dakota prairie. I set fire to a pile o' guns and remembered how Lulu's pups looked after the blizzard . . . I went over and sot down aside Dandy fur a spell o' restin' . . . Then all of a sudden it come to me that I wouldn't never again hear the General laughin' and jokin'. Seemed like they want no use me goin' on."

It is the authentic emotion, the truth to character, the speaking details in such passages that give *Old Neutriment* its claim on us. The book is at its best as history when, like Burkman himself, it is most plain-spoken.[8]

Glendolin Wagner's contribution is at once substantial and problematical. A Billings writer born in 1894, she had an interest in the history of the region that resulted in magazine articles and two books, *Old Neutriment* and (with Dr. William A. Allen) *Blankets and Moccasins: Plenty Coups and His People, the Crows* (1933). Both are first-person accounts told at second hand (Burkman to O'Donnell, Plenty Coups and others to Dr. Allen), then reworked into finished form by Wagner. In both, she adopted fictional techniques that altered her sources. O'Donnell's notes of his conversations with Burkman were unembellished by dialect:

BISON INTRODUCTION

Dan Neally . . . known as Cracker Box Dan. He kept behind a cracker box at Reno Hill. . . . Captain Miles Moylan . . . was called Aparoho Michie, because he was laying behind an Aparoho pack mule aparajo all the time. . . . Billy Blake, a private, made believe he was hurt and lay with the wounded at Reno Hill. Fact was he was not hurt. He was very much ashamed of it afterward and could not stand the scorn of his comrades and joined another company.

The corresponding passage in *Old Neutriment* reads:

Dan Neally . . . he's been goin' all these years as 'Cracker-box Dan' on account of durin' the fight he kept hid back of a cracker box. And Captain Miles Morland . . . was known as 'Aparejo Mickie' 'cause all the time he was layin' behind an aparejo. And then they was young Billy Blake, a private. Fur two days up thar he made out like he was wounded and laid with the wounded so's he wouldn't have to fight, and he want hurt atall. Arter it was over and he come to his senses poor Billy was ashamed o' hisself. He couldn't stand the joshin' he got from the rest o' us and so he transferred to another company.*

Wagner added the rich vernacular for flavoring—a device Custer would have thoroughly approved, judging from *My Life on the Plains* (1874) with its broad rendering of border dialect in reporting on the doings of

---

*There was no Dan Neally in the Seventh, but Daniel Nealon (Co. H), Frank Neely (Co. M) and Daniel Newell (Co. M) were with Reno and Benteen; there was no Billy Blake, though many troopers served under aliases and this could be an instance. The officer referred to was Captain Myles Moylan, Co. A.

[xiv]

colorful scouts like California Joe. In the 1930s readers still relished dialect humor as an art form, and Glendolin Wagner delivered what was wanted in *Old Neutriment*. The danger of such a literary technique is distortion where subtle distinctions are involved; the benefit is the readability it imparts to John Burkman's narrative.[9]

Wagner got *Old Neutriment* out just under the wire. Ever since 1926, when the Semicentennial of the Last Stand attracted a huge crowd to the battlefield for the commemorative activities, Custer had been riding high. A biography with the self-explanatory title *Custer: The Last of the Cavaliers* appeared in 1928, and as long as Elizabeth Custer lived her husband's reputation was safe. Her death in 1933 opened the floodgates of criticism. *Old Neutriment* was published the next year, as well as Frederic F. Van de Water's iconoclastic *Glory-Hunter: A Life of General Custer*. The past had met the future in Custer historiography. Americans, mired in a devastating depression, were skeptical of the heroes of happier times and the kind of sentimentalism that, critics charged, Wagner favored in her histories. But sentimentalism was at the core of *Old Neutriment*, and more or less colored the reminiscences and yarns of other veterans of the plains wars, Indian and white alike, whose stories issued from the presses in the 1920s and '30s. Some were autobiographies, edited for publication perhaps but essentially unadorned; others

[xv]

were straightforward narrations as told to someone else; and yet others were literary contrivances in which the teller and the listener were participants in a story, and the reader was invited to join them by the campfire or the stove while the oldtimer reached back in memory to "the Land of Was."[10]

Old Neutriment is of this last variety. It is not a strictly chronological narrative of the life of John Burkman. It is an exploration of old age remembering, and aching with a sense of loss. It is about a simple man for whom the past was real, and the present but a trial—a man, Glendolin Wagner writes, who "fed his soul upon memories, re-experiencing the adventures of the Seventh, hearing, trickling up through the years, faint echoes of bugle call, of clanking saber and tramp of horses' feet, baying of hounds and creak of saddle leather, and, finally, the derisive laughter of those gay young troopers who turned, up on the ridge, to wave farewell to him and then disappeared down into the valley of the Little Big Horn." *Old Neutriment* may not be conventional history, but it is for everyone who thrills to tales of the Land of Was.

NOTES

1. Kenneth Hammer, *Biographies of the Seventh: June 25th 1876* (Fort Collins, Colo.: The Old Army Press, 1972), p. 210.

BISON INTRODUCTION

2. There are many lives of Custer. For a short version, see Brian W. Dippie, "George A. Custer," in Paul Andrew Hutton, ed., *Soldiers West: Biographies from the Military Frontier* (Lincoln: University of Nebraska Press, 1987), 100–114; and for the most recent full-length treatment, Robert M. Utley, *Cavalier in Buckskin: George Armstrong Custer and the Western Military Frontier* (Norman: University of Oklahoma Press, 1988).

3. Elizabeth Bacon Custer, "To the Victor, the Spoils," *Home-maker* (January 1890): 281 (reprinted in John M. Carroll, ed., *A Libbie Custer Gallimaufry!* [Bryan, Tex.: John M. Carroll, 1978]); Jennie Barnitz to Mary Platt, February 26, 1867, in Robert M. Utley, ed., *Life in Custer's Cavalry: Diaries and Letters of Albert and Jennie Barnitz, 1867–1868* (New Haven: Yale University Press, 1977; Lincoln: University of Nebraska Press, Bison Book, 1987), 15; Elizabeth B. Custer, "'Where the Heart Is': A Sketch of Woman's Life on the Frontier," *Lippincott's* (February 1900), reprinted in John M. Carroll, ed., *Another Libbie Custer Gallimaufry!* (Bryan, Tex.: John M. Carroll, 1978), 24–25.

4. Marguerite Merington, ed., *The Custer Story: The Life and Intimate Letters of General George A. Custer and His Wife Elizabeth* (New York: Devin-Adair, 1950; Lincoln: University of Nebraska Press, Bison Book, 1987), p. 232, in an 1871 letter from New York City; Frazier and Robert Hunt, *I Fought with Custer: The Story of Sergeant Windolph, Last Survivor of the Battle of the Little Big Horn* (New York: Charles Scribner's Sons, 1947; Lincoln; University of Nebraska Press, Bison Book, 1987), p. 55. Windolph's recollection of Burkman corresponds so closely to the version in *Old Neutriment* that it may have been prompted by his questioners, the Hunts; they padded Windolph's story with what they called "explanatory material" and included *Old Neutriment* in their bibliography.

BISON INTRODUCTION

5. John Burkman to Elizabeth B. Custer, ca. 1910, in R. Dutch Hardorff, "Faint Images of the Past: Burkman's Last View of Custer," *Little Big Horn Associates Newsletter*, 22 (March 1988): 5–6. For a contemporary report on Burkman's death, see "Veteran of Custer's Time asserts Burkman killed himself while insane," *Billings Gazette*, November 14, 1925.

6. This paragraph is based on the Elizabeth Custer letters in *Old Neutriment* and her manuscript account of the unveiling of the Monroe statue in Lawrence A. Frost, *Boy General in Bronze: Michigan's Hero on Horseback* (Glendale, Calif.: Arthur H. Clark, 1985), p. 136. Elizabeth Custer was born April 8, 1842; she held off telling Burkman her age until 1922.

7. Elizabeth B. Custer, *"Boots and Saddles"; or, Life in Dakota with General Custer* (New York: Harper and Brothers, 1885); *Tenting on the Plains; or, General Custer in Kansas and Texas* (New York: Charles L. Webster, 1887); *Following the Guidon* (New York: Harper and Brothers, 1890); Katherine Gibson Fougera, *With Custer's Cavalry* (Caldwell, Idaho: Caxton Printers, 1940; Lincoln: University of Nebraska Press, Bison Book, 1986). There are many enlisted men's accounts of the Little Bighorn recorded for the most part in the twentieth century, but few covering the entire span of the soldier's service. Sergeant Windolph's story (*I Fought with Custer*) deserves mention, as well as a little-known newspaper series that has been compiled by John M. Carroll, John Ryan's *Ten Years with General Custer among the American Indians* (Bryan, Tex.: John M. Carroll, 1980).

8. Some of the historical shortcomings of Burkman's account of the Little Bighorn battle are discussed in John M. Carroll's introduction, incorporating Fred Dustin's "A Few

Corrections of Old Neutriment," to a 1973 reprinting of *Old Neutriment* (New York: Sol Lewis). Good overviews of Burkman's part of the fight can be found in Edgar I. Stewart, *Custer's Luck* (Norman: University of Oklahoma Press, 1955), chs. 16–17, and the other standard histories. Burkman's account may have got scrambled in the telling since Walter Camp, who interviewed many veterans of the battle, complimented Burkman on his unusually good memory. Burkman did not ordinarily talk to reporters about his experiences, but he was riled to reply to reports making the rounds in 1916 that Custer was entirely responsible for his own defeat: "Veteran Denies that Custer's Rashness Caused Massacre," unidentified clipping (June 1916) in C 96: Custer's Battle, File 2, American Heritage Center, University of Wyoming, Laramie. The historian might wish to consult the newspaper pieces by W. H. Banfill based on O'Donnell's notes ("New Material on Custer and Little Big Horn comes to light in John Burkman notes," *Billings Gazette*, June 21, 1931, and "The Story of John Burkman's experiences with General George Custer and the 7th Cavalry," *Billings Times* [1931 or 1932], clippings in the Custer files, Parmly Billings Library, Billings, Montana); or the original notes themselves in the I. D. O'Donnell Collection, Custer Battlefield National Monument, Crow Agency, Montana.

9. The original O'Donnell notes are quoted in Don Rickey, Jr., *Forty Miles a Day on Beans and Hay: The Enlisted Soldier Fighting the Indian Wars* (Norman: University of Oklahoma Press, 1963), pp. 291, 303; Custer's California Joe-isms are in his *My Life on the Plains; or, Personal Experiences with Indians* (New York: Sheldon, 1874; Lincoln: University of Nebraska Press, Bison Book, 1966), pp. 131–32.

10. Frazier Hunt, *Custer: The Last of the Cavaliers* (New York: Cosmopolitan Book Corporation, 1928); Frederic F.

[xix]

BISON INTRODUCTION

Van de Water, *Glory-Hunter: A Life of General Custer* (Indianapolis: Bobbs-Merrill, 1934); Review of *Blankets and Moccasins, New Republic*, 77 (January 24, 1934): 317; El Comancho [Walter S. Phillips], *The Old-Timer's Tale* (Chicago: Canterbury Press, 1929), p. 1. The following accounts were published in less than a decade's span: Luther S. Kelly, *"Yellowstone Kelly": The Memoirs of Luther S. Kelly,* ed. M. M. Quaife (New Haven: Yale University Press, 1926); Lewis F. Crawford, *Rekindling Camp Fires: The Exploits of Ben Arnold (Connor)* (Bismarck, N. D.: Capitol Book Co., 1926); James Willard Schultz, *William Jackson, Indian Scout: His True Story* (Boston: Houghton Mifflin, 1926); George Bird Grinnell, *Two Great Scouts and Their Pawnee Battalion: The Experiences of Frank J. North and Luther H. North* (Cleveland: Arthur H. Clark, 1928); Luther Standing Bear, *My People the Sioux* (Boston: Houghton Mifflin, 1928); Thomas B. Marquis, *Memoirs of a White Crow Indian (Thomas H. Leforge)* (New York: Century Company, 1928); Frank Bird Linderman, *American: The Life Story of a Great Indian, Plenty-Coups, Chief of the Crows* (New York: John Day, 1930); Thomas B. Marquis, *A Warrior Who Fought Custer* (Minneapolis: Midwest Company, 1931); John G. Niehardt, *Black Elk Speaks: Being the Life Story of a Holy Man of the Ogalala Sioux* (New York: William Morrow, 1932); Frank B. Linderman, *Red Mother* (New York: John Day, 1932); Stanley Vestal, *Warpath: The True Story of the Fighting Sioux Told in a Biography of Chief White Bull* (Boston: Houghton Mifflin, 1934). It is in this rich context that Wagner's *Blankets and Moccasins* and *Old Neutriment* should be placed.

To

Mr. I. D. O'Donnell

NOTE

THE VEHEMENT EXPRESSIONS OF BLAME VOICED BY "OLD NEUTRIMENT" ARE, OF COURSE, MERELY HIS OWN OPINIONS AND ARE PRESENTED AS SUCH. THE AUTHOR

CONTENTS

[7]

LIST OF ILLUSTRATIONS

INTRODUCTION

John Burkman lived in a world by himself with little in common with his comrades, going along a dull-beaten path at a snail's pace while all the wild world of a cavalry camp with its incessant excitements, its exhilarations, its enthusiasms, sung, shouted, and careened about him. Nothing moved him to a laugh and if he had whistled I should have sent for a surgeon, thinking he had gone daft. I have a photograph of John standing between and holding with each hand the bridles of Vic and Dandy. The dogs stand or lie about the group and the soldier with his solemn face looks as if any remark England or America might make about "Duty" to him would be superfluous.

He may have had a past but no reference was made to it. Nor did he seem to wish for a future in which Dandy, Vic, Bleuch, Tuck and Cardigan with their master were not included.

ELIZABETH B. CUSTER, in *"Following the Guidon."*

Copy of letter from Mrs. Custer to John Burkman. Through courtesy of the Billings Library.

> Osceola, Gramatan Inn.
> Daytona, Florida. Jan. 16.

My Dear Burkman:

At last I have got at the letters that I intended to write. Before I left New York I had a summer of such hard work. It has taken me the three months since I have been here to get rested. I wrote you, doubtless, that I bought an apartment in the best street—so that I could rent winters to advantage, when I am obliged to leave on account of the cold.

The apartment is in a large, twelve story building and I am on the ninth floor, so that it is high and quiet and I can see a little of the river. It is rented but I expect to live there this summer.

After April my address will be 71 Park Ave. The club where I meet many friends is near my apartment and I can get my dinner there on the days that the maid goes out. She married a Patrick Flood and I asked them to live with me summers. He was in the late war and is more like one of our 7th Cavalry men than any one that I have met so far. So respectful, so interested in our affairs and ready to help us when he comes from his work as chauffeur for a large furniture firm.

Burkman, I am so sorry that in settling my apartment I forgot to look for the picture you want. I'll try not to forget it when I return. (The picture in question was a photograph taken at Fort Lincoln of John with the Custer hounds.)

I have heard that there is talk of another celebration of the battle of the Little Big Horn in two years. I hope that you will surely be there. I will do everything I can for them. I am so touched that the present generation honors those who fell.

I hear from General Godfrey and regret so that he was so hurt by being knocked down by a taxi that for some time he could not attend the celebrations or army reunions. But he is very uncomplaining and so happily married and goes everywhere now.

Give my love to the O'Donnell's and thanks for the letter about you.

Sincerely yours,
Elizabeth B. Custer.

OLD NEUTRIMENT

CHAPTER I

JOHN BURKMAN

THIS is John Burkman's story of George Armstrong Custer. It is a story of high-spirited, gallant, hopeful youth coming from the heart of a weary old man, one of the lowliest of Custer's servitors, one whose love and loyalty survived the years.

In writing it we have felt no ambitious urge to add to the voluminous history of the last charge of the Seventh Cavalry on the Little Big Horn, nor to attempt to settle any of the moot questions concerning that tragic event. Nor do we claim, through John, authority to decide upon whose shoulders should rest blame for mistakes that led to the massacre of two hundred young soldiers who turned to wave a laughing goodbye to John that June morning in 1876 and then rode across the valley and up the ridge and straight into the maw of death. The whole truth can never be ascertained. Those who knew have been sleeping, for more than fifty years, on Custer Hill.

We can only voice the opinion of John whose judgment may have been warped by love born of nine years of service under the General who was to him not only superior officer but friend as well. We can only view the drama enacted on the Little Big Horn from still another angle, that of an ignorant trooper, a mule-skinner, one of that vast army of unwritten men whose only claim to distinction rests in a fealty that is rare and beautiful.

John knew Custer as possibly no other person except his wife, Miss Libby, could have known him. Much has been written of George Armstrong Custer, the soldier. John remembered him as the man who loved horses and dogs, relished laughter and a joke, who could be stern disciplinarian and friend as well. There existed between them a friendship that disdained barriers of rank and class.

It was in the fall of 1870 that private John Burkman, then twenty-eight years old, joined A Troop, Seventh Cavalry. The Civil War was over. An entire nation, with the long drawn out agony of hating and killing brought to a close, lay dormant in the unwholesome apathy succeeding the abrupt loosening of taut nerves. Men who, from adolescence to maturity, had fed upon excitement were milling about restlessly, seeking the stimulus of fresh adventures. To such the West called. Those vast, fertile, peril-ridden plains were waiting to be peopled. The frontier sent forth its cry for the covered wagon, the barbed wire fences, the locomotive, the plow,

General Custer, "Miss Libby" and Captain Tom Custer.
Courtesy of Parmly Billings Library.

"I Was Holdin' the Bridle."
Courtesy of Custer Highway Association.

The Afternoons He Spent at His Little Shack.
Courtesy of Mr. I. D. O'Donnell.

the shacks of pioneers. But first the plains must be made safe habitations for the pioneers. Before civilization dared begin its western hegira another race must be conquered, another people with slightly different tint of skin who were fighting for their homes, their racial traditions, their rights as they saw them, must be utterly extirpated or else driven back and back. One fireside must be supplanted by another. The tepee must be razed to make room for the log cabin. And so the West sent out its call for men; and John, lately a private in the Civil War, scented adventure and joined the Seventh Cavalry. Just one of the soldiers of Troop A he was, just a lumbering, unlettered fighting man, giving generously of his courage and brawn, just one of the many small pieces that fit into the plan of national progress.

In Mrs. Custer's book: *Following the Guidon,* she has written of him:

The soldier who took care of him (Dandy) was the strangest contrast to the whole body—dashing cavalrymen, mettlesome horses and rollicking dogs. Indeed he seemed so much out of place in a cavalry camp that I always wanted to label him: "Lost, strayed or stolen." Slow of speech, thought and movement, his affectionate fidelity was to be trusted above the gayer and more active troopers. I have a photograph of him standing beween and holding with each hand the bridle of Vic, the general's thoroughbred which was shot in the battle of the Little Big Horn, and Dandy. His horizon was encompassed by two horses, some dogs and one yellow-haired officer.

Custer, at the time John enlisted with the Seventh Cavalry was also twenty-eight years old, West Point graduate, officer in the Civil War, soldier every inch of him, a man so vigorous, so vitally, joyously alive, so teeming with youth, so quick with his laughter, his flashes of temper, his unflinching adherence to duty that he won without conscious effort the allegiance of all who served under him. John became his orderly whose particular duties during the days of peace were to tend the numerous Custer hounds: Bleuch, Tuck, Lulu, Kaiser, Lady, with their progeny, and the thoroughbred Kentucky horses: Victor, Bluegrass, Dandy, Phil Sheridan and Frogtow. (Note 1.)

In *Boots and Saddles* Mrs. Custer wrote of John:

Such a tender heart as that old soldier had! I had noticed this in Kentucky. My horse, which I prized above all I had ever ridden, died during my temporary absence from home. I was too greatly grieved to ask many questions about him, but one day, some time afterwards, while we were riding through a charming bit of country, Burkman approached me from the place where he usually rode behind us and said:

"I'd like to tell Mrs. Custer there's whar poor Phil lies. I picked the purtiest place I could find for him."

JOHN BURKMAN

My husband and I were so deeply attached to him and appreciated so deeply his fidelity we could not thank the good fortune enough that gave us one so loyal to our interests.

To the residents of Billings, Montana, old John Burkman was, for thirty years preceding his death, a familiar figure. Leaning heavily on a stout cane he ambled up and down the streets, a burly man with long, bushy white beard and piercing eyes that flashed defiance upon an inimical world. He could neither read nor write. The long hours of his empty days were fixed in rigid routine. Rising at four every day, summer and winter, he breakfasted at five. Then he lumbered down to the Union Depot where he sat for hours, aloof, unapproachable, watching with wrathful eyes the trains, the coming and going of strangers. Promptly at eleven he lunched. The afternoons he spent at his little shack, beside a sheet-iron stove in winter, in summer in an arm-chair just outside his door. After a light supper at five he went to bed. Thus did the man who had shared fiery adventures with Custer drag out the last, dismal years of his existence.

He was tragically alone. Old age and increasing deafness isolated him. Illiteracy prohibited the companionship of books. His violent and unreasonable outbursts of temper, his loud-voiced, eloquent profanity, his habitual childishly shrewish attitude of suspicion toward any kindness proffered him rendered him quite friendless during the latter days of his life. Confiding in no one he sat, day after day, hugging jealously to himself the precious heritage of memories, and longing for death, yet shrinking from the act whose finality would insure his release.

As a Civil War veteran and veteran of Indian Wars he might have enjoyed the comforts of the state Soldiers' Home. Driven by poverty and, possibly, by loneliness he did enter the Montana institution but left very soon in a rage because some one had insisted upon opening a window when he wanted it closed.

"If they wanted so much air," he reasoned, "why not sleep out o' doors?"

Later he tried the Soldiers' Home in California. His attempt to adapt himself to the rules of the society of that small world within a world contains all the varying elements of tragedy and comedy.

Mr. O'Donnell has a card dictated by John while in California which reads:

Oct. 14, 1925. Dear Bud: I am here but I am not satisfied. You may look for me any day. This is a wild goose chase I had.
JOHN BURKMAN.

Apparently, from the start, things had gone wrong. Upon leaving Montana for California John had discovered an unsuspected outcropping of affection for the state whose cold winters and hot summers he had damned fervently season after season. He became suddenly reluctant to abandon the region where he had spent the vital years of his life, finding that he was rooted deeper than he had known. But behind the bristling armor of hot temper and pride and sturdy independence was a heart that yearned for friendship. Perhaps at the home he might find comrades who would, in part, fill the gaps left by the death of the troopers of the Seventh. Perhaps there, where the atmosphere from mess to bugle call savored of army life, he might regain something of the joy of a soldier's existence. At any rate he would be housed and fed. He need no longer hunt for jobs, mowing other men's lawns, hoeing and weeding other men's gardens, in order to earn the little necessary to keep body and soul together. (John, at this time, was receiving six dollars a month pension.) And so he made the long journey to California with such mingled hope and despair in his lonely, inarticulate heart as we can only imagine.

Arrived at the station the taxi driver charged what seemed to the old man an exorbitant fare for the trip to the Home.

"The fellow robbed me of five dollars," was his way of putting it.

Then the Commander inadvertently touched match to dynamite when he inquired of John how much money he possessed.

"I told him it was none of his damned business," declared the irate child-man, and promptly ordered the taxi driver to take him back to the station.

"And the thief robbed me of another five dollars!"

Homeless, utterly discouraged he returned to Billings, Montana, feeling himself to be a misfit everywhere, a useless encumbrance upon the earth. And, as the train crossed the divide, speeding eastward, and he sat in the day-coach looking out at the familiar panorama of Montana plain and butte and mountain stream, memories surged through him. Here, under Custer, there had been a skirmish with the Sioux. Over there the wagon train had become mired and they had sweated and toiled and sworn all one hot day getting it free. Here he had spent a summer under Custer guarding Stanley's expedition while the Northern Pacific was being laid. Right at the foot of yonder butte Calamity Jane's shack had once stood, and close by they had fought that fine old soldier, Chief Joseph. Here and there, and here and there, while the train sped on through a country whose history the old man in the day-coach had helped to write.

Immediately upon his arrival in Billings, Mr. O'Donnell took measures to secure for him a livable pension. In his files Mr. O'Donnell still has copies of letter after letter written by him to Honorable Thomas Carter, to Honorable W. A. Clark, to Honorable Joseph Dixon, all beginning:

> I am very desirous of obtaining your good offices on behalf of Mr. John Burkman.—Mr. Burkman has an honorable discharge from "A" Troop, Seventh Cavalry, dated May 17, 1879. He is now drawing six dollars per month. He thinks he should receive an increase of two dollars per month. He is sixty-eight years old and is not able to do much work. He was with Custer in the Little Big Horn expedition.

But there were many threads to untangle, many old records to examine, many reports to investigate, and, while the men higher up engaged themselves, in customary leisurely fashion with the matter, a certain old soldier who, in his youth, had given himself unstintingly to his country waited in his little shack day after day, week after week for news from Washington.

Eventually through Mr. O'Donnell's persistent efforts John did receive the two dollar a month increase. During the last years he was awarded, for services rendered, seventy dollars a month.

Mr. O'Donnell treasures a letter from Mrs. Custer which reads:

Mr. I. D. O'Donnell,
Billings, Mont.
My dear Sir:

It is very kind of you to send me the good news with regard to our friend, John Burkman. I am sure the increase in pension was due to the exertions of his townspeople and I don't doubt that you, Mr. O'Donnell, were in the lead. Do tell John that I am very thankful. Now he has his little home and the increased pension and lives in a community where he has many friends his declining days will be comfortable I am sure.

Thanking you for realizing that I would be pleased to hear the good news and with kindest regards to John, I am

Sincerely yours,
Elizabeth Custer.

John was profoundly grateful. The comforting security attendant upon his ample monthly income meant much to him but the assurance that he had a friend meant far more. Little by little he opened up his lonely heart as he had not done since the death of Custer. He called Mr. O'Donnell "Bud" and, with him for audience, re-lived the stirring days when he was young and Custer was young and the West had need of them.

Mrs. Custer has said of John: "His horizon included some hounds, a horse or two and a certain fiery, laughing, yellow-haired officer."

After fifty years it widened ever so little to include Bud O'Donnell.

JOHN BURKMAN

Unlike most old men John was not addicted to garrulity. During his latter lonely years he lived the life of a hermit, and fed his soul upon memories, re-experiencing the adventures of the Seventh, hearing, trickling up through the years, faint echoes of bugle call, of clanking saber and tramp of horses' feet, baying of hounds and creak of saddle leather, and, finally, the derisive laughter of those gay young troopers who turned, up on the ridge, to wave farewell to him and then disappeared down into the valley of the Little Big Horn which was destined to be, for them, the valley of death.

He was reluctant to share those sacred memories with others. Many reporters and ambitious writers had interviewed him, promising him copies of their articles or books, and then had misquoted him and failed to keep their promise, so John had grown wary.

Even Bud O'Donnell, to whom, alone, he opened up his heart, stirred his anger when he was observed taking notes.

"What you doin' thar, Bud? I don't want none o' this should git in the papers. I won't have my talk put in papers."

Later, however, when patient kindness and genuine friendship had somewhat warmed the distrustful, warped soul, he talked freely, quite willing that his reminiscence be recorded.

"So's folks'll git the how of it, Bud. So's they'll know who to blame and who not to blame."

His memory was remarkably clear and dependable. (Note 2.) Doubtless the more so because, unable to read, his brain had remained uncluttered by the lumber 'of other men's opinions. Much that has been written of the Custer Battle he corroborated. But when, in articles read to him, false statements appeared he quivered with wrath. A saint in appearance, with bushy white beard and halo of silvery hair, his temper was anything but saintly. It was a lie—a damned lie—that Victor, the horse Custer rode in the last charge, had four white feet.

"That mare had three white-stockinged legs. Hadn't I orter know, Bud, seein' 's how I've curried her and trimmed her fetlocks and polished her hoofs time and time agin?"

It was also a lie that Custer's yellow hair, upon which writers with a penchant for the picturesque love to dwell, was worn long in the battle.

"The General jist come from Monroe a spell back, him and Miss Libby, and he'd got a hair-cut back thar."

It was a lie that Curly had taken part in the fight and had escaped from the massacre. (Note 3.) Nor did John hesitate, whenever occasion arose, to vent his spleen upon the Indian scout. Often Mr. O'Donnell has witnessed meetings between the two and has seen his old friend shake a belligerent fist in the notorious Indian's face.

"Curly, you lie when you tell folks you fought up on Custer Hill. You was comin' up to the pack train with a bunch of horses whilst the fight was goin' on, and I seen you."

And Curly, although possibly not understanding the words, could not mistake the menace of huge fist and flashing eyes, and backed precipitately away, nodding agreement to the charge, smiling enigmatically, talking rapid sign talk the while.

This book, then, is the fruit of many visits either in the little shack or at the O'Donnell home when John conjured up the past and Mr. O'Donnell listened, notebook at hand. Whatever merit it may possess is due to the prospicience of Mr. O'Donnell who visioned in John's reminiscences, with their savor of the old West, tang of adventurous days forever vanished, and the rare beauty of the devotion of a humble old soldier for a man whose memory will never die, something of merit to be passed on. *Old Neutriment* is built up from material gathered by him through many years. It gives still another glimpse of a "certain yellow-haired young officer" through the eyes of his orderly, his dog-tender, his friend, John Burkman.

CHAPTER II

TAPS

For John Burkman his last week had been unpleasantly eventful, many incidents contributing to that final spurt of desperate courage which brought about his death. Mr. O'Donnell, chancing to meet him on the street the afternoon of his last day, observed that the excitable old fellow was unusually perturbed. He was coming out of a restaurant still wearing the bib he tied around his neck at meal time. Behind the shrubbery of white eyebrows his eyes blazed with wrath. He carried the gun which he had purchased for the express purpose of ending all his troubles and rage shook his burly frame, for he had been cheated, the revolver wouldn't break.

"Look, Bud!" he roared. "Jist take a look!"

John's mildest whisper, tempered by a rare mood of geniality, was a roar. When wrought up his voice fairly boomed its rage. As he displayed the weapon his gnarled, blue-veined old hands shook.

"Look! He charged me seven dollars for the thing and it's no good. I can't make it work."

"What do you want of a gun anyway, John?"

"Goin' to rid the earth of some rubbish."

Since intermittently for the past ten years John had been planning to shoot himself, thus making room for others of more account, Mr. O'Donnell felt little concern. He laughed and patted the old fellow's shoulder.

"Throw the thing away, John. When you come up to dinner Sunday I'll give you one that will work. You are coming, aren't you?"

"No!" John rumbled, scowling down at his boots. "Bought these jist yisterday. They hurt. Paid ten bucks fur 'em. Bud, every time I turn 'round I git robbed."

"Too bad, but Sunday we'll——"

"My glasses don't fit neither. Can't see no better'n I did afore. Eight bucks jist thrown away. And I don't feel none too good neither, Bud. My nozzles is all stopped up. Never slept a wink last night. Coughed all night."

"Well," Mr. O'Donnell soothed, "the girls'll fix you up Sunday. Better give me the gun now, since it doesn't work anyway."

John's eyes flashed suspicious defiance. Quickly he thrust the weapon into his coat pocket. "Hain't heerd a word from Miss Libby this week. Don't reckon she's sick or somethin' do you, Bud?"

"Of course not. If Mrs. Custer were ill we'd have

heard. Now, John, shall I tell the girls you'll be up Sunday?"

Frowning, John pondered the matter of the dinner. He had his pride. His first bellowed: "No!" was invariably tempered by a milder: "Don't know's I kin come. Your girls don't want to be bothered all the time with an old fellow like me."

Today Mr. O'Donnell reproved him. "You know my girls think a lot of you, John."

The glittering eyes became misted over with tender gratitude.

"I know. They been awful good to me allus. I ain't forgot neither. When I kick off there'll be somethin' in my black satchel fur 'em."

For years, week after week, John had taken Sunday dinners at the O'Donnell home, bringing with him always, as a propitiatory offering, a little paper sack of candy. One particular Sunday, not long before his death, he was late. The family waited, more and more anxiously, until their dinner was quite cold. What could have happened to John who was meticulously prompt in keeping appointments? Then one of them, gazing up the street, saw him trudging along, a block away, and headed in the wrong direction, carrying the little bag of candy. His very back and every rap of his cane on the walk were eloquent of anger. He had lost his way and the fact that no one was to blame but himself only incensed him the more. It took the united efforts of the entire O'Donnell family to restore his equanimity.

John, stubbornly refusing, over and over, to permit any photograph of himself to appear in books or magazines, presented one to Mrs. O'Donnell and was manifestly gratified when she gave it a place of honor on the piano. Always, returning to Billings after one of his journeys, he would hasten to the O'Donnell home and, entering the living room unannounced, go direct to the corner where stood the piano, suspecting that, during his absence, they had removed the photograph. Rather pathetic was his childish delight upon finding it invariably in its accustomed place.

Although he was wont to wander in whenever he chose, and although the Sunday dinners had become through the years an established custom, yet a standing invitation upon those occasions did not suffice. He refused to be taken for granted. Each week must bring a special and urgent request for his company and, since he always took a pill two nights prior to the dinner, it was necessary to importune him on Friday. A Saturday's invitation unfailingly brought forth a brusque: "No!"

It was on Friday, however, that Mr. O'Donnell met

him coming out of a restaurant and so John, whose dignity restrained any tendency toward over-eagerness, vouchsafed a curt nod of acceptance and, without a backward glance, went trudging off down the street, his cane rapping smartly on the cement walk.

A few hours later he was found on the porch of his boarding house, dead, a smoking gun gripped in one hand, in the other a paper bag of candy.

John Burkman, who maintained that no coward kills himself, had at last found the courage to rid the world of an encumbrance. One of the last survivors of the famous Seventh Cavalry, one of the last of those men who had marched and suffered and fought under Custer, one of the last who could truthfully say: "I knew him"; John had fired his own salute. And his body was borne along the trail of the Little Big Horn and placed beside the bodies of those others who had served their country well, giving of their youth and strength that the West might be made safe for its home-seekers.

"But," he had said once, wistfully, "I'd like fur to be buried 'longside the rest o' Custer's men even if I want with 'em that last day. It want no ways my fault I was left behind."

"Of course, John, I'll see to that. No man has a better right to a place on Custer Hill than you. But let's hope it'll be a long time before——"

George Armstrong Custer, "The Baby General."
Courtesy of Parmly Billings Library.

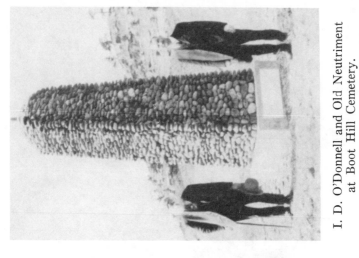

I. D. O'Donnell and Old Neutriment
at Boot Hill Cemetery.

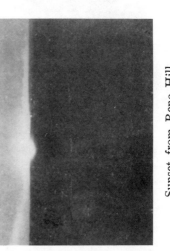

Sunset from **Reno Hill.**

Photograph by Mr. I. D. O'Donnell.

John scowled his impatience. "Let's hope *not*. I'd like, if it's anyway possible, fur it to be a military funeral, taps and the flag and a bugler, maybe. I recollect Custer's bugler, John Martin (Martini). A great bugler he was, one o' the best Voss, the head bugler, ever had. But he didn't bugle fur Custer that last day. A Dago he was and Custer said, kinda laughin':

" 'Today I want a bugler that kin understand the English language.' So another fellow—a German—took Martin's place. Speakin' about Germans——"

John had paused, irresolute, for a second. "Bud, thar's somethin' weighin' on my mind. Somethin' I'd like to tell you, only you won't darst ever repeat it, leastways not till arter I'm gone. Do you promise, Bud?"

"I give you my word, John."

"Wall, it's this." John edged nearer, lowered his voice to a booming whisper. "Bud, it's this. I said I was born in Pennsylvania. Wall, that's a damn lie. I was born in Germany. Do you think that 'ud make any difference 'bout me bein' classed as an American citizen, seein's how I fit through the Civil War, and then fur nine years under Custer?"

"Certainly I do not. No one could question your loyalty."

"Wall then, that wouldn't stand in the way of me

[33]

havin' a military funeral up on Custer Hill, with the flag and sich, would it? It'll cost, Bud, takin' me so fur, but I've been savin' toward it. Here's two hundred dollars in gold pieces. You keep it fur to bury me up thar."

Deeply touched by this expression of the old man's trust in him, Mr. O'Donnell took the money and deposited it in a bank, receiving a deposit check for the amount. A few days later John came to him:

"That money I give you a spell back—I want it. When you need it you'll find it in the black satchel 'long with somethin' fur the girls and my letters from Miss Libby and sich."

"I told you you were a bit hasty," Mr. O'Donnell remarked cheerfully. "Two hundred dollars, wasn't it?"

John nodded assent. "Two twenties they was among 'em and five ten's."

Counting the amount in bills Mr. O'Donnell proffered it to John. The old man flew into a rage. "That ain't my money. I give you gold pieces, two twenties and——"

"But what difference does it make, John? Money is money. I deposited your money in a bank. It was safer that way and could be drawing interest and——"

"You put my gold pieces in a bank? If I'd wanted

'em in a bank I could have put 'em thar myself. You go git 'em back, every identical piece."

"Well, I'm afraid I can't do that—not the same coins. But I'll get the amount in gold for you if you'd rather have it that way."

"No!" John thundered. "You go git me the same ones. Bud, I trusted you. I been keepin' 'em fur years. One of 'em had on it the date of Custer's birth. One of 'em had on it 1876, when Custer died. I want 'em back. I want 'em fur to pay fur puttin' me 'longside the rest o' the Seventh."

John was very angry but, more than that, he was deeply hurt. His holy of holies had been desecrated and his friend, Bud, had failed him. In his eyes was the baffled, inarticulate pain of a wounded animal.

Vainly Mr. O'Donnell endeavored to appease the old man. "I'm sorry, John. Honestly I didn't understand. You see I thought it was just money and that it could be drawing interest and——"

"One of 'em had 1876 on it," John muttered. "'Tother was the year Custer was born."

Mr. O'Donnell made such amends as he could. Fortunately he knew of a friend whose hobby was the collecting of old coins. In his predicament he went to him. "You've got to help me out. John's awfully mad at me.

If you've got a gold piece with the date 1876 on it I'll gladly give you twice what it's worth."

As the result of his efforts Mr. O'Donnell did finally secure two gold coins with proper dates and thus regained the confidence of the irate old child-man.

It chanced that, after his visit with John that last day, Mr. O'Donnell drove out to his ranch. News of his friend's death reached him there. At once he started to town but, on the way, a mishap occurred to his car that delayed him. When finally he reached the boarding house which, for the past year, had been John's home, the latter had been dead more than an hour and the black satchel had been emptied, not only of the gold coins, but also of treasures which John prized more than money: the bundle of weekly letters from Mrs. Custer, a lock of Custer's hair, a photograph of John and Custer with some of the hounds.

He was taken to Custer Hill, however, and placed beside his comrades of the Seventh, all those young troopers who had followed Custer that June morning more than half a century ago, laughing, joking, down into the valley of the Little Big Horn and up the ridge where Sioux and Cheyenne lay in ambush awaiting them.

John had wanted to go along. The hurt of having been left behind had rankled up to the last hour of his last day. He had trembled with eager desire as he hurriedly slipped the saddle off of Dandy and onto Vic while Custer snatched a bite of breakfast. But he had been doing guard duty the night before and Custer decreed otherwise.

"I think we're going into a real fight, John, and you're tired. Besides your place is with McDougal and the pack train. But if I should send for more ammunition be sure to come along. You'll get in at the tail end and share in the glory. There'll be plenty of Indians for us all."

And so, sullen with misery and anger and love, John watched Custer leap into his saddle and ride away at the head of his troops. Never again was he to see his beloved friend either in life or in death.

"So long, Old Neutriment," the gay young troopers had shouted back. "We'll bring you a scalp or maybe a little papoose."

"We'll catch a pretty, young squaw for you, Neutriment."

Forty-eight hours later, by trick of fate, laughter had been wiped forever from their lips and Gibbon's men were digging shallow graves in the hard-baked earth in which to place their bodies: Teeman, unmutilated and covered with Indian blanket; handsome Jack Victor, regimental color-bearer, right arm cut off at the shoulder; Lieutenant Cook, whose black sideburns had been "scalped," with whom John had arranged a horse race upon their return to Fort Lincoln.

Immediately after the fight John had wanted to go up on the hill.

"I jist wanted to see him once more. I wanted to cut off a lock o' his hair to send to Miss Libby."

But neither was that privilege vouchsafed him. While others were burying the dead John was ordered to make litters to help carry Reno's wounded from Reno Hill to the Far West.

"Agin," he mourned bitterly, "I was left behind."

When, finally, he did stand upon the hill bathed in bright, June sunshine and viewed the pitfully inadequate graves, with an arm protruding here, a leg there, knowing the awful sacrifice to have been avoidable, something went out of John, the last trace of his youth, the resilience that had kept him alert in service. At that moment he could think of no reason why he should survive. Years stretched before him, barren. Custer's dogs, Custer's horses, his laughter, his quick flares of temper and quicker repentance—all those things had colored John's existence, had made it worth the living. He went stumbling away from the scene of carnage, a lonely, broken-hearted man.

CHAPTER III

"THE General and me didn't allus git along," John remarked, spitting in the direction of the red-hot, sheet-iron stove. It was a chilly fall day and raining, but he and Mr. O'Donnell were cozy and comfortable in his little shack, smoking and visiting. He got up and set a pail to catch the drip from a leak in his roof.

"Got to git that fixed," he muttered.

For a time he sat, watching the smoke curl upwards from his pipe. "The General had a temper. Maybe in my younger days I was sorta spunky too. When he got mad I usually got mad. Oncst he seen me with a keg. It was jist Jamaica Ginger but he thought it was whiskey. He thought I bought it off'n *The Far West* when she come up the Missouri to Fort Lincoln. He said somethin', quick and stern-like, and his eyes flashed. I disremember what but I recollect it riled me up considerable. Somethin' about me disobeying orders. The General was all-fired strict about his men drinkin' liquor. I said I didn't. He said I did. I said I didn't. He said I did. I got purty het up, Bud. 'Course I could've shown him what was in the keg but I was a leetle mite stubborn and it 'peared to me, arter all the years he'd knowed me, he orter know I wouldn't lie to him.

"Wall, we stood eyeing one another, mad as wet hens. He threatened to have me put in the guard house which was whar I orter gone by rights, me answerin' back to a superior officer. I felt glum, not about the guard house so much, but because he didn't believe me. Wall, I went to Miss Libby, same's all o' us allus did when we was in hot water.

"I says to her: 'I'm goin' to ask fur a transfer to another company.'

"She said: 'Why, John, you wouldn't leave the General, would you?'

"I said: 'I been with him off'n on comin' nine years and he don't believe me when I tell the truth.'

"Wall, arter she'd heerd the hull thing she talked to me and she talked to Custer. She says to me:

" 'Why, John, you mustn't think o' leavin'. Why, who'd take keer o' the hounds, and who'd look arter Vic and Dandy and Phil?'

"Which was what I was thinkin' perxactly but I didn't say nothin'.

"She went on in her purty, coaxin' way: 'You know how sot the General is agin drinkin', John, and how hard he tries to keep order at the Post. P'raps he was a leetle hasty, you know he often is, but if he's mis-judged you he'll be glad to make it right.'

"Wall, I didn't say much, went on 'bout my work, feelin' glum, feedin' the hounds, curryin' Vic and Dandy, thinkin' maybe I'd have to go, now I'd made my threat. Then, one mornin' whilst I was givin' Vic her oats, Custer come to me. He was smilin' and he looked straight in my eyes. He says, 'John, how 'bout this transfer to another company? Do you want it?'

"I turned from him and begun combin' Vic's mane. 'Don't know's I want it, perxactly,' I told him.

"He laughed and held out his hand. 'And I don't want you to git it neither,' he says. 'Vic'd miss you, and Dandy and Bleuch and Tuck, not to mention Mrs. Custer and myself. Are we friends agin, John?'

"My hand gripped his right quick. 'Yes, sir!' I says.

"Fur a spell he stood strokin' Vic's neck. 'John,' he says, 'I was in the wrong. I know the only way to gov-ern men is to trust 'em.'

"Then thar was another time we quarreled and this time it was about a cow. It was whilst we was campin' near Yankton. Some one o' the Seventh stole a cow from a man in town and brung it out to the Post and every night and every mornin' he milked it and us who was his friends guzzled fresh milk which was a treat them days.

"Wall, the man that owned the cow complained to Custer and he looked into the matter and the upshot was, he accused me of stealin' that cow. One o' the troopers told him I was the thief.

"I got purty hot about that and at supper I called the mess to order and pointed to the man that had squealed. 'Fore long he apologized. Not long arter that he deserted and none o' us ever heerd o' him agin.

"But Custer's blamin' me rankled. I said I didn't. He said I did. He got mad and I got mad too. The General, fur all his kind ways, could be awful stern on occasion. But Miss Libby, she fixed things up fur us agin. She said we orter be ashamed, two grown men actin' like a couple o' boys. She allus laughed when she scolded which sorta took the sting out o' her words.

"The women often ask me, Bud, was I ever married. I tell 'em: 'Yes, often.' "

John's eyes twinkled. His big frame shook with silent laughter. He went on: "Fur a short time. Jist whilst my money lasted. Then 'twas all off.

"Speakin' of women, Bud, ain't they wearin' their dresses awful short these days?"

"I thought you couldn't see very well, John."

"Wall, I ain't so blind I can't see women's legs when they don't keep 'em covered. Bud, if I could've been lucky enough to git a woman like Miss Libby! But I reckon they ain't any sich any more. She was one to stand by her man through thick and thin. Campin'; long, hot marches across Dakota prairie; rattlesnakes; Indians; nothin' was ever too hard fur her so long's she could be with the General. Allus smilin' and purty and sweet she was, too, and good to everything, from the Post kittens to us men. Sorta mothered everything, even though she want no bigger herself than a pint o' soft soap on wash day.

"I can see her yet, ridin' aside the General at the head o' the Seventh, him on Vic or Dandy, her on Phil Sheridan, and the two of 'em laughin' and jokin'.

"They want no trees out in Dakota and the sun shone down hot as blazes. When we stopped fur noon mess—that was whilst we was marchin' from Yankton to Fort Lincoln—they'd be a lot o' scurryin' 'round to do fust to make camp, trompin' down the grass and killing rattlesnakes. (Note 4.) Then I'd stretch a blanket from one wagon to another so's she'd have a shady spot to rest. I can see how she'd look up and smile and say: 'Thank you, John.' And she'd lay down and drop off to sleep with Tuck and Bleuch and Lady curled up aside her.

"More'n oncst she took little hound pups to bed with her 'cause they was orphans and sorta hankerin' fur their mother."

John got up to pour a scuttle of coal into his stove. "Reckon I'm gittin' old, Bud. I feel the cold more'n I used to. I'll be eighty-five years old my next birthday. Custer'd be the same age if he was living. That don' seem no way possible. I can't think of him except as he looked the last time I seen him, that mornin' when he led his troops to the charge, settin' Vic so straight, lookin' so young and strong. But he'd be an old man now, same's me.

"Bud, did I ever tell you how I come to git the name: 'Old Neutriment'? We all had nicknames at the Post."

Mr. O'Donnell settled himself comfortably for the story. "Tell me about it, John."

"Wall, it was this way. It was oncst when I was ailin'. Nothin' much the matter with me, I reckon, but vittals didn't taste good and my knees was wobbly and I was kinda pale 'round the gills. Miss Libby noticed it. I was splittin' some fire wood back o' their quarters and she come out and said to me:

" 'Don't you feel well, John?'

"I says: 'Jist fair to middlin', Miss Libby.'

"She told me: 'You go right straight to the doctor. We can't have you gittin' sick 'round here. Maybe you orter go to the horsepital fur a spell.'

"The General was writin' inside. He stuck his head

out the window and laughed and said: 'All John needs is some brandy with a lot o' pepper in it.'

"But I acted accordin' to Miss Libby and Dr. Porter told me what I needed was a change of vittals and sich. The upshot was Miss Libby had me come and eat in the kitchen with Mary fur a spell. Bud, the stewed tomatoes that Mary fixed! I can taste 'em yet. And the dried apple pie! Ain't no pies you git in a restaurant tastes like them used to. I want in no hurry to git well and go back to mess, livin' on hardtack and rice and beans and bacon. My appetite come back somethin' terrible and I got to feelin' frisky as a young colt but I kept on goin' to the kitchen fur my meals. I eat and I eat. My bunkie joshed me. He got to callin' me: 'Old Neutriment.' And arter that, when I come out o' the kitchen, pickin' my teeth, the men 'ud say, 'Here comes Old Neutriment.'

"I jist let 'em josh. I knowed they'd give their right arms fur the pie and stuff Mary was handin' out to me. (Note 5.)

"Miss Libby and me allus had our jokes. I took keer o' Phil Sheridan fur her, o' course, and usually when her and the General went huntin' I'd ride along with 'em, across the plains. And allus, when I was helpin' her on or off her horse, I'd say, 'How old be you, Miss Libby?'

"And she'd laugh and say, 'The General don't think it proper I should tell gentlemen my age, John.'

"When I was at Monroe awhile back, Bud, when they had the unveilin' of the monument fur General Custer, she was thar too, o' course, and I stood right aside her, and arter she'd pulled the ribbon and all the crowd was cheerin' and the band was playin' Gary Owen— that was Custer's favorite tune—I whispered to her and says, 'How old be you, Miss Libby?'

"The tears come to her eyes and she whispered back, kinda smilin', kinda cryin': 'I don't think the General would want me to tell gentlemen my age, John.'

"Wall, jist this winter, in one o' her letters to me, she writ:

" 'John, I think it would be quite proper fur me to tell you my age now, and I don't think the General would mind. I am eighty years old today.' *

"Wall, life goes on. To me she'll allus be jist Miss Libby, young and purty and sweet.

"Did you ever drink champagne, Bud?"

"Yes. Do you like it, John?"

The old man chuckled. "I got drunk on it oncst. One time when *The Key West*—that was one o' the boats under Captain Marsh—come up the river it

* See Mrs. Custer's letter at the end of the Chapter.

[46]

brung the usual supplies o' Jamaica Ginger which was sure welcome to us men, the water 'round thar bein' full o' alkali. And if brung kegs of whiskey and some bottles o' champagne.

"General Custer give a poker party that night and though he never tiched a drop hisself—not since Civil War days—he served champagne to his company. Doctor Burleigh was thar, I recollect, and Captain Marsh and 'Boss' Custer and young Autie Reed, the General's nephew and some others I disremember. All night I was kept on the jump bringin' in wood fur the fire and openin' bottles and sich. Oncst Custer nudged me and whispered:

" 'Save a bottle of champagne fur Mrs. Custer.'

"I knowed that was the only drink she liked. Wall, 'long 'bout two o'clock the party broke up. Whilst I was straightenin' things up I tasted some liquor that was left in a glass. I never tasted nothin' so good, Bud. They was several bottles left. I opened one and poured me out a drink and my innards begun to feel warm and nice. So I took another drink. I emptied that bottle and opened another. Purty soon I was tight as a hoot owl. I kept openin' bottles and drinkin'. But all the while I was worryin' 'bout somethin'. I knowed thar was somethin' I orter do or else orter not do and I curled up on the floor under the table still worryin' 'bout somethin'.

"Wall, by'n by I woke up and it was broad daylight and I had the damnedest headache and a queer feelin' that somethin' awful'd happened. I lay thar fur a spell, worryin', tryin' to figger things out. Then, sudden-like, it all come back to me, how the General had said: 'Be sure and save a bottle fur Mrs. Custer.'

"I felt awful glum, Bud. I looked 'round. Every bottle was empty. Custer could be purty stern when he was good and mad. Fur all his kind ways he expected his orders to be carried out. I begun to plan maybe I'd best git a transfer to another company. Then I rolled over on the floor whar I was layin' and I felt somethin' hard under me and I opened my coat and thar was a hull bottle o' champagne. Funny, want it, Bud, how I'd saved it fur Miss Libby and then disremembered everything?

"Wall, whilst they was at breakfast I took it in to her and put it aside her plate. She looked up smilin'—she had a purty smile—and she says:

" 'Oh, thank you, John!'

"But Custer looked me over, kinda stern but with his eyes a-twinklin', and he says:

" 'Better take the dogs out fur exercise, John.'

"We kept 'em chained up so's they wouldn't kill the

[48]

General Custer on a Hunting Trip.
Courtesy of Custer Highway Association.

Custer's Three Scouts at the Battlefield.
Courtesy of Custer Highway Association.

I. D. O'Donnell Beside Old Neutriment's Grave.

Post cats and sich. I reckon he was thinkin' more o' me than the dogs jist then, guessin' maybe a leetle fresh air'd be good fur me, too.

"Bud, I git all hot under the collar when I hear folks say nowadays that Custer was a drinkin' man, hintin' that maybe he'd been drinkin' too much jist afore his last charge. That's a damn lie, Bud. They was jist one man drunk whilst we was on the Little Big Horn expedition and that was Reno. If Reno hadn't been drunk and a coward to boot maybe Custer and most o' the other two hundred men'd be livin' today. (Note 6.)

"Life's so damned full o' 'if's,' Bud.

"Oncst I thought fur sure I'd caught the General at it. Jist arter *The Key West* come in I seen him drinkin' out of a bottle, so I sneaks up behind him, quiet-like, but he heerd me and he turned 'round. His eyes shone the way they did when he was laughin' inside and he says:

" 'Have a drink, John?' and offered me the bottle and it want nothin' but Jamaica Ginger.

"Custer loved his men. I reckon they ain't no father more proud of his kids than he was of his men of the Seventh. And I reckon they ain't no regiment in the hull world made a better showin' than we did on parade, horses feelin' their oats and prancin', colors flyin', band playin', every damned thing about us spic and span clean down to the horses' hoofs. Them was great days. It was great, seein' Custer smilin' and his eyes twinklin' whilst he sat on Dandy watchin' us parade by. We was proud o' him, too. We'd o' gone through hell fur him, every last man of us. Sorta like one big family we was, havin' some quarrels betwixt ourselves, but stickin' together thicker'n molasses in January agin the infantry or the citizens.

"We was allus playin' pranks on the infantry. And, fur all the gray horse troop bein' Custer's favorite, they give him more trouble than all the rest put together. Oncst whilst we was in Kentuck the gray horse troop got tired o' the rations handed out and made plans to go foragin'. So one night they stole the infantry uniforms and put 'em on and went out. When they come back they was loaded to the brim with fresh vegetables and eggs and sich stuff from the farms 'round about. 'Course, when the complaints come in to the General from the farmers it was agin the infantry. They swore they seen the infantry prowlin' durin' the night. And the infantry had to do kitchen duty fur a week to pay fur what the cavalry did.

"Us that knowed the rights o' things wouldn't squeal 'cause the gray horse troops paid us in fresh onions and eggs to keep still.

"Wall, we got orders to move sudden, and then they

found the cellar under the gray horse troop full o' chicken feathers and they was two live hogs down thar. We had a lot o' fun them days. The gray horse troop was one o' the five that went along with Custer on the last charge.

"I told you they called me: 'Old Neutriment.' Most of us had nicknames. Custer they called 'Yellow-hair.' Varnum went by the name o' 'Crazy Horse.' Charlie Reynolds, the scout, was known as 'Silent Charlie,' 'count o' his never talkin' much. Russell and Scott wore glasses and so we called 'em 'Star-gazers.' Jack Victor, our regimental pall-bearer—he carried the colors up on the Little Big Horn. When they found him his right arm was amputized at the shoulder—him we called 'Handsome Jack.' Captain Wallace was nick-named 'Tony Soldier.' He was killed at Wounded Knee. When they found him in a tepee they was five dead Indians scattered close by, showin' as how he could fight fur all he was so slick and tony.

"As I says, Bud, Custer set great store by his men, allus lookin' out fur our comfort, never askin' nothin' of us beyond reason, and proud as hell of us all. But when he give an order we was expected to toe the mark which we usually did, accordin', he watchin' to see that we did.

"Oncst whilst we was marchin' from Yankton to

Fort Lincoln he sent one o' his scouts out to meet some troop he was expectin' and conduct 'em back to camp. Then he climbed a hill and watched with his field glasses to see that the man obeyed. It want no joke goin' out alone across the plains in them days, I can tell you, what with Indians hidin' 'round about. So this scout, bein' somethin' of a coward, rid jist a leetle ways off 'til he reckoned he was out o' eyesight o' the camp and then he hid and waited fur the troop to come up. When he got back to the garrison Custer called him to his quarters. I was there and I heerd the conflab. Custer said, 'How fur out was you when you met the troop?'

"The man told him about two days' ride out, which was a lie. Bud, I never will forgit the lecture that man got, Custer talkin' to him, quick and stern, about duty and a soldier's honor and sich. When he got through the scout kinda wilted and went slinkin' off like a whipped dog.

"The General was allus that way, settin' great store on honor and expectin' every one o' his men to do likewise.

"Whilst I was in the Soldiers' Home a spell back Sergeant Knipe (Kanipe) visited me thar. We had a great time talkin' over old days. I remember, same's if it was yisterday, how he come dashin' up to Mc-

Dougal with the last message from Custer. If Mc-Dougal's mules hadn't got mired or if Benteen had acted accordin' to orders, 'stead o' joinin' Reno up on the hill, Custer might be livin'. Life's jist one big 'if' ain't it, Bud?

"Wall, we set and talked, me and Knipe, thar at the Home, and he said to me:

" 'Thar never was a better, braver, truer officer ever lived than General Custer.'

"Which are my sentiments and the sentiments of most every man that ever served under him."

Thus did old John wander on along the trails of the past, re-living bitter-sweet memories. Often Mr. O'Donnell must wait patiently, biding his time, while the old soldier, white head sunk low, crossed the inexorable bridge of years, back to the days when he was young and Custer was young and life was filled to the brim with adventure and hope.

Copy of letter from Mrs. Custer to John Burkman. Through courtesy of the Billings Library.

71 Park Ave., New York, July 13, 1916.
My Dear Burkman:

It was such a pleasure to see Mrs. O'Donnell and hear directly from you. She gives a good account of you—(Note 7) and please thank Mr. O'Donnell for his kind letter. How fortunate you are to have such friends! God send them such faithful friends if there should ever any trouble or need come their way. Please thank Mr. O'Donnell for his letter telling me about you. I wish that I had some one to talk over the old days with.

General Godfrey lives in New Jersey with his very devoted wife, on an estate that she inherited. He was often in New York at reunions and at West Point but the last time he was here he was knocked down in the street—not badly hurt, but I expect that his wife is anxious and tries not to have him come here.

General Edgerly has prolonged his life—for he was far from well—by going to some Springs with his wife——

He is so straight, so fine in the way he carries himself that he does not look his age at all.

Talking about *age*, Burkman, I find that I don't mind being eighty and more nearly as much as I feared I would, since I go everywhere and do everything I did at forty, except riding. I don't realize that time has been on the wing. I am trying to write some things of the Civil War and of the General and I got quite a start in Florida where there is little to do.——

I went to see the distinguished Senator Walsh of Montana when I passed through Washington, to ask him if he would be interested in some kind of a building on the battle field where there could be articles, books and pictures of frontier men and soldiers. (Note 8.) He was already interested in a building for those who go there now to lay their dead, but I hope that he will be interested in my scheme. He took my sketch, plans and specifications that an architect made for me and I am trying to be patient until he is ready to do something toward getting a bill passed. (This is a secret with you and your good friends, the O'Donnell's, for fear he may drop the plan.)

I hope that you will keep well, Burkman, and always be sure of the friendship of your

Sincere friend,

Elizabeth B. Custer.

(Kindest regards to the O'Donnells.)

CHAPTER IV

SOLDIER—DOG-TENDER—FRIEND

"The General's hounds give me considerable trouble most the time," John remarked mildly one sunny day when he chanced to be in a conversational mood. He sat, chair tilted back against the outside walls of his shack, immersed in clouds of tobacco smoke and reminiscences.

"Tell me about them," Mr. O'Donnell encouraged.

John puffed thoughtfully for a moment. "They was the orneriest pups you ever shook a stick at," he chuckled. "Seemed like they could think of more ways of gittin' into mischief and raisin' hell general. But Custer and Miss Libby set great store by 'em. You never seen him anywhar without half a dozen trailin' at his heels or fightin' fur a place on his lap. Wharever he went they went too, pesterin' us considerable. Some of 'em was with us on the Stanley expedition to the Yellowstone in 1873. And they went with us whilst we was in the Black Hills in 1874.

"Custer claimed he took 'em along fur to help catch the elk and antelope and sich he was allus mountin' and sendin' back to Monroe. (Note 9.) But I knowed it

[56]

was partly 'cause he couldn't stand the look in their eyes when they was left behind. A few of 'em, Bleuch and Tuck and Lady, was with us that last day on the Little Big Horn. They whined and couldn't understand why I held 'em back when Custer went ridin' away at the head of the Seventh.

"I got to havin' a sorta tender feelin' fur 'em myself, seein' 's how I had the tendin' of 'em, raisin' some o' the pesky pups by hand when the mother died. Bud, they ain't nothin' so helpless as a baby pup, unless it be a new-born colt without a mother. It gives you a kinda funny feelin' in your innards when it nozzles agin you, trustin' you to keer fur it.

"Wall, the General started out with one hound, a thoroughbred bitch some Englishman sent him as a present. Custer thought it'd be great to breed pedigreed dogs and sell 'em. Wall, he raised 'em. By the time we left Kentuck fur Yankton we musta had 'round 'bout eighty. Trouble was when come time to sell 'em. 'Peared like he never could bear to part with one o' 'em hounds. Bein' full-blooded they could've made him a lot o' money, but if a buyer 'ud come along Custer'd git red in the face and hedge and stall, talkin' fast, tellin' a dozen reasons why he couldn't sell jist then.

"Maybe he'd have to talk things over with Miss Libby fust, or maybe this or maybe that. Then, arter

[57]

the fellow'd left, the General 'ud look at me kinda sheepish and take the pup up in his arms.

" 'John,' he says, 'you'd miss the little tike, wouldn't you, if I'd let it go?'

"And I told him as fur as missin' the pup was concerned, likely I would, but if we kept on keepin' every litter we'd soon have to buy a farm fur to raise 'em on.

"He jist laughed. Custer laughed a lot them days. That was whilst we was in Kentuck, followin' Civil War days, jist arter him and Miss Libby got married, and afore he had the trouble at Washington that got him in Dutch with the government. (Note 10.) You know, Bud, I never did git the hang of things but Custer orter been General of the hull army of the West 'stead o' jist the Seventh Cavalry. He would o' been if he hadn't writ the truth right out too many times and made Grant mad at him.

"But I git to wanderin'. We was talkin' about his hounds. Oncst a fellow offered him five hundred dollars fur one o' the pups. 'Peared like Custer was goin' to take the money, then, sudden-like he spoke up, sharp and stern:

" 'The pup ain't fur sale,' he says.

"And arter we was alone he says: 'John, did you see the look in Lulu's eyes? Jist as if she was beggin' me not to sell her baby?'

[58]

"I says: 'Yes, sir, but beggin' your pardon, that ain't no way to make money and if'n you don't seduce the litters they'll eat us out o' house and home.'

"I recollect the look in his eyes whilst he stood pattin' Lulu's head. He says: 'They's more in life than jist money, John. They's friendship, too, and faith. Lulu trusts us.'

"Miss Libby was jist as foolish about the hounds as he was. Their quarters was allus full o' dogs. Most the time they was two or three sleepin' cross the foot o' their bed. I've knowed her to take some o' the pups to bed with her. That was arter we got up into Dakota and the leetle things, bein' thin-skinned, want used to the cold and suffered considerable.

"But, most the time, the ornery critters kept me in hot water. Oncst, whilst we was in Kentuck, I had 'em out fur exercise and they killed a bull pup belongin' to a woman that was one o' the camp trailers. The woman raised hell but I didn't say nothin' about it to Miss Libby 'cause whenever thar was trouble she'd give away one o' the pups to settle the matter and I didn't think it fittin' that that woman should own one o' our hounds. Oncst they killed a cat belongin' to a negro wench livin' down on Suds Row. I fixed things up thar too without tellin' no one.

"It was my special duty to exercise 'em every day, me

[59]

ridin' my horse, the dogs trottin' 'long aside me, chained in twos. They was a purty sight, so slick and slim, eighty of 'em canterin 'along. And they behaved peaceful unless we met another dog. Then all hell couldn't 've held 'em back. Bleuch in particular, him bein' a vicious dog.

"Oncst down in Kentuck I passed a man in a buggy with a fine bird dog trottin' 'long aside him. Bud, I seen trouble ahead and my heart went right up into my mouth. Things begun to happen quick. Sich bayin' and yelpin', horses rarin', dust you couldn't see through, the fellow cursin' and swearin', me tryin' to hold in the hounds. Might's well try to hold in a hurricane.

"Wall, Bud, when things kinda settled down our hounds was lickin' their chops and the bird dog was chewed into leetle pieces. I felt sorry. He'd looked purty a minute afore, trottin' 'longside the buggy. I started to tell the fellow I was sorry but he was madder'n blue blazes and he come at me with a buggy whip.

" 'Them thar hell-hounds belong to you?' he says.

"Right away I got mad too. I reckon in them days I had some temper myself. I says, 'No.'

"He says, 'Whose be they?'

"I wouldn't tell. I kept gittin' madder. I was young and strong and it took more'n a fellow with a horse whip to skeer me. It was my business to stand betwixt the General and trouble and I was goin' to do it. The man said he'd find out and sue fur damages. I was plumb worried and soon's I got back to camp I told Miss Libby.

"She says, 'We'll try and keep this from the General, John, if we can. He's got enough to worry about.'

"Which was my idee perxactly. Wall, she made me take her to the man and arter she got through talkin' to him and sorta smilin' and lookin' up at him the purty way she had, he want mad no more.

"He says to me, 'Why didn't you tell me the hounds belonged to General Custer?'

"I didn't say nothin' fur fear I'd be sayin' too much, me bein' purty mad yet 'bout the buggy whip.

"He says to Miss Libby, 'I'm sorry I lost my temper, Mrs. Custer. If I'd knowed the dogs belonged to the General I wouldn't 've made no trouble. Him and me are friends. We'll jist consume that nothin' ever happened.'

"But Miss Libby wouldn't have it that way. She said, sorta soft-like—you know, Bud, how soft women can talk sometimes—she said, 'I don't blame you. If your dog had killed one o' our dogs I'd felt bad too.'

"But she want satisfied till she made him promise to take one o' the pups out o' Lulu's fust litter when they come. Never guessin' that when they did come Lulu'd be wanderin' alone out on the Dakota praries in a blizzard, hunderds of miles away.

"I reckon it's a good thing we don't allus know what's in store fur us, Bud, else we wouldn't have the guts to go on.

"Oncst whilst I was at mess chewin' my vittals and listenin' to the jabberin' 'round about, some one come rushin' in and says, 'Neutriment, your hounds is gone.'

"Sure enough they want whar I'd tied 'em to feed 'em and they want nowhar about the Post. Them eighty hounds vamoosed all in a jerk of a lamb's tail and nary hide nor hair of 'em anywhar.

"Till plumb dark I hunted and called and hunted and called, gittin' more'n more anxious all the while. I know'd if them dogs was lost I might jist's well be thinkin' about a transfer to another company. Me and Custer was close friends but he wouldn't stand fur no one neglectin' his duty—not even me. I sauntered up to his quarters, wonderin' should I best tell him or not, but him and Miss Libby was havin' company. I could hear 'em all laughin' and talkin' inside. So I got on a horse and went ridin' up and down the roads and off across the prairie in the dark, callin': 'Bleuch! Tuck!' 'cause them two was allus the leaders whenever mischief was afoot.

"Wall, the night got still and dark whilst I rid along.

[62]

Couldn't see my hand afore me. But purty soon, from fur away, I heerd some pigs squealin' somethin' turrible. The sound was enough to wake the dead, it bein' so still. I galloped off in that direction fur them pigs was in trouble and whar trouble was the dogs was sure to be.

"Want long till they come tearin' across the country to meet me, all eighty of 'em, actin' tickled to death and proud-like, as though they'd done somethin' smart. But when they begun lickin' my hand I seen their chops was covered with blood.

"Early next mornin', settin' out to locate what'd happened, I met a nigger. Bud, he was the maddest nigger I ever hope to see. He yelled at me: 'Hey, you white man! Them dogs of your'n kilt my pig last night and eat it.'

"Jist one pig! I was some relieved. Judgin' by the sound o' things I'd expected 'bout a million dead hogs scattered over the prarie. Wall, it jist happened that a few nights afore I'd made a little playin' poker and so I paid fur the pig and never said nothin' to nobody. I figgered that keepin' trouble away from the General was what I was thar fur. He had plenty as 'twas, some o' the officers hatin' him and actin' accordin'. Fur all he and Captain Tom and Miss Libby and Autie was allus laughin' and jokin' and cuttin' up pranks they was times when we was alone together I seen a kinda un-

[63]

happy look in his eyes that worried me considerable.

"But about the dogs. When they run out o' mischief they set to killin' cats. One time a woman—wife o' one o' the privates—she come to me and she was so mad she couldn't hardly talk and she was cryin' too and she said our dogs had killed her cat and his name was 'Tip.' I couldn't see nothin' in that to make a fuss over, thar bein' already too many cats around the Post, gittin' under our feet and eatin' up good dog rations. Whilst I was arguin' and the woman was cryin' Miss Libby heerd us and she come up. She said, kinda soft-like:

" 'John, maybe she loved her Tip as much as we love our dogs.'

"She put her arm around the woman's waist and kept talkin' to her, sayin' how sorry she was, and by 'bye she made her stop cryin' by offerin' her one o' the pups.

"I spoke up and says: 'Beggin' your pardon, Miss Libby, them pups is worth a lot o' money, and you can't give cats away.'

"Bud, I never will forgit the look that she give me then. She was smilin' but they was tears in her eyes. She says: 'John, seems like us women here at the Post has jist got to have somethin' little and helpless to take keer of.'

"That set me to thinkin', Bud, about how maybe Miss Libby got lonesome sometimes, she bein' so little and

[64]

Seventh Cavalry Camp. Black Hills Expedition.
Courtesy of Custer Highway Association.

Seventh Cavalry Camp.
Courtesy of Custer Highway Association.

They Buried Their Dead.
Photograph taken one year after the massacre.
Courtesy of Judge Goddard.

The First Monument Erected in Memory of General
Custer, on the Spot Where He Fell.
Photograph taken in 1876.
Courtesy of Judge Goddard.

young,—no home, no kids, pullin' up stakes at a minute's notice and off fur somewhar else, skeered continual, too, about Indians and rattlesnakes and sich. It want the natural way fur a woman to live. But she was happy. Whar the General was, that was home to her, even if 'twas only a camp stool sot on the shady side a wagon out on the prarie. Wall, life goes on.

"I could keep you up the rest o' the night, talkin' over old times, tellin' stories 'bout Custer's dogs and the way they allus kept me in hot water. The feedin' of 'em was some problem. They was days arter a hunt when they gorged on buffalo meat but they was more days when their ribs caved in and they looked at me with a kinda reproachful look in their eyes that made me plumb miserable. But they was army dogs and army life means bein' tired and footsore and thirsty and hungry and jist marchin' on.

"Tuck was the General's favorite, I reckon 'cause that dog didn't have no time fur any one but Custer. He was a one-man hound and Custer was the man. Did you ever notice, Bud, how we git to havin' a tender feelin' fur the things that like us best? (Note 11.) Tuck, as I says, was with us up on the Little Big Horn. He was in the tent with Custer the last night we camped. He was the damnedest dog to run. Could ketch a jack-rabbit single-handed. Oncst he ketched an antelope

[65]

and held it till the General and me could kill it. Sometimes jist Tuck and me and Custer'd ride fur miles ahead o' the line, scoutin' or huntin'. Them times is when we got to be close friends. Then he was like a boy, gittin' all het up over every new thing he seen, ridin' Dandy up steep cliffs that no other horse could've took. We had fun. Noons we'd stop by a stream, maybe ten miles ahead o' the command, and 'ud build a fire and cook fish or antelope meat if we'd ketched any, and then we'd jist lay a spell, restin', smokin', with the dogs sprawled 'long side us, and the horses munchin' grass, and he'd talk to me same's if we was jist two common men, 'stead o' private and superior officer.

"Custer liked to talk. If I dropped off to sleep he'd throw clods at me to wake me up and then I'd see him laughin'. Seemed like he never did git tired.

"He never thought of danger fur himself. It worried Miss Libby considerable, him bein' reckless and scoutin' so fur away from the lines. 'Cause no tellin' whar an Indian might be lurkin' them days. I allus aimed to go with the General, havin' give her my word to look arter him best I could.

"But we was talkin' about Custer's dogs. Me and Miss Libby liked Bleuch best. Arter mess when I gathered up scraps to feed the hounds I allus seen that he got a leetle more'n his share. He was a funny dog, fierce as hell towards anyone he didn't like, and not afeared o' nothin' except one thing. You could shake any kind o' a club at him and he'd jist stand lookin' at you, waggin' his tail, ready fur a game, unless that club had metal on it. Anything with iron—a saber, a pitchfork, a gun—'ud set him to whimperin' and he'd crouch on his belly, whinin' like a baby. We never could figger out why metal on a stick skeered him plumb to death.

"Bleuch liked me. We had good times together, him and me. Many's the time we've gone off across the plains together, me on my horse, Bleuch streakin' it ahead till he was jist a speck. Then he'd come trottin' back, pantin', a gopher in his mouth, and proud as hell.

"But, I never will forget our trip from Kentuck up to Yankton which was the end o' the railroad in them days. We was all tickled to go. Arter the Civil War, whilst we was in Kentuck, they want much to do except keep the Ku Kluxers quiet and we'd been hearin' 'bout the Indians stirrin' up trouble out in the West and we was all itchin' to go out thar. As fur's Cairo our regiment traveled by steamboat and then we unloaded everything and loaded up agin onto trains.

"That was sure some job, Bud, hunderds o' horses and mules and wagons, to say nothin' o' the men and officers and the women-folks and dogs. The regiment had been considerable seduced but at that they was more'n nine hunderd of us. If they's anything ornerier'n a mule when you're tryin' to hist him onto a train I don't want to see it. The critters seemed to know that want their natural mode of locomotion and acted accordin'. And course every day arter we got onto the plains we'd have to stop and take every animal off'n the train and water him and load him on agin. If they was grateful they didn't show it none, except the dogs. Them times when we stopped Custer and Miss Libby'd allus come back to talk to me and Vic and Dandy and Lulu and Bleuch and Tuck.

"Whilst we was travelin', arter we'd got into Dakota, somethin' dreadful happened. I want to blame but I got blamed fur it. Lulu give birth to a litter o' pups on the train, nine o' 'em. They was the cutest pups I ever seen, and I made a bed fur her, comfortable, and fed her extra, and when the General and Miss Libby come back I took 'em to her. They talked to her, praisin' her some, and she lay waggin' her tail, 's though she'd done somethin' smart. But arter we was on the move agin I slid open the car door jist a leetle ways fur air and and 'fore I could say 'Jack Robinson' Lulu jumped off. Wall, I run fur Custer and he stopped the train soon's he could and we hunted and called fur her but we never seen hide nor hair o' her agin. She'd got swallowed up by the prarie.

"That was one o' the times when the General and me got into a row and come purty near havin' a bust-up. He was riled up at fust, bein' natural hot tempered and he looked at me and his eyes was sharp and he talked quick and stern. He said:

" 'Was you asleep?'

"I said: 'No, sir, I wasn't asleep.'

"He snapped out: 'If we can't depend on you, John, we'll find some one we kin depend on.'

"His sayin' that, 'long with the loss o' Lulu, worked me up considerable. Course I didn't say much, him bein' my superior officer, but I was thinkin' plenty and Custer knowed it. I got back into the car and sot down longside the pups and we rid along. Next stop, whilst I was busy helpin' water the horses and mules, he come huntin' me up.

"He says: 'How's the pups, John?' And his voice was warm and friendly and he was smilin'.

"But I answered him gruff. I told him well's could be expected, considerin', but I kept my back turned to him. D'you ever notice, Bud, how you can't look a man straight in the eye whilst you're mad at him? Funny, ain't it?

"Wall, he kept on smilin' and then he held out his

[69]

hand to me and I took it. He said, 'John, I knowed damned wall you keer fur them hounds as much as we do. What happened to Lulu want anyways your fault.'

"Then I looked him straight in the eye and he said, 'Everything right between us, John?'

"And I told him, 'Yes, sir, it was.'

"Seemed like you couldn't hold a grudge agin Custer when he kept lookin' at you that way and smilin'.'"

Copy of letter from Mrs. Custer to John Burkman. Through courtesy of the Billings Library.

71 Park Ave., New York, June 28.

My Dear Burkman:

I have just been reading Mr. O'Donnell's letter telling me that you were as well as usual, that you were worried a little because you had not heard from me for some little time.

Well, Burkman, I had an attack of neuritis which quite used up my strength and I suffered also. It was so unusual for me for I am usually so well.——I bought an apartment in this big house last year—rented it while I had to go South to escape the severe winter and now I am here again with the friend with whom I began to work in New York over forty years ago. She says that she has been visiting me for ten years off and on. She has no home.

The Irish Margaret I have had so long keeps house for me. She married and I was so troubled fearing I had lost her but Patrick consented to come also and as he is an old soldier I feel

[70]

as if it was like the old days on the frontier. He goes to his work early and in the evening he has his dinner and his pipe and the evening paper with all the sporting news and it seems like an army kitchen. He was in the late war.

My address after October will be care of the Osceola Inn, Daytona, Florida. Do write me at any time if there is anything that I can do for you.

How faithful you were to the General, Burkman and how he trusted you! And how happy he was with the horses and dogs!

And do you remember, Burkman, how he used to want to have all the new puppies and "Ginnie" in the corner of my bedroom? And if by chance I stepped on one and the puppy squealed the General looked up as if he would like to send me to the guard house!

And what good care you took of the dogs! And when you used to come in, salute the General, and say:

"I have the honor, General, to say that Ginnie has nine puppies," the General would look so solemn and ask:

"Did any of them get away?"

And you would go off trying not to let him see you laugh! Oh, those were merry days!

Take good care of yourself, Burkman, and tell me if there is anything that I can do for you.

Your sincere friend,
Elizabeth B. Custer.

CHAPTER V

"Bud, it makes me feel young agin, talkin' over old times, and sorta funny in my innards, half glad and half glum. Here I am an old man jist clutterin' up the earth, and it don't seem no time atall since we made that trip from Kentuck to Yankton on our way to Fort Lincoln, with Miss Libby so purty and sweet, allus laughin', and me and the General young and spry and strong.

"The train took us as fur's Yankton and thar we had to unload, preparatin' fur the five hunderd mile march across the plains to Lincoln. It was long the last part o' April we got to Yankton, but colder'n blue blazes. Leastways, seemed so to us, havin' jist come from the south. And sich a God-forsaken country! Nary a tree. Nary a bush. Jist bare brown plains fur miles and miles rollin' on and on to the skyline. And so terrible still, Bud! That everlasting quiet creeps into your bones. You stop and listen and you git kinda skeered and you git to thinkin' queer things—about whar you come from and whar you're goin' to and what you're here fur and whar heaven is, if any, and sich. Did you ever git to thinkin' like that, Bud, sorta solemn?

[72]

A DAKOTA BLIZZARD

"I'll never forgit the look in Miss Libby's eyes when fust she got· off the train thar at Yankton and stood lookin' 'round—jist lookin'. She seemed so little and so young to buck up agin them plains. Cactus and prarie dogs and rattlesnakes and the wind—allus and furever the wind. But, like I says, she was a born campaigner and wherever her and the General spread canvas over a couple o' poles and sot under it boilin' coffee, with the dogs round about, thar was home. In a minute the lonesome look went out o' her eyes and she was laughin' at the way the pesky mules was actin', gittin' off the train.

"And us men want given no time to loiter 'round, gittin' homesick. We was ordered to unload everything and set up camp, which we did accordin'. It was some job, what with camp equipment fur nine hunderd men, as many horses and mules, wagons loaded with forage and rations and ammunition, dogs, puppies, canary birds, and even a few cats some fool women'd lugged along. Sich brayin' and bayin' and whinerin' and hollerin' and cussin' you never heerd, the men workin', the officers gallopin' back and forth, givin' orders. Fast as we set up tents the wind blew 'em down agin. Even yet I kin see Custer in his fringed buckskins, wearin' his big, white hat, his red tie and his long, yellow hair flutterin' in the wind, settin' so straight on

Dandy, and Dandy prancin' like a colt, tickled to death to be stretchin' his legs.

"Custer come to whar me and some others was lockin' wagon wheels together, making a half-circle barricade, and he says to me, 'John, I want you should look arter Mrs. Custer. 'Pears like a storm's comin' up. Most o' the women's goin' to Yankton fur the night but she aims to stay in that cabin over thar. Go see what you kin do to make her comfortable.'

"He talked hoarse and his face was redder'n usual and he was coughin' considerable.

" 'General,' I says, 'if I kin find the brandy and fix you up a drink with pepper it'll warm your innards.'

"But he jist laughed and dashed off, shoutin', 'I'm all right, John. You go to Mrs. Custer.'

"Which I did accordin'. The cabin want no sort o' shelter fur a cold night, jist an empty hut, dirt floor, no stove—nothin', and the logs so fur apart you could throw a cat through. Dark was settlin' down and it begun to rain.

" 'Miss Libby,' I says, 'you're goin' to git good and cold 'fore the night's over.'

"But she jist smiled, bright and pert. Mary and her was bustlin' 'round, huntin' fur blankets and quilts in the trunks.

" 'What the General kin stand I kin too,' she told me.

[74]

'We'll soon be as cozy as a bug in a rug. You'll see. If you'll jist start a fire so's we kin boil some coffee fur the General.'

"I looked around and in all that hunderds o' miles of bare plains I couldn't see a tree or a bush or even one blasted stick fur firewood. So I split up a packin' box and tried to start a fire on the floor o' the shack—thar bein' no stove—but the smoke choked us out. So then I built one jist outside the door but that want no use neither. The rain was pourin' by that time and the flame couldn't git a start. We was plumb discouraged, me and Miss Libby and Mary, and stood lookin' at each other, shiverin' till our teeth chattered, and the wind went shriekin' 'round the corners of the cabin like it was mad 'cause it couldn't git in.

"Some women 'ud broke down and cried, what with bein' hungry and cold and homesick, but not Miss Libby. She smiled best she could, her lips so stiff with cold, and hung a quilt up to the winder, and right away we felt cheered, 's though that quilt could keep out the night. Me and Mary made beds on the dirt floor whilst Miss Libby hunted up a lamp and lit it and sot it so's the light would shine out. A beacon light, she called it, to show the General the way home. That lamp helped to save my life, arterwards, and the lives of a good many o' the men.

"Miss Libby asked me, had I seen the General, and I told her I had. She asked, how was he, and I said he 'peared fair to middlin', not wantin' to worry her none.

"Oncst I peered out the winder and then I called to her. 'Look, Miss Libby,' I says.

"She come and stood aside me. I heerd her say: 'Oh!' soft-like, and then she didn't say nothin' more. Our train was jist pullin' out, goin' back to God's country, leavin' us on the prarie. We watched it. Fur miles we could see it. It looked like a long, red snake crawlin' away through the dark. It give me a kinda lonesome feelin', watchin' it go, but if Miss Libby felt that way too she didn't show it none. She spoke up, brisk, 'John, go tell the General to come straight home. He'll be down sick, ridin' 'round in this rain.'

"I'd been thinkin' about him and about Lulu's pups. So arter I'd done what I could fur Miss Libby I went back to camp. Jist whilst I was walkin' that leetle ways —not more'n a quarter mile—the rain changed to sleet and snow, comin' down thicker'n molasses in January. I found the pups whimperin' whar I'd left 'em in a basket under a wagon. Most likely they was hankerin' fur their mother. You know how a pup is, Bud, so damned soft and helpless. I soaked hardtack in water and fed 'em best I could and then I made a nest fur 'em with an army blanket in a packin' box, and shut 'em in, leavin' jist a leetle crack open fur air.

"The men was trompin' around in the snow, pitchin' tents which the wind tore down agin, glum and swearin' considerable. They was tired and wet and cold and hungry. Some of 'em was kneelin' on the ground, shelterin' leetle flames with their hats, hopin' to cook bacon and coffee, but it want no use. The snow pelted down constant, puttin' out the fires. Some of 'em was munchin' hardtack whilst they cussed. The lucky ones, when the General want lookin', was warmin' their innards with whiskey.

"But the horses and mules was most pitiful, hunched up agin the storm, too plumb discouraged to graze, jist standin' thar, heads droopin', like's not thinkin' of warm, sunny pastures back in Kentuck. Most of 'em bein' Bluegrass thoroughbreds, what was left o' government stock arter the war, hadn't never seen snow afore. Vic and Phil Sheridan perked up a bit, kinda hopeful, when they seen me, and begun to nicker, but they want nothin' I could do fur 'em.

"All of a sudden a bugler sounded officer's call and when we was at attention Custer come ridin' up.

" 'Boys,' he says, 'we'll break camp. You may ride into Yankton. You kin git a hot meal thar and maybe some sort o' shelter fur you and your mounts.'

"Then the men set up a cheer and waved their hats and the bugler sounded: Mount! Forward! and in a jiffy the cantonment was plumb empty o' men. The General rid to whar I was waterin' my horse down at the river. He saluted. 'Nice country, John,' he says.

"His voice was jist a croak. It want so dark yet but I could see icicles hangin' from his long moustache. He scowled when he coughed and put his hand to his chest. Salutin', I says, 'You look 's if you feel like hell, General.'

"He laughed, 'You've expressed my feelin's per-xactly, John,' he says. He asked me how was Mrs. Custer. I told him last I seen her she was settin' on a mess chest, wrapped in a quilt, swingin' her feet to keep 'em warm. I give him her message 'bout him comin' straight home.

"He looked over to whar the light of the lamp showed through the dark and he smiled kinda sad and said, soft-like, 'Home—home,' and he didn't speak fur a spell. Arter while he says, 'Better start fur Yankton, John, afore it gits too dark to find the way.'

" 'Is that an order, General?' I asked him.

"He laughed. 'No, John,' he says. 'Jist a suggestion from one friend to another.'

"So I picketed my horse and rummaged 'round till I found oats fur him and Vic. They nickered when I

left 'em like they was skeered to be alone in the storm.
It bothered me considerable, not takin' 'em on to Yankton but I figured like's not Miss Libby'd be needin' me.

"The hounds was crouched here and thar under
wagons or wharever they could git a leetle shelter. I
managed to snitch a leetle bacon and hardtack fur 'em
from the mess wagon, jist enough to stay their hunger.
I didn't chain 'em, thinkin' they could best take keer o'
theirselves if left free, which turned out to be a lucky
thing fur me. Saved my life, more'n likely.

"By that time it was as dark as a nigger in a haystack
and the cantonment was plumb empty, every man
havin' started fur Yankton. I sot out fur the cabin,
sorta hankerin' fur the sight of humans agin. 'Twant
very fur. I walked aways, figurin' every step 'ud bring
me to the shack, but I couldn't see nothin' ahead, not
even the light of the lamp, and the snow kept whippin'
agin my face, whirlin' this way and that, till I was all
bemuddled. And I hardly couldn't breathe, the cold
feelin' like fire pourin' down my throat. I walked and
I walked, Bud, and it got so dark and still it skeered
me. 'Peared like I was the only one left on earth. I'm
substitious as hell, Bud. I thought the dark was full o'
things out to git me. Fust I could o' cried with the
cold but arterwards my hands and feet got numb and
stopped achin' and then—funny thing—I begun to feel

[79]

warm and sleepy and so damned tired I jist wanted to drop down in my tracks, thar alone on the prarie, and go to sleep. But I had gumption enough left to keep trompin' on, fur I knowed what ailed me. I was freezin' to death. I ain't a prayin' man, not havin' no religion worth mentionin' but I prayed that the snow'd let up jist fur one second so's I could git my breath, or that I could see the light from the cabin or hear a human voice. But they want no sound except the wind, with the dark so thick 'round me you could cut it.

"Arter while, stumblin' along, I said to myself, 'What difference if you do stretch out and let the snow kiver you up? Maybe they'll find you, maybe not. You'll be jist one more heap o' bones to help fertilize the prarie. Nobody'll keer much, exceptin' Vic and Dandy and Bleuch and the General and Miss Libby.'

"But I kept trompin' on and on through the dark, the wind shriekin' like she-devils past my ears and the snow stoppin' up my nozzles and my feet heavy, frozen lumps. Bud, I blubbered like a baby, I was so lonesome and so tired and skeered.

"Then sudden I felt somethin' brush agin my leg. I heerd a whine. It was a dog. It was one o' the hounds. I felt him over and knowed it was Bleuch. He'd fought his way through the blizzard, huntin' me. He keered enough fur me to do that. Arter that I want lonesome any more. I wallowed along behind lettin' him lead and purty soon I spied a light ahead and I knowed it was the lamp Miss Libby had sot in the winder. I hollered with all the strength I had left and they opened the door and I fell in, not keerin' particular what happened arter that.

"The cabin was full o' men with frozen hands and feet that'd lost their way goin' to Yankton. Miss Libby and Mary was tendin' 'em. They begun fussin' over me. All I hankered fur was to sleep and sleep but they rubbed snow on my hands and feet and kept wishin' fur hot coffee.

"The shack was cold as hell but I recollect snoozin' off, wrapped in a quilt on the floor, Bleuch cuddled close, thinkin' how cozy it was in thar, with the dark and storm shut off. Last thing I remember was seein' Miss Libby bendin' over the General whar he lay and sayin':

"'You ain't goin' to git ammonia, Autie, 'cause I won't let you.'

"That was a terrible blizzard. Some o' the men had to have toes and fingers amputized but I got through. We lost a lot o' horses and mules, froze to death. The rest, when we could git out to feed 'em, was nigh starved. We pitched hay fur 'em and I fed the hounds raw bacon and hardtack. All the while I'd been worry-

[81]

in' considerable about Lulu's pups. Soon's I could I plowed through to 'em—neck deep the snow was. Their box was all covered with snow and I thought they'd been nice and warm inside but when I peeked in they was dead, every last pup. Such leetle mites, no bigger'n a pint o' soft soap on washday. They'd smothered to death.

"Kinda pitiful they was, dyin' out thar alone in the night. But it was best they went the way they did, 'cause life wouldn't 've been none too easy fur 'em, havin' no mother. I didn't tell Miss Libby, not right then, and I couldn't bury 'em proper, the way she'd like, the ground bein' froze, but I wrapped 'em in a blanket and shoved 'em way back into a snowdrift whar the coyotes couldn't git at 'em fur a spell. Many a man I knowed never had no fitter burial. Thar's many a shallow grave on the plains, Bud, with no stone to mark the place. We'd leave 'em whar they fell, usually, and cover 'em up with dirt and sagebrush and drive the mules across to hide the spot so's the Redskins couldn't find the bodies and mutilize 'em. Not that it mattered much. Bleached bones ain't men.

"If the old buttes and plains could talk they'd have stories to tell that'd beat anything ever writ in books. Bud, I git to thinkin' funny thoughts, settin' here alone day arter day. Git to thinkin' how us and the Indians was fightin' fur the same thing—our homes, our land, both believin' ourselves in the right. But who knows? The color o' the skin ain't so damned important. Ain't nothin' about bones scattered over the plains to tell which was red and which was white.

"But we was talkin' about the blizzard. I recollect how queer things looked arter the storm, all white and still fur's eye could see. Eleven o' our hounds aside the pups died and we was plumb discouraged. Had to make the best o' things though. Custer was some better and could lay a-bed, givin' orders and purty soon the sun come out hot, it bein' April, and the snow blockation went fast. By noon the tents was up, animals fed and us men hangin' 'round the mess tents thick as bees 'round clover. How the smell o' beans and bacon and coffee did tantalize our nozzles that day!

"Bud, since you got me my pension I've been what you might say real comfortable here in my shack but it ain't never seemed home to me, not like a army tent pitched on the plains fur a month or a week or a day was home. Can't make this old fellow with the bushy white whiskers seem like the young trooper in camp whar all was hustle and bustle, hounds and horses and Miss Libby needin' me, men cuttin' up jokes, Custer dashin' by on Vic or Dandy, bands playin', mules brayin' and sich. I reckon when he died somethin' went out o' me. 'Course I kept on fightin'. Right arter the Little Big Horn expedition I fought agin Chief Joseph but things never seemed the same to me agin. All these years I been sorta driftin', lost-like.

"Thar was plenty o' drinkin' the days arter the blizzard. The men had got their liquor in Yankton and Custer was sick abed and couldn't watch 'em. I mixed a drink accordin' to his own receipt—hot brandy with lots o' pepper—and took it to him. He looked purty white and gaunt layin' thar but he laughed.

" 'Doctors don't never take their own medicine, John,' he said. 'Mrs. Custer's fixin' me up fine with hot coffee.'

"As I says the General had drunk some durin' the Civil War but arter him and Miss Libby was married he was a total refrainer. I recollect one time when the Seventh under Custer was guardin' the locatin' engineers for the Northern Pacific under Stanley out in Montana Territory. That was in 1873. Custer caught some men drinkin' and bein' quick-tempered and easy riled he poured four barrels o' whiskey onto the ground. Stanley reprimanded him fur wastin' good liquor.

" 'Good liquor don't make good soldiers,' Custer said.

"Fur that act Stanley placed him under arrest fur three days. On 'count o' things like that, 'cause Custer

[84]

was dead set agin drinkin' and graft and sich, they was some officers and a few men that didn't like him. They was jealous o' him. They hated him and went out o' their way time and agin to make life miserable fur him, up to the day they left him to fight his last battle alone."

CHAPTER VI

JOHN sat bathed in June sunshine outside his shack, eyes half closed, musing aloud upon the events of vanished years.

"If I was to tell you, Bud, all the things that happened whilst we was marchin' the five hunderd miles from Yankton to Fort Rice and then on to Fort Lincoln it'd make a book. No use takin' down what I say. Folks wouldn't be interested. Same thing day arter day. Hard work. Cricks to ford and it want no joke gittin' a whole regiment across—mules, mess wagons, ammunition, horses, women. Sometimes we had to stop and make bridges. It don't sound much in the tellin' to say a wheel come off'n a wagon or a wagon got stuck in the mud but fur us that had to tug and sweat and cuss in the blazin' sun fur maybe half a day it meant a lot. It meant a lot jist makin' camp at night. Trompin' a place clean o' rattlesnakes, pitchin' tents, feedin' and waterin' the animals, gettin' together at mess, eatin' rice and beans and hardtack, then droppin' off to sleep dead tired.

"Seemed like reveille sounded afore we hit the hay.

Then a hurry-up breakfast, tearin' down tents and off again. Day arter day windin' across them bare, brown hot Dakota plains. I kin close my eyes and see us as we rid along, flags flyin', horses prancin', scouts to either side and in front, mess and ammunition wagons and pack mules bringin' up the rear. I kin see Jack Victor, our regiment pall-bearer, carryin' the colors and Kellogg on his little gray saddle mule and Lieutenant Cook with his black whiskers and me with some half grown pups danglin' either side my horse. I kin see Custer on Vic or Dandy in his buckskin coat and big white hat with Miss Libby aside him on Phil Sheridan and the hounds scamperin' along, scarin' up jack rabbits which none could catch except Tuck. I kin hear the rumble o' wagons and the creak o' saddle leather and tromp o' horses' feet. I kin hear the swish o' wind through prarie grass. Don't seem but yisterday that we was all young and strong and marchin' on to Lincoln.

"Hard work, but we had fun too. Them days the plains was alive with wild game, antelope, prarie chickens, buffalo and sich. More'n once we'd break lines to go chasin' somethin' and if we was lucky enough to git it then fur mess that night we had a feast. And sometimes we'd take time off fur fishin'. You could see men lined up both sides a crick, solemn and quiet, with the damnedest contraptions fur fishin', a pole made out o' a cottonwood stick and bent nail fur a hook, holdin' their pole with one hand, fightin' mosquitoes with the other. And proud as Lucifer if they ketched a leetle fish.

" 'Course they was allus Indians to look out fur. In that part o' the country they was supposed to be friendly but on 'count o' their treaties bein' broke time and agin and crooked agents holdin' back their rations they was some riled up. Not knowin' when an arrow or bullet might come whizzin' at us from back of a butte sorta kept the days from gittin' monotonous.

"Custer allus rid at the head o' the regiment, not bein' the kind of officer that'd hide behind his men when danger was lurkin'. He did a lot o' scoutin', sometimes alone, which worried Miss Libby considerable, and sometimes with Tuttle, his orderly. Many times jist him and me went off over the hills together. I like to think over them times when Custer and me was alone together out on the plains. We got close the way men do when they ain't nothin' around but sky and earth. We got to understandin' one another without sayin' much. Barrin' three months we was the same age but I felt, allus, as if I had to take keer o' him and look arter him. It's bothered me considerable all these years, Bud, that at the last, when maybe he needed me, I couldn't be aside him.

"Wall, life goes on. Oncst when one o' the men was chasin' an antelope he got excited and rid too fur away from the line and he was killed. They was an arrow stickin' in his back when we found him. We dug a shallow grave between two cottonwoods and buried him thar and driv the horses back and forth so's the spot wouldn't look like a grave.

"Isaiah Dorman, a nigger, was one o' our scouts. He fell with Custer in the last charge. When he was found his body was mutilized and pinned to the ground with arrows. Another o' our scouts was Charlie Reynolds—Silent Charlie. He want given to jabberin' much but everybody liked him. He was a great favorite of the General's. Charlie fell at Reno Hill. One time Custer sent him ahead the lines on a scoutin' expedition whar he had to travel through hostile country. A day and a night passed and he didn't come back and we begun to worry considerable. Then one o' us spied a lone rider comin' toward us from far away. He got closer and we seen it was Charlie but his horse was walkin' slow and queer. Purty soon we knowed why. Arter the scout'd eat and rested a spell he told us the story.

"'I met up with some Redskins off in the hills,' he said, 'and they chased me aways, me stoppin' occasional back of a tree to shoot at 'em and them shootin' continual at me. We played hide-and-seek till my horse got winded and I had to stop.'

" 'But how'd you git away?' we asked him.

"He looked at us with a twinkle in his eye. 'Wall,' he said, 'it jist happened that I had got out o' sight behind a hill. So, whilst they was huntin' fur me, I took the shoes off'n my horse and put 'em on backwards.'

"Backwards?" we said, not gittin' the idee right off the bat.

"Charlie laughed. 'Sure,' he said. 'Then I rid along aways and hid in some cottonwoods and stood thar watchin' them Redskins followin' my trail the wrong direction. Soon's it got dark I hit fur camp.'

"Reynolds was one o' the best scouts on the plains. He could outwit any Indian that was ever born. He had a sore on his thumb the mornin' of the Battle. But I git to wanderin'——

"Reckon it sounds dull to you, our long march up to Fort Lincoln but it want dull in the livin'. Captain Tom Custer and Boss Custer and Autie Reed and Crittendon and Hodgson and McIntosh and the General was allus cuttin' up jokes. They was horse racin' and poker playin' among the men, and they was allus the hounds to tend to, their feet gittin' full o' prickly pear thorns till me and Miss Libby got tired pullin' 'em out and made mittens fur 'em out o' leather from old boots. Then, long towards night, when we was tired and ready fur mess they was the worry huntin' fur a stream. Time and agin we had to make dry camp, the horses and mules goin' without water arter a hard day's march and eatin' cottonwood bark we stripped fur 'em. Army life's hard on troopers, Bud, but it's a darned sight harder on the animals, they understandin' nothin' about the glory of fightin' and sufferin' fur the flag and sich. Sometimes I hardly couldn't stand the look in their eyes.

"One time when *The Key West* passed us it forgot to leave off the bacon and we marched three days on beans. 'Nother time it left off wormy hardtack, held over from Civil War days, I reckon. But when the steamer did come they was allus good times. The officers and their wives took dinner on board with champagne and music and dancin'. The men got their pay those times and sot up all night playin' poker, drinkin' Jamaica Ginger or stronger. I was allus one o' the lucky ones at cards.

"Bud, the band music from the boat sounded so damned purty nights, creepin' off across them bare, still plains. Folks is good to me here. I don't make no complaint but I git tired o' the chug o' gasmobile cars and all the noise and clatter and git homesick, hankerin' fur the plains, with nothin' on 'em but sagebrush and cactus and prarie dogs, maybe a buffalo grazin' fur away, or an antelope standin' purty agin the sky up on a hill.

"Wall, we was all young then and on edge to git to Fort Lincoln. We never thought of death in them days. Never thought that when it come time to fight the Indians we'd be defeated. Funny, with death hangin' close to the edge of things we never give it a thought.

"I've heerd it said that Custer played poker with his troopers and took their money. That's a lie and I orter know, bein' closer to him than any other man, private or ñicer. Him and the officers did play poker some, th .y bein' no other amusement but he was allus preachin' to us men to save our money, tryin' to git us to leave it on the boat in a sorta bank.

"I was one o' them that spent mine soon's I got it, figgerin' that's what money was fur. One night I was in a tent with some fellows that was playin' poker— Tuttle and some others. (Note 12.) Bein' tired I stretched out on the floor and went to sleep and they used me fur a table and played cards on me all night. When I woke up next mornin' they was gone and I found a two dollar bill and a ten cent piece they'd left to pay fur the use of me.

"As I say, Custer never touched liquor or tobacco in any form but he did like to play poker. Oncst I watched a game he was in. That night luck was agin him. He kept losin' heavy and he laughed but I could tell he was some worried. Arter while, when his money was all gone he got up. One of the fellows said, 'You quittin', General?' He said, 'No, I'll be right back.'

"Soon's he come back they dealt. They was playin' stud. Fust card up Custer drew an ace. The man next to him a four spot. Custer threw in a thousand dollars and he was called. Next time 'round the other fellow paired his four and it turned out the fours was good. Custer threw down his cards and laughed kinda shaky and got up and left. Next mornin' I was in his tent puttin' things to rights and I heerd him tellin' Miss Libby the hull thing.

" 'Oh, Autie,' she says, 'you took that money we been savin'? Now I can't have any new clothes when we go back East.'

"She allus called him 'Autie' when she was feelin' extra glum or else extra glad.

" 'I'm sorry, Libby,' was all the General said. She want cross but they was tears in her eyes which worried him considerable. Fur a long spell arter that he was unusual quiet, not laughin' or jokin' to speak of. A few days later he come to me.

" 'John,' he says, 'I want you should arrange to fix a race fur me, Vic agin any horse in the regiment, fur five hunderd dollars.'

"His face was gaunt-like. They was an anxious look in his eyes. I understood. He was trustin' to Vic and me to raise some money so's he could git Miss Libby the purty things she'd been wantin'. So I acted accordin' though feelin' doubtful. Vic was the fastest horse in the regiment barrin' none but she hadn't been none too well the last few days. Her and the General had taken a fall awhile back, comin' down a steep hill at a gallop. Maybe she'd hurt her innards. Leastways she acted sorta droopy. I says to the General, hadn't he better run Dandy.

"Custer shook his head. 'I been noticin' lately,' he says, 'that Dandy's feelin' his age.'

"So, whilst I curried Vic, I talked to her. 'Vic,' I says, 'me and the General expects you to win. It's fur Miss Libby. You gotta do it fur her.'

"Then Vic looked at me—she had kinda sad eyes. She fell with Custer in the last charge. She looked at me and rubbed her nose agin my cheek as much as to say, 'I'll do my best.'

"That ain't foolishness. You been 'round horses, Bud. You know they git to understandin' most every thing you say to 'em.

"Vic was a purty horse, sorrel with three white stockinged legs, neck arched proud and dainty. I knowed we could depend on her. Wall, a race was arranged

[94]

fur next arternoon, between the General on Vic and Lieutenant McIntosh on a big, rangy bay. The hull regiment gathered 'round to watch. I marked off two hunderd yards. Charlie Reynolds stood ready to fire the signal to start. The band played Gary Owen whilst the two horses was nosin' agin the starting rope. Vic danced about on her little white feet, her nozzles quiverin'. Then Silent Charlie fired the shot, I dropped the rope and they was off. I seen Miss Libby smile and wave at the General.

"From the fust the big bay took the lead. He was a nose ahead, then a neck. Things begun to look bad fur us. Looked like Miss Libby wouldn't git her new dresses and fixin's. Custer never touched whip to Vic nor spurred her none. He jist leaned low over her neck and I knowed he was talkin' into her ear, and I knowed she'd understand. I knowed she'd run till it killed her, run till her heart burst, fur the man on her back. And I knowed the General want thinkin' of the five hunderd dollar stake whilst he was coaxin' her on. He was thinkin' of the tears he'd seen in Miss Libby's eyes. To me, watchin', it seemed like hours they run. 'Til the race was half over Vic favored her left front leg, laggin' a leetle. Then, all of a sudden, I seen her spurt forward, strainin' every muscle of her body and her flyin' hoofs hardly didn't seem to touch the dust of the track and she crept up and up, and it was neck and neck and then it was nose and nose and then she jist give one long leap plumb through the air and crossed the line a length ahead.

"I was holdin' the bridle whilst Custer dismounted and I seen the stake-holder give him the purse. Miss Libby come runnin' up, eyes shinin', all excited. She put her arms 'round Vic's neck.

" 'Good, old Vic!' she kept sayin'. I seen Custer turn to her, smilin', and slip the money into her hand and I seen the look that passed between them. They was tears in her eyes agin but this time they want the kind o' tears that hurts a man. Everybody was cheerin' and Vic was prancin' 'round and tossin' her head, proud-like, and the band struck up Custer's favorite tune, Gary Owen, and him and Miss Libby walked away together.

"I heerd him sayin', 'Now you kin have your new dresses, Libby.'

"And I heerd her say, soft, 'Oh, Autie, I didn't keer so much, really. I was jist mean and cross.'

"I heerd him laughin' as they went away, which was natural, 'cause Miss Libby couldn't be mean or cross ever.

TIME-DIMMED TRAILS

Copy of letter from Mrs. Custer to John Burkman. Through courtesy of the Billings Library.

Address care of Burke Stone Inc.,

41 East 42nd St., New York, Jan. 20.

My Dear Burkman:

I am at the South—(Daytona, Florida) near the friends of my childhood who lived in Monroe, the Lawrences and Wellington's. Mrs. Wellington was a Miss Agnes Bates. She is the greatest possible comfort to me in my lonely life for, having visited us at Fort Lincoln when a girl, I find it such a privilege to talk over the old life in Dakota.

It is a beautiful place here. The oranges make the orchard perfectly golden in color and the flowers and fruit are wonderful, but I miss New York and its constant interest. I am liable to bronchial trouble so I must stay South winters.

I have a picture of you that Mr. O'Donnell sent me and I cannot believe that the veteran with the heavy white beard and almost closed eyes is the active, slim young athlete that used to fling himself in the saddle and tear after his young general, over those Dakota fields. But though your eyes and your beard are no longer young, Burkman, I find that you stand as straight as ever. (I am also glad to say that in growing old I have not grown stout or crooked either.) (Note 13.)

Thank you for the picture of the General, Dandy, Bloody Knife and Reynolds. Give my kindest and most grateful remembrance to the O'Donnell's for their unfailing interest and kindness to you. I am very glad that you decided to go to California. It is very hard to stand up against the hard winters. Tho' I am grateful to be well I am glad to come South with my Monroe friends (who now live in New York).

With kindest regards to the good friends, the O'Donnells, I am

Your sincere friend,

Elizabeth B. Custer.

CHAPTER VII

"WALL, the five hunderd mile march ended at last and we got to Fort Rice. From thar, if I remember correct, Miss Libby took her trip East and we set out into Montana on the Stanley expedition whar nothin' of account happened, exceptin' a few Indian skirmishes and sich. It was the duty of the Seventh to clear the way fur the railroad engineers, 'cause the Redskins want takin' kind to the idee of a road bein' run through their huntin' grounds and acted accordin'. We had Varnum and his Ree * scouts with us, and Charlie Reynolds and Bloody Knife. Bloody Knife was Custer's favorite Indian scout. He had a mother and brother with the Sioux.

"Oncst we had a fight with the Sioux close to Pompey's Pillar. It might o' turned out purty serious, they bein' about two thousand Redskins agin four hunderd o' us. They tried to lead us into a trap whar we'd o' been completely surrounded but Custer outwitted 'em. It was Bloody Knife fired the fust shot, killin' a Sioux. Custer had his horse shot from under him but he want

* Arikaree.

hurt none hisself. Settin' Bull led the charge agin us and fur a spell looked like they was goin' to have things their own way. Then we charged full tilt agin 'em, regimental colors flyin', band playin' Garry Owen, and they turned and run like hell. Four o' our men was killed. We buried 'em near Pompey's Pillar. Ain't no stone to mark their graves. Funny, settin' in a train, with it rollin' so peaceful along steel rails, to think back on them stirrin' times. Reckon folks nowadays don't allus figger how much they owe to sich men as Varnum and Braden and Moylan and Custer and the army of common privates under 'em. It was in this fight that Tuttle—him that used me fur a card table—was killed.

"Bud, they ain't no better Indian fighter ever lived than Custer was or one that understood Indian warfare better. Time and agin, his forces outnumbered four to one—ten to one—he's licked 'em. He knowed all about their tricks and traps. He knowed you had to take 'em by surprise. That's what he aimed to do up on the Little Big Horn and we'd licked 'em thar too, if Reno and Benteen hadn't turned yellow and left him to fight it out alone. I hear as how some folks say nowadays that he rushed into things pellmell. Why, that's how he won every big battle agin the Redskins aimin', whenever possible fur night or early morning attack. (Note 14.) They blame him fur this and they blame him fur that.

Some say he'd orter found out fust what a big force he was buckin' up agin. Sich folks don't stop to think how things was in them days. Hunderds of miles from telephone or telegraph or railroads. No way to git messages to and fro except by messenger on horseback. Then we was invaders in hostile country which the Indians knowed every inch by heart. Custer was cautious. He scouted continual hisself. He had Ree scouts and Crows on the lookout every minute. But Montana bein' so rough, what with buttes and coulees, a hull regiment, horses and men, could hide a mile away and never be seen. (Note 15.)

"Wall, I'm gittin' ahead o' my story. Them was happy days we spent at the Fort (Lincoln) arter the 1873 expedition, winterin' and summerin' thar. I recollect how, when we was fust sighted comin' 'cross the plains, the band at the Fort struck up Garry Owen and the regiment flags was a-flyin' and everybody was cheerin' us, laughin' and jabberin' and shakin' hands. Down in Kentuck our regiment had been considerable seduced. Now, fur the fust time fur a long spell, we was all together agin. Men that hadn't met since Civil War days was all talkin' at oncst, askin': 'Do you remember this and do you remember that?' I'm glad fur them happy days to remember, Bud, bein' the last, you might say, a lot o' us was ever to know.

"The Fort was like a little town, jist squat buildings set down helterskelter on the prarie. On one side the parade ground was the officers' quarters. Tother side, down by the river was the men's barracks and futher on was 'Suds Row' whar some married privates lived with their wives. The hull thing comes back to me. I kin close my eyes and see it all, wagons, hounds, mules, horses. Privates lazyin' 'round 'most o' the day. Officers and their wives saunterin' up and down. Ladies on porches talkin' and laughin' whilst they sewed. Garrison flags a-flyin'. Time and agin now I spring out o' bed early in the mornin', thinkin' I hear the bugler soundin' reveille, and time and agin in the night I think I hear the sentry callin' 'All's well.'

"We had good times fur a spell, nothin' much to do except guard duty and tendin' the horses and mules and paradin', keepin' the officers' quarters supplied with firewood and water and sich. Plenty o' time fur huntin' and fishin' which we done considerable. Many and many a time Custer and Miss Libby'd go off fur an all day's hunt with jist me along to look arter the hounds and preparate their campfire and maybe cook prarie chicken or fish if they caught any. Ain't no meal nowadays, Bud, tastes like coffee and prarie chicken cooked over an open fire under a cottonwood on Dakota praries used to taste. Sometimes the three of us 'ud run races,

[101]

the General on Vic, Miss Libby on Phil Sheridan and me on Bluegrass. Those times Custer'd forgit he was my superior officer and we was jist like friends.

"Then arter while (1874) come orders to go to the Black Hills which was Sioux country whar gold had been discovered. The Sioux was raisin' hell general on 'count o' the government breakin' a treaty with 'em and we was sent to quiet 'em down and protect the miners. Which we did accordin'. Nothin' in particular that I recollect happened. A few skirmishes, a few men killed.

"Whilst we was thar Calamity Jane hung 'round our camp, pesterin' us considerable. She dressed in men's clothes and was allus beggin' some one fur a drink. We didn't like her. She was dirty. She was lousy. The men wouldn't have nothin' to do with her. Some of 'em hired her to wash their clothes, payin' her in whiskey. One time a fellow bunked with her all night and never knowed she was a woman till some one told him next day. He come to me, his eyes a-poppin'. He says, 'Hell, Neutriment, I slept with a woman!'

"Takes a good many kinds to make up a world, don't it, Bud? Thar's the Calamity Jane kind and then thar's the kind like your wife and Miss Libby. (Note 16.) Don't know's a man orter even mention 'em in the same breath.

"Reckon you hardly can't git head nor tail out o' what I'm tellin', Bud, I ramble on so. Thar was many hardships durin' the long march from Yankton to Fort Lincoln. (Bismark) It took weeks. Us men was tuckered out completely. It must o' been awful hard fur Miss Libby, she so little and young, but she never complained. She was allus ridin' up in front longside Custer, him on Vic or Dandy, her on Phil Sheridan which was a little, trottin' bay, and the two laughin' and jokin' continual. They often took side trips with the hounds whilst the long column—men, horses, mules, wagons—went stragglin' 'cross the plains. I can close my eyes and see 'em yet, dashin' away, hounds all around 'em, she so slim, her long skirts spreadin' over Phil's flank, Custer in his fringed buckskin, with red tie and big, white hat. The General was a good shot. On that trip he got a black-tailed deer and an antelope and a bear and a buffalo. When he mounted 'em they looked jist like life. His quarters was allus full o' sich things.

"One time I went with 'em on a huntin' trip and Bleuch—the dog that was affeard of a stick with any kind o' metal on it—Bleuch caught and held a big elk single-handed till Custer killed it. The elk put up an awful fight. Bleuch was a vicious dog and he hung on even arter he was torn up considerable. Arter the

[103]

General shot the elk Bleuch lay limp, bleedin' at the nozzles, and we thought fur sure he was goin' to die. Miss Libby run and got water from a crick near by and poured it down Bleuch's throat and she held his big head on her lap and talked soft comfortin' talk to him, and then he wagged his tail a mite, feeble but grateful like.

"We had a hard time gittin' him back to camp, him bein' too big to carry on our saddles. He had to walk all the way but we went slow fur him and we finally got thar. Then me and Miss Libby washed his cuts and fixed him up comfortable as possible on her bed. By next day he was real pert agin. Bleuch was with Custer on the last trip up the Little Big Horn.

"A sad thing happened whilst we was on the march. Phil Sheridan died. Each night, when the oats was bein' rationed out, I allus seen to it that my own horse and Vic and Dandy and Phil got a leetle mite more'n their share, which was a job sometimes, every man lookin' out, the same way, fur his own mount. One night I noticed that Phil was off'n his feed. He jist nozzled his oats but he wouldn't eat none to speak of. I don't know what was the matter. I never did. Same as usual that night I went to bed and dropped right off to sleep but I woke up sudden thinkin' of Phil. So I got up and felt 'round in the dark to whar he was picketed and he was layin' down and he was dead.

"Next mornin' I hunted up the General and told him. Me and him went over to whar Phil was stretched out, same's if he was sleepin'. Custer stroked his neck.

" 'Poor old boy,' he said. 'You've been a faithful friend.' Then he said to me, and his voice was husky, 'John, you tell Miss Libby. I can't. I'm busy. I got things to do.'

"Which want true. He jist couldn't bear to hurt her none. So I acted accordin'. Fust I hunted till I found a purty spot, the kind o' place Miss Libby admired, under cottonwoods down by a stream, and I dragged Phil over and buried him thar. 'Peared like it'd be easier fur her if she knowed he was restin' whar it was purty. Then I went and told her. I took her over to the place. She cried some, lovin' Phil and bein' young and tender-hearted. I could find that very spot now, Bud, I know I could. If I was to git back to Dakota I could go straight to the spot whar poor Phil was buried. Wall, he jist went a leetle sooner than Vic and the rest, and he died easy, 'stead of on the battlefield with bullets whizzin' all 'round and arrows plungin' into his body. He was lucky but we didn't know that then."

CHAPTER VIII

"ARTER we got back to Fort Lincoln from the Black Hills expedition things went on same's usual. I kin remember how Miss Libby run out to meet us and how she flung herself into the General's arms almost afore he was off'n his horse. And the tears rolled down her cheeks, she was so tickled to have him safe agin.

"The months of waitin', thar at the Post, musta been purty hard fur her and the other women whenever we went out on an expedition, letters bein' so few and seldom and them not knowin' would they ever see their men agin. It takes guts to go into action, fightin', but I reckon it takes a heap sight more to jist set wonderin', waitin', worryin'.

"Wall, life went on. Custer and me had some fallin' outs that year but we allus made up agin. As I says he was quick-tempered and I reckon when I was young I could git riled on occasion. Oncst when his own horse was knocked out he borrowed mine fur a scoutin' trip. A man gits to carin' a lot fur his horse, tendin' it and feedin' it, thar bein' nothin' much else to care fur. So when the General brung mine back and its legs was

[106]

cut and scratched bad from a fall on some rocks, I was mad. I didn't say nothin' to him, natural, him bein' my superior officer, but I told Miss Libby and I showed her Bluegrass' legs. Wall, that night whilst I was rubbin' intment on 'em Custer come huntin' me up and he brung an extra ration o' oats fur him and stroked his neck. He didn't say nothin'. That was his way o' tellin' me he was sorry. So we was friends agin.

"Another time our trouble was more serious and I come purty near gittin' a transfer to another company. It was this way. It want till later I got all the ins and outs o' the matter. You see fur some spell I'd been wearin' a big, white felt hat that belonged to the General. He havin' several I didn't figger he'd care. The men all joshed me and called me 'General' and I took their joshin' good-natured but seems like Custer got tired seein' his hat on another man's head. So, fur a joke, he told the officer of the day to arrest the fust man he seen walkin' by wearin' a big white felt hat. So the officer acted accordin' and took my hat away from me and put me in the guard house fur an hour or so. All the regiment knowed it was jist a joke except me and I was purty riled. That night I went to Custer's quarters and I says to him:

" 'General, I'd like to be transferred to another company.'

"He set fur a spell, quiet. 'Very well, John,' he says.

"Him bein' so willin' surprised me some 'cause I didn't know's he could git along without me to take keer o' the hounds and his and Miss Libby's horses and look arter them general. Fur nine years I'd been you might say one o' his family. But when he jist looked up from his writin' and says, 'Very well, John,' I preparated to leave.

"Then Mary—she was Miss Libby's cook—she come to me and says, 'John, you gotta leave your horse when you git transferred.'

"'You mean I can't take my own horse along?' I says.

"'Yes, John,' she said. 'Them's the General's orders.'

"Wall, Bud, I was flabbergasted. It was like tearin' an arm off, a man bein' separated from his horse. How'd I know Bluegrass'd be treated right? Maybe he'd sicken fur me, him bein' used to me talkin' to him whilst I curried him. It took a man that understood his ways to handle him proper. He had a habit of kickin', playful like, whilst I polished his hind hoofs. I thought the hull matter over and then I went to Custer.

"'General,' I says, 'I've decided to stay.'

"And then he laughed. 'I thought,' he said, 'I knowed the right way to keep you with us. Why, John,' he said, 'you're one o' us and Mrs. Custer feels jist as I do about it. Here! Take this and wear it.'

"It was one o' his big, white hats. I wore it whilst we was at Fort Lincoln and I wore it on that last trip up the Little Big Horn. A bullet went through it up on Reno Hill whilst I was layin' back of a rifle-pit.

"The General and me was allus havin' squabbles like that. Sometimes he was to blame and then he was quick to own up. More'n likely, though, it was me in the wrong. Many and many a time Miss Libby's kept me out o' the guard house by talkin' to Custer soft and laughin'.

"Custer want strict exactly but he did expect his men to do what was right. The only time I ever heerd him roundup or argue with one of his officers was when he sent a Lieutenant up the Yellowstone to drive a bunch of Indians back over the river near Pease Bottom. The Lieutenant did drive 'em back but Custer thought he should have captured some of 'em and he said so quick and sharp to the officer. He allus said the best way to govern men was to trust 'em. He said, 'the man that trusts men will make fewer mistakes than the one that distrusts 'em.'

"Things didn't allus run smooth o' course and he worried considerable over graft goin' on. The government agents stole rations from the Indians and sold to the soldiers and civilians. The soldiers 'ud git things cheap from the sutler and sell to the civilians. The sutler had to keep count o' his provisions. He'd tear a shirt in two and report he had so many pieces and then sell the extra shirt to privates in Bismark. Sich things got under Custer's skin. So one time he took a troop and marched into Bismark and rounded up hunderds of dollars worth o' stuff that had been sold from his regiment and declared the town under martial law. With 'most nine hunderd men to look arter, all kinds, good and bad, it was natural there'd be some trouble. But the men respected Custer 'cause they knowed he was straight and honest. They knowed he wouldn't ask more of them than he was willing to do hisself. Most of 'em loved him. They loved Miss Libby too. She knew every single man in the regiment by name. She was allus stoppin' to talk to one or another, askin' about his health and his family and sich. And when any one was in trouble he allus went to her with it. Like one time when Billy Blake got word his mother'd died back in the States. He was jist a young kid and he took it hard. Fur days he was so glum he hardly couldn't eat or sleep. I told Miss Libby about it and she went to him and set down aside him on his cot and listened whilst he told her all the little things he could remember about his mother and he cried some and arter that he was hisself agin.

"Come Christmas at the Fort a lot o' men felt sorta blue bein' so fur away from their folks. Some of 'em drank and raised hell jist to keep from thinkin'. I was all right 'cause the regiment was the only home I ever knowed and seemed like Custer and Miss Libby was my own folks. She give me that year fur Christmas a potograp o' her with the General. (Note 17.) That same time Lieutenant Smith made a leetle playin' poker and he bought a cow fur a present fur Miss Libby and he wanted I should take it to her. So fust him and me fixed it up. We brushed it and curried it and tied ribbons on its horns and he writ a note which we fastened round its neck with another ribbon. The note said: 'Compliments of Lieutenant Smith to Mrs. Custer.'

"We led the cow up to her door early Christmas mornin' and knocked and then we run and hid whar we could see when she opened the door. Wish you could o' seen her face, Bud. She jist looked and looked and then she begun laughin' and she read the note and called to the General and he come out and he laughed too. But they was awful tickled, fresh milk bein' so hard to git thar at the Fort. It was one o' my jobs arter that to milk the cow which they named Daisy.

"Wall, life went on that winter with one thing and

another. One time Vic fell into a well and we had to pull her out with a block and tackle. She want hurt to speak of but she was plumb skeered.

"Bud, did I ever tell you about Mrs. Nash? Wall, that was funny but it was some sad too. As I said, across from the parade ground was 'Sud's Row,' which was the quarters whar the washwomen fur the regiment lived, some bein' the wives o' privates. A woman by name o' Mrs. Nash lived thar. She was half Mexican, I reckon. Leastways she was funny-lookin' and allus wore a shawl over her head, pinned under her chin. She was an extra good washer and she was a good nurse too, allus in demand to chase the rabbit when some woman was expectin' a baby.

"She was a queer woman. Takin' my washin' to her regular I got to know her real well. She didn't jabber much though. Oncst she said to me, 'John,' she says, 'are you havin' good luck playin' poker?'

"I had to remit that lately I hadn't been havin' any luck to speak of.

"She says, 'Give me your deck.'

"Which I did accordin'. She took my cards and spread 'em out on her table and passed her hands over 'em and spoke some gibberish I couldn't understand and then give 'em back to me.

" 'Thar!' she said. 'Now you'll win.'

"Bud, I'm blessed if I didn't win every game I went into arter that, mostly from civilians. I offered to divide my winnings with her which appeared to me the fair and honest thing to do, but she said, 'No, she didn't want my money.'

"I never could figger out what she did to my deck to make it lucky. I reckoned she was a witch maybe. Anyway I kept still about it, lest some o' the others 'ud go to her and git their cards fixed lucky too.

"Wall, time went on and arter while she married a man in the Seventh by name o' Clifton. He was a smart young fellow from the east, Clifton was, actin' as quartermaster clerk. He'd allus been jolly, laughin' and cuttin' up jokes, but arter he'd been married a spell he got to bein' glum and jist a few days afore his time expired he deserted, sayin' nothin' to nobody. We never seen hide nor hair o' him agin and so Mrs. Nash was a widow. She stayed on with the Seventh, washin', mendin' helpin' to bring babies into the world, and by'n by she got married agin to a private in the Seventh by name o' Nonan and her and Nonan lived together over in Sud's Row.

"It want very long arter that, oncst when Nonan was away on scout duty, she took sick and died sudden. The hull Fort felt bad, her havin' been sich a friend in trouble and a couple o' women was delegated to fix her up nice fur burial, whilst me and some others went out and picked prarie flowers so's Miss Libby could make a wreath. Sudden one o' the two, a great big woman, come runnin' out o' Nonan's quarters, all excited and pantin' and stutterin'.

" 'Mrs. Nonan want no woman atall,' she said. 'She was a man!'

"We was flabbergasted. When Nonan come back from scout duty we told him about his wife dyin' and all. He was a quiet man. He didn't say much, but his face went white and kinda jerked. Arter that everywhere he went the regiment joshed him. We'd say, 'Ain't you lonesome without your wife?' We'd say, 'When I want a girl I'll git Nonan to pick her out fur me.' Things like that all the time till we purty nigh drove him crazy. He quit playin' poker any more with the rest. He took long walks out across the prarie alone. He'd git up nights and walk. At mess we'd josh him till it seemed like his vittals choked him. He lost flesh and looked awful sickish and miserable.

Wall, things went on that way fur quite a spell. Then one day I was in the balcksmith shop whar the blacksmith and the carpenter worked. They was the ones that was killed later fightin' agin Chief Joseph on Canon Crick. (Note 18.) Nonan walked in. His face was gaunt and sorta set. The carpenter looked up.

" 'Hello, Nonan!' he says. 'Say, you and Mrs. Nonan never had no children, did you?'

"We all started laughin' and then we stopped sudden. Nonan was standin', lookin' at us, fust one and then another, jist lookin', and his eyes was wild, like an animal that's bein' hurt. Then, afore we had sense to stop him he pulled out his gun and shot hisself dead, right thar at our feet.

"We was ashamed, Bud, terrible ashamed. Layin' thar, he looked like a kid, and we remembered how oncst he'd been so full o' pranks, allus smilin' and jolly. They give him a nice funeral with the flag and sich, and John Martin (Martini), the bugler, sounded taps. All that didn't bring Nonan back though. It was the best we could do but it didn't ease the sore place we'd made in his heart. His bones is out on the Dakota prarie somewhar under a cottonwood yet, I reckon.

"It takes all kinds o' men to make up an army. Officers, o' course, whose doin's is writ up in books, but it takes a lot o' common fellows too, like me and Tuttle and Billy Blake and Nonan—jist privates, men that don't know nothin' except what they're told to do, that kills and gits killed, and that the world never hears about. Jist privates we was, jist rough, strong young fellows ready to march all day, tired, hungry, thirsty, to go here, go thar, without understandin' why or nothin'

[115]

except to shoot and shoot to kill. And yet to ourselves we seemed important, Bud. Nonan's troubles meant jist as much to him as though he'd been a Major. Hunderds of graves scattered over Dakota and Montana of men that's never been missed, never been writ up, but they was good soldiers jist the same, and without 'em thar wouldn't've been no country, maybe.

"Wall, we all felt purty bad about Nonan but if he hadn't killed hisself more'n likely an Indian bullet'd got him a few months later, up on the Little Big Horn. He didn't miss nothin', goin' whilst he was young. It ain't easy lingerin' on and on arter the others when you ain't no use to nobody any more.

"Life went on at Fort Lincoln that last winter and spring, jist one day arter another. A good many things happened that I disremember, it bein' more'n fifty years ago. Happy days they was in the main, lookin' back on 'em now. Killin' rattlesnakes, choppin' firewood, goin' fishin' or huntin' with the hounds, gittin' up at reveille, goin' to bed at taps, cussin' our vittals, playin' poker, scoutin' round about fur Redskins. They was allus excitement when one o' the boats—*The Key West* or *The Far West*—come up the river. Then we got Jamaica Ginger and letters and news from the outside world and the men was paid off and they was a lot o' drinkin', spite o' the General and Miss Libby. Some o' the fellows built a dance hall that winter which was attended by the washwomen and officers' wives and a few civilian women from Bismark. Me bein' heavy on my feet I want none too popular with the ladies and mostly I set back and listened to the band. Miss Libby and the General looked nice dancin' together. She was a purty little woman.

"Early that spring (1876) it got winded 'round that they was havin' some trouble at Washington. I never did git the hang of it exactly, but they sent fur Custer and he went back East. I've heerd of how in books they writ about Custer bein' found on the battlefield arter the last charge and about his long, yellow, curly hair. That want true 'cause I remember him comin' from the East with his hair cut short and how he looked so unnatural arter that wearin' his big, white hats.

"Afore he went he said goodbye to me. 'You'll take good keer o' Mrs. Custer,' he said, 'same as usual, won't you, John?'

"I told him I would. He looked awful sober I recollect. Him and Miss Libby seemed worried 'bout somethin' but he laughed and joked a leetle at the last. I'd been busy the last few days spadin' up a vegetable garden back of their quarters.

" 'Now, John,' he says, 'no matter what Mrs. Custer

[117]

tells you whilst I'm gone be sure and put in lots o' onions.'

"So I acted accordin', but afore they was ready to pull the Seventh had started on its march up the Little Big Horn.

" 'Long in the spring afore Custer come back from the East the news got spread around that we was maybe goin' out on an expedition into Montana Territory whar the Indians was raisin' a rumpus. It was reported a good many Sioux had left their reservation and was runnin' 'round loose under Rain-in-the-face. They was good and mad at the whites on 'count o' several things that'd happened. One thing the government agents was stealin' their rations and the buffalo was run off their range and they was half starved. Then the government broke a treaty with 'em by lettin' the whites open up mines in the Black Hills. Rain-in-the-face was arrested by Captain Tom Custer fur somethin' or other and put in the guard house. Arter Teeman helped the chief escape he led a lot o' the Sioux over into Montana and it was our business to herd 'em back.

"Durin' that time, whilst we was waitin' fur Custer to come back from Washington, they was a good many confabs amongst the officers of the Seventh and a lot o' wranglin' and us men got an inkling that things want goin' smooth. It was even hinted 'round that maybe

Custer wouldn't git to command his Seventh. Anyway we got the feelin' that things was serious and that we was more'n likely goin' to have some real fightin'. (Note H.)

"Wall Custer come back with his hair cut short as I says and lookin' awful quiet and stern and we begun preparatin' fur the expedition. I remember them last days at Fort Lincoln how white Miss Libby was and how she couldn't talk without her voice shakin' and her lips quiverin' and how, when she tried to joke and laugh with the General same's usual her eyes'd git full o' tears. Oncst I was in the kitchen eatin' a piece o' pie Mary'd saved fur me and I heerd them talkin'.

" 'Why, Libby!' the General said, 'is this the way fur the bravest leetle wife a soldier ever had to act?'

"And she cried right out. 'I can't help it, Autie. I jist can't help it. I wish Grant hadn't let you go.'

" 'Libby!' Custer spoke her name stern-like.

" 'Oh, I don't mean that,' she said. 'I'm sorry I said that, Autie.'

"Arter that she was brisk and lively, not cryin' no more when the General could see, tryin' to help him by bein' brave.

"The last day at the Fort Custer come to me. 'John,' he said, 'I want you should preparate fur a race fur Vic. We'll have it soon's we git back from the Big Horn.

"He was settin' on Vic then, whilst he talked, and I can see 'em both plain's though it was yesterday, Vic prancin' same's usual, sich a purty horse with her three stockinged legs, and the General, in his fringed buckskin and red tie and big, white hat, sorta sideways in the saddle, strokin' Vic's neck and plannin' fur the race. His moustache was long. You couldn't hardly tell when he was smilin' except fur the twinkle in his eye.

" 'Of course Vic'll win,' he said. 'She's got to 'cause Mrs. Custer and me spent all our money on our trip East and we're broke.'

"So I acted accordin'. I hunted up Lieutenant Cook who owned the fastest horse in the regiment except Vic and Dandy.

" 'Lieutenant Cook,' I says, salutin', 'the General wants to arrange fur a race between Vic and your horse, a thousand yards, five hunderd dollars stake.'

" 'When?' he asked, quick-like. 'Today?'

" 'No,' I says. 'Soon's we git back from the Little Big Horn.'

" 'I'll call it,' he said. 'You may tell General Custer we'll have that race *if* we git back from the Little Big Horn.'

"And none of 'em ever did git back, either horses or men. Lieutenant Cook had long, black side whiskers.

Arter the fight he was found on the battlefield with his whiskers scalped. (Note 19.)

"Wall, the next mornin'—it was about the middle of May, 1876,—everything bein' ready, we started out from Fort Lincoln headed fur the Powder River in Montana. The Seventh was filled up, most o' them Civil War veterans that had since been with Custer on the Stanley expedition and the Black Hills expedition. They was twelve troops o' cavalry, 'bout sixty men to a troop, under Custer, besides Varnum with his forty Ree scouts and three troops o' infantry from Fort Rice. It 'peared like sich a force o' experienced Indian fighters could lick all the Redskins in the hull world. We didn't know then that Crook had jist been licked. And we didn't know that 'most every able-bodied Indian from all the reservations was banded agin us. We didn't know that jist a few o' the Seventh 'ud be left to fight 'em all. And still we was glum that day, Bud. I can't ever forgit it. I reckon no living man o' the Seventh can ever furgit how the leetle fort looked as we marched away from it, so lonesome and quiet, the mornin' sun shinin' over everything, the flag flutterin' high up on its pole, the women and children standin' thar, wavin' their handkerchiefs and cryin', squaws down in Indian village wailin' and beatin' tomtoms. Thinkin' to cheer the women folks some Custer had the band strike up

Gary Owen whilst we marched 'round and 'round the parade grounds afore we left and the soldiers looked trim and the horses pranced and Jack Victor carried the regimental colors, but spite o' our tryin' to seem pert and gay we was downhearted.

"I'd seen the General sayin' 'Goodbye' to the hounds early in the mornin' and that made me know things was serious 'cause usually he'd been takin' them with us on expeditions into hostile country. I seen him pat Tuck's head.

" 'Be a good dog,' I heerd him say, 'whilst I'm gone and don't git into no prickly pears.' Which was Tuck's failin'. He was allus limpin' up to Miss Libby or me, whinin', holdin' up a paw fur us to pull the thorns out of.

"Miss Libby rid out with us one day's march. She'd wanted to go the hull way but Custer said, 'No!' Then she'd coaxed to go on *The Far West* up the river but Captain Marsh and Custer said, 'No!' So she rid at the head o' the column aside the General the fust day, settin' on Dandy. Dandy was a purty little brown horse. He never could brook no horse bein' in front o' him. I heerd Custer say to Miss Libby that mornin' as they rid along:

" 'Dandy's age is beginnin' to tell on him a leetle. He ain't got the stamina he used to have. I'll baby him

[122]

some on this expedition and when we git back he can have a good long rest.'

"Dandy was wounded up on Reno Hill. Arterwards he was sent to Custer's father back in Monroe.

"Oncst durin' the day Miss Libby looked back and she cried:

" 'Autie, look!"

"Thar was Tuck and Bleuch racin' to ketch up with the General, their tongues hangin' out, tails waggin', tickled to death to see him agin, skeered they'd be sent back. They went with him on into the valley of the Little Big Horn.

"It bein' more'n fifty years ago I ain't clear on some points. I disremember how fur we got that fust day. Next mornin' the General sent Miss Libby back to Fort Lincoln with scouts and the paymaster from the boat to protect her. I was standin' holdin' her horse ready to help her mount. Even now, arter all these years, it brings a lump into my throat, rememberin' how she clung to Custer at the last, her arms tight 'round his neck, and how she cried. She want one to take on usually but seemed like she jist couldn't go back and leave him that day. Thar was tears in his eyes too and he kept tellin' her she was a soldier's wife, she must be a brave little woman, soon he'd be back and then we'd all have good times at Fort Lincoln agin.

[123]

"Thinkin' to cheer her a leetle as I helped her mount, 'Miss Libby,' I says, 'how old be you?'

"That was a standin' joke between us, me allus tryin' to find out how old she was and she never tellin'.

"She sat in the saddle lookin' down at me and her purty eyes was plum full o' tears and her lips was quiverin'. Then she said, kinda laughin', kinda sobbin':

" 'The General don't think it proper that I tell gentlemen my age, John.'

"Then she leaned over and put her hand on my shoulder.

" 'Goodbye, John,' she said, 'you'll look arter the General, won't you?'

"Then we stood watchin' her ride away across the prarie, the General and me. She looked so little and so young and she was leanin' way over with her head bent and we knowed she was cryin'. We watched till she was jist a speck way off on the plains.

"Custer's face went white and he was awful sober. 'A good soldier,' he said, low and quiet, 'has to serve two mistresses. Whilst he's loyal to one the other must suffer.' "

CHAPTER IX

CUSTER—HUSBAND AND SOLDIER

"Fur the next few weeks arter that the General was all soldier. I've heerd folks sayin' Custer rushed into things headlong, specially in that last campaign on the Little Big Horn. That ain't true. Thar never was a man took things more serious. Thar never was a man worked harder than he did those last few weeks. Why, Bud, he cared fur us men o' the Seventh. He was brave hisself. He expected us to be brave. But he wouldn't endanger our lives by makin' an attack pellmell. And life was dear to him. He was young, him and Miss Libby was so happy. He didn't want to die. I was with him a lot whilst we was marchin' on and I can't see whar he made a single mistake, or whar he could o' done different. He had scouts out continual. Day arter day he'd take a few men and go off into the hills hisself, ridin' hard, miles more'n the rest of us did, scoutin', huntin' fur Indian signs. And arter a fifty mile march, when we was all dead tired, ready to flop down jist anywhar fur a spell o' restin', he'd be settin' in his tent, thinkin' things over, plannin' manœuvres, writing reports, preparatin' fur the fight. He asked a lot o' horses

and men on that march but he never spared hisself none.
I know, doin' guard duty outside his tent most o' the
time. I'd see him inside, Tuck and Bleuch curled up
aside him, thinkin'—thinkin'. He was sent out with
the Seventh to lick the Redskins. That was his job. He
meant to do it. And, Bud, he could o' done it, too, if
Reno'd supported him, out-numbered ten to one though
he was. (Note 20.) Or if Benteen'd jined Custer 'stead
of Reno or if they'd sent ammunition from the pack
train when they fust got Custer's hurry-up order, or
even if the guns 'ud worked proper. Sich a lot o' 'if's',
Bud, betwixt life and death.

"Custer made jist one mistake, fur's I can see, and
that want due to poor judgment accordin' to what he
already knowed of Indian warfare. He was offered
three extra troops of the 2nd Cavalry and the three
Gatling guns under Lieutenant Low. The three extra
troops, as things turned out wouldn't o' made a speck
o' difference—jist a hunderd fifty more men agin the
thousands o' Redskins and the Gatling guns was heavy
to haul. The mules was already tuckered out completely from the scouting expedition under Reno. If
Custer had taken the guns he'd had to march slow
which ain't proper when you're plannin' a surprise attack on the hostiles. O' course, if he'd had them guns
up on the hill he could've mowed down the Indians like

hail mows down saplings but the idee is he could never've got 'em up thar. The Indians was on the warpath. They was out to git us, same's we was to git them and they watched every move we made from the time we left *The Far West* at the mouth o' the Rosebud on the 22nd till Custer attacked the village on the 25th. They was sharp eyes peerin' out at us from behind every butte and boulder and tree and coulee whilst we was marchin' along. And they had the advantage, not only in numbers and guns and sich, but 'cause they knowed every inch o' the land by heart and it was all new territory to us. Seems like, lookin' back at it all, now, that we was rushin' hellbent right into death with our eyes shut.

"Sich a thing as Custer's defeat couldn't 've happened these days, what with telephones and telegrap and sich. We'd o' knowed that Crook'd been licked jist a hunderd miles away. We'd o' got wind that the Indians was supplied with plenty ammunition and the best guns our government had. We'd o' got Sheridan's warning in time that thousands o' Indians had left the agencies and was on the warpath. (Note 21.) But no word reached us and we kept on, out o' Dakota and into Montana, the hull o' the Seventh Cavalry, horses and men and mules and wagons, with Terry's men and Gib-

bon's men close by, and *The Far West* steamin' up the
river bringin' extra rations.

"I disremember all the partic'lars of our march across
Montana Territory, it bein' so long ago, more'n fifty
years ago, Bud. Time flies. In some ways it seems jist
like yisterday. We was about a month gittin' from
Fort Lincoln to the mouth of the Rosebud whar we met
Gibbon and Terry and *The Far West*. The days was
all purty much alike, ridin' on and on, blazin' our own
trail, havin' a hell of a time, sometimes, when wagons
'ud git mired in mud, or when we'd have to double up
climbin' a butte. They'd be days when we'd make forty
miles, other days when we'd have to plow through mud
and not make more'n ten. Times we'd march in the
rain. Twice we got caught in hail storms that beat the
tar out o' us and left the horses bleedin' considerable.
Often we wouldn't make noon camp, jist takin' time off
fur a snitch o' raw bacon and hardtack, whilst the horses
eat their oats out o' nose bags. And the horses got gaunt
and when they stood their heads dropped and they had
a tired, hungry look in their eyes. They was days they
didn't have nothin' except bark we stripped off'n cottonwood trees fur 'em. And they was times when we had
to make dry camp at night arter a long march under a
sun's hot as all blazes, a leetle mite o' water fur us that
we carried in our canteens but none fur the dumb

"Some of Us Was Scrambling up the Cliff."

A Deep Ravine Led from Our Hill.

First Monument Marking Grave of Captain Keogh.
Courtesy of Judge Goddard.

Phantom Hosts on Custer Hill.
Photograph Taken in 1876.
Courtesy of Judge Goddard.

brutes. It kinda took the tuck out o' a man, Bud, seein' the sufferin' look in their eyes. And then nights, when we was all tired out, horses and men, they was the damned mosquitoes to fight. It all comes back to me, the nights so dark and still, no sound except men cursin' and moanin' and slappin' whilst they lay sprawled on the ground, tryin' to sleep, and horses picketed out to graze, fidgetin' and stompin' and shiverin' off the mosquitoes, and the crunch of night guards' feet on dry grass, and their call, regular, 'All's well!' or maybe, occasional, a sharp: 'Who's thar?' when they seen a shadder movin' from behind a tree or rock, which more'n likely was a scout creepin' in to camp.

"It want never no Indians, and that seemed mighty peculiar to us, knowin' we was in infected country. But they was movin' on, steady, slow, toward the west, jist a leetle ahead o' us, more'n ten thousand of 'em, savin' their strength and ammunition fur the big fight.

"Our line strung out fur miles, the color bearers, the Cavalry band, the troopers ridin' four abreast in formation, scouts both sides and in front and rear, watchin' continual fur signs of the enemy, and Custer, settin' on fust Dandy and then Vic, tryin' to be everywhar at oncst keepin' up the spirits of the men, seein' to it that they want no drinkin' goin' on, and behind come the pack mules and the wagons rumblin' along.

"Arter we got aways into Montana the band didn't play nights no more and we was mighty careful about campfires, boilin' coffee quick and puttin' out the fires instant, lest the smoke give the enemy inklin' of our whereabouts. And nights we lay on the ground, not settin' up no tents except fur the officers, each trooper by his horse, and we kept the horses saddled and bridled ready to mount instant at command.

"All about us was the mountains and buttes and coulees and they was still—too damned still, Bud, no sign of life anywhar, and yet we knowed that from peaks sharp eyes was watchin' us, and whilst we rid along, quiet, no laughin' and shoutin' and singin' of songs, no sound but the thud o' our horses' feet and creak o' saddle leather and rumble o' wagons, our nerves got on edge. We had a feelin' that somethin' more serious than usual was goin' to happen and we was all anxious fur it to happen quick.

"Many and many a time we rid through a rain and laid down at night in our wet clothes and got up at reveille wet and cold and stiff to ride on agin. Don't know which was worse, that, or marchin' under hot sun fur hours and hours, sufferin' from thirst and findin' no stream. Sometimes we'd come to buffalo wallows with a leetle water so muddy we'd have to chew it, and awful glad to git it too.

"Don't know's you care fur what I'm tellin' you, Bud. Maybe it ain't what you'd properly put into a book but it's sich things that makes up army life. Fightin' ain't so hard. You git all excited and kinda like it but the jist endurin' this and that, day in and day out, mile arter mile, seein' horses droppin' in their tracks, petered out, shootin' 'em and goin' on, that's what takes guts. One time one o' the horses broke it's leg scramblin' down a steep place and had to be shot. The fellow that owned him broke down and cried like a baby.

"Wall, by'n by, long 'bout the middle o' June, we reached the mouth o' the Rosebud whar it empties into the Yellowstone. Whilst we was a long ways off we could look down and see *The Far West* anchored thar. It gave us a kinda comfortin' feelin' and cheered us up considerable, gittin' in touch with the outside agin, arter more'n a month marchin' through wild, lonesome country. Soon's they spied us they begun to cheer and Custer had our band strike up Gary Owen. Captain Marsh was thar and General Gibbon and General Terry. *The Far West* was loaded with provisions and ammunition and forage and Jamaica Ginger and some liquor. They was letters for some o' the men from Fort Lincoln and even from the East. None fur me, me havin' no kin nowhar. Custer got a lot o' letters from Miss Libby. He went over and set under a tree, alone, to read 'em. Arter while he called to me.

" 'John,' he said, 'Miss Libby wants I should tell you the hounds are missin' you.'

"Which o' course I knowed without tellin'.

"That same day, unless I disremember, Reno and his troops come in from a scoutin' expedition, him and his men and horses and pack mules tuckered out complete. They'd scouted up the Rosebud and found a big, deserted Sioux camp, all signs pointin' to about a thousand warriors. Reno followed their trail till he was sure they was makin' tracks fur the Big Horn then he come back. I often think if he'd gone on jist a leetle further he might o' found out they was ten thousand Indians 'stead o' one and then the hull plan o' campaign 'ud been different, but I ain't blamin' him none fur that.

"That evening I seen Custer go into the cabin of *The Far West* whar Gibbon and Terry was. It was late when he left the boat and come to his tent, Terry and Gibbon walkin' longside him. They all stood jabberin' awhile jist outside the tent. I was inside puttin' things to rights. I heerd their voices mumblin', laughin' occasional, but I couldn't catch much they said fur reason Tuck, layin' on Custer's cot, heerd his voice too and set up a bark.

"One of 'em—I think it was Terry—said, 'Goodbye and good luck.'

"And then Custer laughed kinda excited and said, 'Thanks. We may be needin' a lot o' luck.'

"Then the other two left and the General come into his tent. He stood fur a minute, jist starin' straight ahead, frowin', not seein' me or Tuck or Bleuch or nothin', and then he turned and went out quick and right away officer's call was sounded. When we was lined up at attention he give his orders. By that time it was dark but we could see his face a leetle. It was awful sober. He talked quick and short. We was to start early in the morning fur a fifteen day's march. We was to carry, each, one hunderd rounds of ammunition and twelve pounds of oats in our saddle bags. We had a feelin', whilst he talked, that things was serious. Already we was tired from our long march, horses and men and mules. The pack mules of Reno's command, partic'lar, jist back from the scoutin' trip was nigh petered out. Custer want like some officers, never thinkin' of the feelin's of his men. We knowed, when he hustled us on that way, without rest, it was purty serious. That was the night of June twenty-first.

"Arter we fell out I went back to Custer's tent whar I was doin' guard duty till twelve. Purty soon he come along and they was two officers with him and they was all talkin' kinda quick and excited, arguin' over some-thin'. One of 'em, General Godfrey, 'peared to think the mules couldn't carry so much. At the door Custer turned as if he was mad and he said, 'We'll more'n likely have to live on horsemeat 'fore we git through.'

"Godfrey and Custer was friends. Whatever they was arguin' about they want mad at one another. When the General come into his tent, knowin' him so well, I seen he was purty much worked up over somethin'. He didn't joke none with me. He didn't pay no at-tention to the dogs, even when Tuck tried to worm his way up onto his lap. He set on the edge of his cot, frownin', starin' ahead. I don't think he went to bed atall that night. I went outside and patroled my beat. Purty soon Boss—that was the General's brother—he come and asked was Custer inside. I told him yes and he went in and talked jist a minute and left. Then Autie Reed, Custer's nephew, come rushin' in. He was all excited. 'Is Uncle George inside?' he asked me. When he come out Custer stood fur a minute in the door with him and put a hand on his shoulder.

" 'You ain't goin' with us, Autie,' he said. 'You're goin' up on *The Far West* with Captain Marsh.'

"The boy didn't say nothin'. He went away, walkin' slow, his head hangin'.

"Most the night Custer set up writin'. Oncst he

called to me. 'John,' he said, 'I'm writin' to Mrs. Custer. What shall I say fur you?'

"I stuck my head inside the flap o' the tent. 'Tell her, General,' I said, 'that I'm aimin' to take care o' Tuck and you and Bleuch and Vic and Dandy best I kin.'

" 'She knows that, John,' he said, 'without my tellin'.'

" 'And tell her not to worry 'bout the hounds killin' the regiment cats, they bein' too many anyhow, and not to give away any o' our pups in exchange.'

"Custer laughed. 'I'll tell her, John,' he said

"I tried to think of other things that'd make him laugh. 'Tell her, General, that when we git back to Fort Lincoln I want she should tell me how old she is.'

"He said, 'All right,' and I went back outside and took up my beat, back and forth. I'll never forgit that night, Bud, as long as I live. In front of every officer's tent some guard was patrolling. Off in the shadows clear 'round the camp was other guards patrollin', back and forth, back and forth. Fur a while, across the river, in the cabin of *The Far West* they was a light twinklin'. They was probably playin' poker down thar and maybe drinkin' some. Thar'd been a lot o' drinkin' goin' on that day amongst the troopers and some officers, they bein' human and liquor tastin' good to their innards arter so much alkali water. Some of them, though, havin' given their word to Miss Libby afore we left Fort Lincoln, never touched a drop. Two officers in partic'lar, that was under pledge to Miss Libby, fell with Custer in the last charge.

"The night was dark and cloudy, I recollect; no moon, jist a few stars showin'. They was some drops o' rain spatterin' on the tents and wind sorta hissin' and shiverin' through the cottonwoods, then the light went out on *The Far West* and all got still. Here and thar was blotches whar men was layin' asleep on the ground. You couldn't hear nothin' except horses munchin' their feed or nickerin' soft to one another. From fur away, down at the Indian camp, whar the Ree scouts and Crow scouts was, they was dancin' their death dances and havin' their death powwows. The Indians is like dogs. They can sorta smell death a long ways off. The beat o' their tomtoms, when everything else was so still, sent cold chills up and down my spine. Arter while Tuck come out the tent and nozzled his nose agin my hand and took to marchin' with me, back and forth, kinda like he wanted to help guard the General.

"I was tickled to have him along fur company. Queer thoughts git to runnin' through a fellow's head, Bud, all alone under the shadow of the mountains with the stars blinkin' down at him. He gits to wonderin' jist whar he come from and whar he'll go to when he dies.

I was brung up a Catholic but I shied away from religion arter I got out into the world. Seemed like bein'
honest and doin' my duty as I seen it was about all the
religion I had time fur. Wall, I got to wonderin' how
fur away the stars was and how long they'd been a-shin-
in'. Got to wonderin' was they folks up in the stars
lookin' down at us same's we was lookin' up at 'em and
was they on the war path aimin' to kill one another
same's we. A fellow gits to feelin' skeered and lonesome and sorta little and helpless like out alone in the
night with plenty time to think.

"Purty soon Tuck set down on his haunches and
stretched up his muzzle and begun to howl. It sounded
like the death howl. Maybe it was the sound o' the tomtoms set him goin' but I'm substitious as hell, Bud, and
I didn't like fur him to do that. I tried to shut him up.

"Arter him and me'd been patrollin' fur what seemed
years 'stead o' one night thar come streaks of light
across the sky and I went in to wake the General accordin' to orders. He must o' jist dropped off. He was
hunched over on the cot, jist his coat and boots off, and
the pen still in his hand. I hated to 'rouse him, he
looked so peaked and tired. We was the same age,
Custer and me, lackin' three months, but he allus
seemed like a boy to me. He was the youngest officer
in the command.

"When I spoke to him he jumped up, spry as a cricket, wide awake. He was awful strong, not needin' much rest, like most men does. He said, 'What's the day like outside?'

He was glad when I told him it was clear and shiny. It'd be easier on us not havin' to march in the rain.

Purty soon the buglers sounded reveille. That was allus a nice sound, Bud, floatin' in the mornin' air, even though it meant gittin' up and stirrin' when we was all dead tired. Right away all was hustle and bustle, officers and men rushin' 'round camp, horses nickerin' fur their oats and sich. All over the valley they was little camp fires started and men runnin' down to the river fur water and choppin' wood and squattin' aside the fires, cookin' coffee and bacon. The smell of bacon and wood smoke was good to a man's nozzles that mornin'.

"Oncst whilst I was takin' down the General's tent and packin' his belongin's Silent Charles—Charlie Reynolds, the scout (Note 22)—he come to me and his face was gaunt.

" 'This damned hand,' he said, 'kept me awake all night. Dr. Porter says it's a felon. He says I ain't fit to march but I'm goin' along. Do you know anything to do fur it?'

"I knowed a bread-and-milk poultice was good fur a

[138]

felon, but not havin' no milk and not havin' no bread I mixed up some hardtack and water and plastered it on his thumb and wrapped it up fur him. When Silent Charlie rid out of camp with the Seventh the mornin' of the twenty-fifth he was still wearin' that bandage but when I seen his body at the foot o' Reno Hill it want on his hand."

CHAPTER X

A JOUST WITH WAITING DEATH

"WALL, if I recollect right it was 'long about noon of the twenty-second that we had the officers' tents down and packed, horses and mules watered, fifteen days' rations and ammunition passed out and we was ready to start on our march to the Little Big Horn whar, accordin' to Reno's scouts, the Indians was congregated. We had a guide with us now, Muggins Taylor, besides six Crow scouts—Curly, White Swan, Half-Yellow Face and three others whose names I disremember. This was Crow country and they knowed every inch of it and we was tickled to have 'em along.

"I can't say as any o' the Seventh felt specially glum that morning, except maybe some that'd lost in poker the night afore. We knowed we was goin' into a big fight and that out o' the six hunderd of us thar was some wouldn't come back, but that sort o' thing a soldier takes fur granted. Jist afore we started they was a lot squattin' on their haunches scribblin' letters to send on the boat that was goin' down the river. Fur most o' them they was the last letters they ever writ. But the feelin' in general was that we was proud as hell 'cause it was the Seventh bein' sent out to git the Indians 'stead o' Gibbon's men or Terry's.

"Bud, I reckon they ain't never been no regiment looked so fit as we did that day. Six hunderd of us, besides Crow and Ree scouts and Custer's brother and Autie Reed and the newspaper man, Mark Kellog. (Note 23.) Our horses all pranced excited like, as though they was hankerin' to git into a fight and the regimental colors flowed in the breeze and the band was a-playin'. I can see Custer in his broad-rimmed hat and buckskin hat settin' on Dandy so proud and Dandy frettin' and dancin'. I can see young Autie Reed tickled to death 'cause he was havin' his own way and goin' along spite of the General. I can see our hull column, four abreast, passin' in review afore Gibbon and Terry to the tune o' Garry Owen and I can hear the cheer Gibbon's men set up whilst we marched by.

"I'd saddled Dandy fur Custer and held the bridle whilst he mounted. At the last I seen him lean from the saddle to shake hands with Terry and, at something they said, I heerd 'em laugh. Then the bugle sounded 'Forward!' and I took my place along side the pack train under McDougal which was whar the officer of the day ordered me, and Custer dashed on ahead and we was off.

"That fust day arter leaving the Yellowstone we followed the Rosebud fur a short spell and camped early. I hear thar's a lot o' talk about Custer makin' forced marches in a hurry to git to the Indian village and attack ahead o' Terry and Gibbon. That's a damned lie. It bein' so long ago I disremember the exact number o' miles we marched each day but I know till up to the last day and night we went slow, havin' good nights' rest and takin' plenty o' time off whilst the scouts examined the country.

They was signs all along tellin' us we was on the trail o' the redskins. We seen buffaloes with arrows stickin' in their hides. We seen places whar the Indians 'ud camped and held their Sun Dances. One place we found a scalp of a white man tied to a tree. We didn't know who he was. A trapper, maybe, or a lone scout. Nothin' left of what was once a man but that hank o' hair danglin' from a tree.

That fust day out whilst we was followin' the Rosebud the General and me had one o' our quarrels, the last we was ever to have. An orderly come ridin' to me and said as how Custer wanted to see me, so I rid up to him. He said to me, quick and short, 'Why ain't you in your proper place in line?'

"Bein' hot-headed myself I saluted and said, jist as quick and short, that I was whar the officer of the day had put me, guardin' the wagon train. Then I went back and rid along fur a spell, feelin' glum as hell. Purty soon Custer come dashin' back to me, on Dandy, and he said, 'Everything's all right, John. It was my mistake. I'm sorry.'

"That's the way he allus was, flyin' off the handle sudden, maybe sometimes without occasion, but quick to own up when he was in the wrong. Even then, Bud, goin' into battle, with so much on his mind worryin' him, he could take time off to think o' my feelin's, knowin' how his bein' mad at me would rankle.

'I'm glad he did that, Bud. All these years I've had that to be glad fur, that between him and me at the last they want no hard feelin's.

"Fur two days we marched along, keepin' sharp lookout fur stray Indians and seein' none. The days was hot. The sun blazed down on us. Arter we left the Rosebud and struck across toward the Big Horn they want many streams, mostly dry runs. Often, arter marchin' all day, we had to make dry camp at night which was hard on the animals. Some places the mosquitoes pestered us considerable so's we couldn't sleep nights. Oncst, I remember, we got caught in a hail storm that purty nigh caused a stampede. When it was over they was stones big as bullets a foot deep on the ground and the backs of the horses and mules was bleedin'.

"Arter the second day, gittin' closer to whar we surmised the Indian village was located, Custer ordered that they be no bugle calls or band music and that all orders be by signs, and that there be no singin' or shoutin' up and down the line, same's we'd been used to doin' whilst we rid along. He didn't have to tell us that last. Everything was still, the hills, the valleys and the men. A queer sort o' glumness hung over us. Not 'cause we knowed we was goin' into battle, the thought o' fightin' the Redskins didn't skeer us none. All they ever did was shoot a few arrows from behind trees and then run. The idee of the Seventh gittin' licked never entered our minds. But, for all that—maybe you think I'm substitious, Bud—but I believe we had a—a— what's the word?—a kind of presentment of what we was headin' toward. Maybe 'cause Custer was unusual quiet and stern, not cuttin' up tricks with Captain Tom or Boss Custer or Autie Reed the way he'd been doin' ever since we left Fort Lincoln. Not laughin' and jokin' but jist ridin' on and on toward the Indian village in the Little Big Horn. That steady, quiet ridin' through them quiet hills kinda got on a man's nerves. Our column went marchin' four abreast now,

Sitting Bull.

Chief Gall.

Smoky, U. S. Marshall on Crow Reservation.

William White, F Troop, 2nd Cavalry.

but scattered out, lest the dust we stirred up 'ud give the enemy inklin' to our whereabouts.

"Often the General with three or four men 'ud go way ahead the troops, scoutin'. Oncst he took me with him. We seen a good many deserted camps with the grass all tromped down showin' whar they'd been a lot o' horses grazing. We seen trails made by lodge poles draggin' through the dust. Custer said to me, 'We're close on their heels and looks like they's a lot of 'em, more'n we figgered on.'

"I says, 'Not too many to lick, though.'

"He turned then, quick, and flashed a smile at me over his shoulder. 'What the Seventh can't lick,' he said, proud-like, 'the hull U. S. army couldn't lick.'

"We dismounted and let our horses rest and graze whilst we waited fur the troops to catch up. We lay stretched under a tree. Custer didn't talk none, he jist lay starin' up into the sky. That's the last time we was alone together.

"I was one of those detailed to do stable guard duty. Soon's we hit camp, arter rubbin' down and waterin' our own mounts, we was to herd the horses and mules a long way off from camp whilst they grazed, leavin' the grass close by fur night. The night of the twenty-third we kept the mules corralled, which seemed a pity, they bein' somewhat gaunt and they bein' so much grass fur grazin' and we left our horses saddled and bridled and stretched out on the ground aside 'em, the reins linked through our arms, our rifles close by. The camp fires was put out quick. The buglers didn't sound taps. When we talked it was in whispers. Long arter everyone else was asleep I seen a candle light shinin' from Custer's tent.

" 'Long 'bout midnight officers come creepin' through the dark, feelin' their way from man to man, waking us up and we was on the march agin. All day of the twenty-fourth we marched, havin' hardtack and coffee and bacon fur breakfast but takin' no time off fur noonin'. We rid along slow, givin' the scouts plenty o' time to search the hills. We probably didn't git more'n twenty-five miles that day. All the way along Custer showed hisself anxious to save the strength of men and horses. He didn't rush us forward till we was exhausted as some folks nowadays say he did. Then and allus he was fur savin' our feelin's when he could. But I know, Bud, they was some officers in the regiment that want above spreadin' discontent among the men, makin' 'em feel Custer was hard on 'em 'cause he punished 'em fur drinkin' and sich. No man o' the Seventh that come nigh doin' his duty ever complained about Custer bein' too strict.

"Wall, late on the evenin' of the twenty-fourth we

made camp, fed and watered the animals or doin' sich camp duties as fell to us, carryin' water, gittin' firewood and sich. About eight-thirty we bedded down and went to sleep right off. Seems as though I can remember, plain as if 'twas yisterday, how still everything was, valleys and hills, and how I'd think I seen somethin' movin' up on a hill and then find out it was only the shadow of a tree rustlin' in the breeze. Long shadows of the buttes stretched across the plains, makin' all look queer.

"In a leetle while, arter three or four hours, officers come waking us quiet, without soundin' reveille, and we was on the march agin. We marched all night at a slow trot, movin' quiet through the dark, not in formation, but helter skelter, scattered out, and we advanced the best way we could, every man fur hisself. It was pitch dark. We couldn't see one another. When we got strayed too fur away we didn't dast yell. Some of us got lost. Some fell, horse and all, into ravines and had to get out alone the best way they could. The moon had gone under a cloud.

"At daybreak of the twenty-fifth, long about three o'clock I reckon, we had orders to halt. We was in a deep ravine between two high ridges purty well hid from the enemy and thar we made camp—our last all together—unsaddlin' the horses, startin' fires with sage brush and buffalo chips and boilin' coffee. Some o' the men jist laid down and dropped off to sleep, without carin' fur breakfast, they was that tired. We all understood that we'd come to the end o' the march and that it was Custer's intentions to wait here till the twenty-sixth and then jine Terry and Gibbon in the attack. (Note 24.)

"I seen Custer layin' in the brush a leetle ways off, his hat pulled over his eyes. I took him some hot coffee and hardtack. When I spoke to him he didn't answer. He was sound asleep. I woke him up though, and gave him the coffee, thinkin' he needed it, maybe, more'n sleep. The way things turned out I was allus glad I did that.

"When he drunk it he handed me back the cup and smiled. 'Thanks, John,' he says to me, 'I'll tell Miss Libby when we git back how well you've been takin' keer o' me.'

"Then he closed his eyes agin.

"A leetle later whilst I was eatin' my own breakfast the nigger scout, Isaiah Dorman, come to me from whar Varnum was posted with the Ree scouts. He 'peered considerable excited. 'Whar's General Custer?' he asked me.

"I told him the General was restin' and couldn't be

disturbed. The nigger said, 'This is important, Boss. I got a message from Varnum fur the General.'

"So I pointed to the brush whar Custer was layin' and Isaiah went over to him. I didn't hear what they said. I seen Custer get to his feet quick. Purty soon he come rushin' to me. 'Saddle Dandy quick!' he said.

"I acted accordin' and Custer mounted and rid away with Varnum and his scouts. He was gone about two hours. When he come back to camp I seen he'd been ridin' hard. Dandy was pantin' and all white with foam and his nozzles was a-quiverin'. Whilst I rubbed him down Custer had officer's call sounded, jist one low call, and the officers confabbed together fur a spell. We didn't hear what they said, o' course, but it got rumored round that the Indians had got an inklin' of our whereabouts and we was goin' to attack right away, without waitin' fur Gibbon and Terry.

"Then we was lined up and jist accordin' to when the troops answered roll call they was divided, three to Reno, three to Benteen, the pack train to McDougal and five to Custer. I've heerd it said that Custer took his pick of the troops that mornin' but that want so. They was assigned jist as they answered to roll call and it was only happenstance that among the troops fallin' to Custer was his favorite, the grays.

"Bud, I can see the Seventh yet, lined up, as they

was that mornin', ready to start off. Fust Lieutenant Varnum with his scouts, includin' Charlie Reynolds and Isaiah Dorman, then General Custer and his staff, then the hull Seventh. The regiment colors was flyin' and the horses prancin'. The men was joshin' and laughin'. They was bettin' which one'd git the most scalps. They was sayin' they'd be back by noon, ready fur a good feed. Young Autie Reed was tickled pink 'cause he was goin' to git to see real Indian fightin'. He was only a kid, jist seventeen. I went over to him whar he was settin' his horse close to Captain Tom Custer.

" 'Autie,' I says, 'don't go with the General today. Pears like they's goin' to be considerable fightin'. You stay and guard camp.'

"The youngster threw back his head and laughed. He pulled his foot from the stirrup and give me a friendly kick. 'Me stay!' he says. 'When they's goin' to be a fight! Why, John, you're crazy! That's what I come out West fur, to see an Indian fight.'

"I kept on arguin' with him. Bud, I coaxed him with tears in my eyes. Seemed like I couldn't bear his goin' into battle that mornin'. But it want no use. He jist laughed. 'You're mad,' he said, ' 'cause you can't go along.'

"When the battle was over he was found close to his

uncle, Boss Custer, jist a leetle below whar General Custer was layin'.

"Custer called to me then and ordered me to saddle Vic. (Dandy was in the fight up on Reno Hill. I disremember who rid him. He was wounded in the neck but he got well and was arterwards sent back to the General's father.)

"Whilst I was holdin' Vic's bridle, him prancin' considerable, I said to Custer, ' 'Pears like I ought to be goin' along, General.'

"He leaped into the saddle and then he leaned over and put his hand fur a minute on my shoulder. He smiled at me. His moustache was long, almost hidin' his mouth. He was wearin' one of his big, white hats, o' course, and a fringed, buckskin coat.

" 'No, John,' he says to me. 'You've been doin' guard duty three nights in recession. You're tired out. Your place is with McDougal and the pack train. But if we should have to send fur more ammunition you can come in on the home stretch.'

"Them's the last words he ever spoke to me.

"He rid over to Chief Bugler Voss and I heerd him say, laughin', 'Martin's a good bugler, Voss, but today I'm goin' to need one that can understand the English language, since I can't talk Italian.' So Martin (Martini) was replaced by another bugler, a German, whose name I disremember.

"Wall, long 'bout eight o'clock, everythin' bein' ready, the bugler sounded 'Mount!' and 'Forward!' and they all started off along the ridge, lookin' fine, ridin' in columns of four, with Jack Victor, who had the name o' bein' the handsomest pall bearer in the regiment, carryin' the regiment colors. When they found him his right arm, the one that carried our colors, was cut off.

"I can close my eyes, even now, Bud, and see 'em— all o' the Seventh—ridin' off so gay, down into the valley of the Little Big Horn. One of 'em—I think it was Martin—turned in his saddle and hollered back at me, 'Shall we bring you a scalp, John, or do you want a live squaw?'

"Bleuch and Tuck started to follow but I called 'em back and held 'em by the collar. They whimpered and whined considerable whilst we stood, watchin' Custer ridin' out o' sight at the head of his men. They was a little yellow dog, though, that trotted off with the troops. I whistled to him but he didn't pay no attention. Two days arterwards, when they begun buryin' the dead, that little bulldog was still up on the hill, sniffin' 'round among the mutilized bodies fur his master. I never heerd what become of him. Off and on fur years I git to thinkin' about the leetle fellow, wishin' I could've held him back." (Note 25.)

CHAPTER XI

With tattered guidons spectral thin
Above their swaying ranks
With carbine swung and sabres slung
And the gray dust on their flanks
They march again as they marched then
The gloom trail, the doom trail,
The trail they came not back.

"FUR awhile the mornin' of the twenty-fifth the Seventh all rid along together, the men talkin' low and keerful but laughin' a lot. We was headin' fur the valley of the Little Big Horn and we was headin' fur hell but we didn't know it then. Strung all along the river jist over the ridge and down below us was the big Indian village, the biggest Indian force ever gathered to fight the pale faces and they was armed with government rifles, better'n any the Seventh had, and they was headed by sich warriors as Rain-in-the-Face and Chief Gall and Crazy Horse and Crow King. They was waitin' fur us down thar, hid by the trees, ten thousand of 'em, waitin' to put it to a test fur good and all who was to rule their land. But our scouts had only seen a

[153]

few tepees, the rest hid by the trees, and they'd reported about a thousand Indians and so we acted accordin', joggin' along across the plains in the sunshine
sorta easy and keerless.

"Arter while, actin' accordin' to Custer's orders, we
divided. Bein' to the rear with the pack train I didn't
hear what Custer said to Reno, but I know Benteen and
his troops went to the left to scout through the hills.
Reno kept straight ahead with the idee of attacking the
village from the rear whilst Custer and his troops went
to the right, up on top the ridge, to attack the village
from that direction. And McDougal with the pack train
strung along behind, supposed to be on hand to supply
reserve ammunition when needed.

"Bud, circlin' out like that we had the village plumb
surrounded. If the four divisions had acted together
the way they was supposed to do I consume we'd had
the Indians licked and scattered afore night. Custer
knowed Indians and their ways. He knowed they
won't never stand up afore a regiment in formation
and fight 'em face to face. They'd 've fired a few shots
and then escaped, guardin' their women and children,
which was what they started out to do till they seen
Reno retreatin' up the hill.

"Wall, I was one o' the men detailed to guard the
pack train and so I didn't git to hear Custer's last words,

but I seen him ridin' off to the right, up onto the ridge, settin' on Vic, and I seen his face lookin' kinda white and sober-like. He want laughin' none. He knowed he was leadin' his men into a helluva big fight but he didn't figger then that they'd be left to fight and die alone jist two miles further on, up on top the hill. I seen him ridin' away at the head of his troops. I seen his red tie flutter over his shoulder whilst Vic went gallopin' off. And that was the last. I never seen him agin.

"Fur a spell arter that my 'tention was purty much took up with the mules. The night afore we'd made dry camp. It'd been most twenty-four hours since they'd had a drink. So when we come to a water hole the mules stampeded fur it and got out of control. All hell couldn't hold 'em back. Some of their packs fell off. It was boggy thar and a lot of 'em got mired. Sunk into the mud clean down to their bellies. We worked and cussed fur a spell, maybe a couple o' hours or so, gittin' 'em out, and then we watered 'em. That took a leetle more time, not more'n an hour. I know that whilst we was workin' with the mules Benteen come back from out in the hills reportin' that the country was too rough fur travelin' in comfort and he hadn't seen hide nor hair of the enemy. Then he begun waterin' his horses at the same place. He asked whar was Reno and whar was Custer? None of us knowed perxactly, but by that time we knowed thar was fightin' goin' on, ahead o' us in the direction of Reno and to the right beyond the ridge whar Custer had gone. We couldn't hardly see an arm's length away, what with the dust and with the smoke from the grass the Indians had set fire to, but we did hear rifle shots comin' from the direction of Custer. Benteen's troops and Mc-Dougal's was still back whar they couldn't see down into the valley. Fur quite a spell Benteen kept back o' our slow-movin' pack train. Finally he went ahead.

"Now the ravines and the hills was covered with men on horses and with riderless horses but through the smoke and dust we couldn't make out whether 'twas Reno's men or Custer's, or whether 'twas the Redskins. We couldn't make out nothin'. We heerd a warwhoop: 'Hi-yah! Hi-yah!'

"One o' the men tendin' the mules aside me says to me, 'Yellow Hair's givin' 'em hell.'

"We thought Reno and Custer was attackin' the two ends o' the village accordin' to Custer's plans.

"Whilst we was at the water hole waitin' fur the mules to drink, some officer—I consumed from Reno—come dashin' back and cut out one o' the pack mules and rushed it forward.

"Then, whilst we was still waterin' the mules, a man

[156]

on horseback come dashin' to us. It was Martin, the bugler. He come straight from Custer. He was excited. His horse's nozzles was a-quiverin'. He waved his hat and yelled, 'Hurry up, boys. We got 'em.'

"Purty soon another message come from Custer. This time it was Sergeant Knipe. Bein' at the head o' the string of pack mules I was close to McDougal and I heerd the message. Knipe said, 'You're to bring the pack mules straight across the country. Come quick. Thar's a big Indian camp. Tell Benteen to come quick. Custer's runnin' out o' ammunition up thar. Hurry up!'

"But, Bud, we didn't hurry. We finished waterin' the mules. I don't know whether that message ever got to Benteen or not. I never heerd the rights of that. I do know that Benteen jined Reno 'stead o' Custer, and I do know that when we did git started our pack outfit was strung out fur a long ways, jist stragglin' along, and that us that was in the lead had orders to hold up and wait fur the rear to catch up. We waited thar when twenty minutes' ride would got us to Custer with ammunition and guns and fresh horses and six troops. Maybe, had we gone to him then, 'stead o' loiterin' and then jinin' Reno, the hull story of Custer's last charge would be writ different. But we didn't hurry. We in advance jist stood thar waitin' fur the rear to catch up, whilst up on the hill whar we could 've seen if we'd gone to the top o' the ridge Custer and his men was firin' their last bullets, maybe lookin' continual fur the reenforcements that never come.

"Bud, did you ever try to figger out how those men must've felt up thar, what must a gone through their heads, the Indians surroundin' them, and then waitin' fur us, lookin' fur us comin' across the ridge, then firin' at a Redskin, backin' up and backin' up, men fallin' here and fallin' thar, in leetle groups or all alone, their guns stickin', then feelin' in their belts and findin' their last cattrige gone, and still no sight o' us comin'?

"Wall, thinkin' won't bring any one o' the two hunderd back agin. It bothers me considerable, even yet, rememberin' how Martin looked when he give Benteen the message and went dashin' past us, yellin', 'Fur God's sake, boys, hurry to Custer. He's run out o' ammunition.' I yelled at him. I tried to git him to stop and tell how things was goin' up thar. He wouldn't stop. He wouldn't listen.

"More'n likely Custer died thinkin' that neither one o' his messengers got through to us. I hope so. He'd ruther think that, than that part of the Seventh failed him.

"Jist about that time along come some Ree scouts with Billy Cross and a half-breed scout and Curly.

[158]

They driv about eighty head o' Sioux horses they'd captured and they was bein' followed by some Sioux. One of the officers yelled out, 'Let them damned horses go or you'll have the hull pack of Indians down on us.'

"Curly didn't want to let his horses go. One of 'em, I recollect, was a buckskin with a white face. But some soldiers rounded up the bunch and driv 'em back. This was when we was hearin' the fust shots over on Custer Hill so you can see by that, Bud, that Curly lies when he says he was in the fight.

"Then McDougal and Benteen jined and we had orders to advance double quick. We did advance, rifles drawn, most of us thinkin' we was goin' to Custer. I ain't never blamed McDougal fur nothin'. He was a brave man and a good officer and he was Custer's friend. He wouldn't never have failed his general on purpose.

"Wall, we dashed ahead and topped a raise and thar, down below us, we seen Reno's men retreatin' from the valley. Some of 'em was fordin' the river. Some of 'em was scramblin' up the cliff whar it was awful steep, hell bent fur Sunday, horses and men all mixed to-gether, and the Indians arter them. They didn't all git to the top. About forty o' Reno's men fell on the river bottom. Silent Charlie was hit jist at the foot of the cliff. Some fell half way up. Lieutenant Hodgson tumbled off his horse jist as he was on top.

"The men was skeered, bein' human. Their main idee jist then was to git away from the Indian bullets and Reno was leadin' 'em all in the retreat. They want cowards, them men, none of 'em. With a brave general at the head they'd stood and faced the enemy to the last man but excitement and fear is contagious. And Reno was excited, he was skeered out o' his wits and he was half drunk. Under him, his men was like stampeded cattle. (Note 26.)

"Bud, maybe you've heerd tell as how Reno had to use his six-shooter to keep his men from retreating. Bud, that's a damn lie. He led the retreat. Penwell was Reno's bugler. He was close to Reno most o' the time. He backs me up in what I say. Burdick was thar too, and Godfrey. They'll tell you the same thing. He had a red handkerchief tied round his head. His face was smeared with blood—some other fellow's blood, not his—and he kept yellin' orders nobody could understand. His eyes was a-bulgin' and he was shoutin', 'Do this,' and then, 'Do that.' And we didn't know what to do or whar to go.

"McDougal's fust question when we got to the ridge and seen Reno's men scramblin' up the tother side was, 'Whar's Custer?' But Reno was thinkin' more of his own hide than anything else jist then and he didn't answer.

"Some one else said, 'How do you s'pose Custer's makin' it?'

"Then I heerd Wallace answer, snappy-like, 'That's jist one way to find out.'

"I seen his eyes flash when he said that. We was all under Reno. Wallace knowed actin' agin him meant maybe courtmartial. But he argued with him. So did Weir and Edgerly and McDougal. They wanted to fight, to go to help Custer, to do anything 'cept hide behind rifle pits like cowards.

"McDougal says, 'Can't we reconnoitre?'

"But Reno yelled, 'No! Stay whar you be. Them Indians has got some trap planned fur us.'

"Every one kept sayin', 'We ought to go to Custer.' And Reno'd appear to agree. Then, when we'd git started, he'd order us back.

"Then Wallace said, 'Commander or no commander, I'm goin'!' He yelled to his men, orderin' 'em to mount and charge, and they acted accordin', every man of 'em, prompt, and they went chargin' down into the valley which was all a-fire and filled with smoke and with Indians firin' and yellin'. Him and his men went right down into that hell, aimin' to cross the valley and git to Custer, but by that time it was too late. He couldn't git through, but even if he'd made it across the valley

and up onto tother ridge I reckon they want nothin'
left fur him or any other man to do fur Custer.

"We didn't know that then, though. We set up a
cheer whilst we watched him and his men plungin'
down into that awful bunch o' shootin' Indians.

"Then, bein' kept purty busy with this and that, we
forgot him fur a spell. The top o' that thar hill was
shaped like a wash basin. We could crouch down and
shoot over the ridge and duck agin, purty well per-
tected from the enemy, 'cept from them occupyin' a
higher hill. Most o' the enemy was down below us
at the foot o' the steep cliff. Our idee was to keep 'em
thar. If they'd circled the hill and attacked us from
the rear, whar they want nothin' fur miles but a wide,
open sweep o' plains, they could 've got us, every man,
like they did Custer. They talk a lot about them chiefs
bein' sich good generals. Seems like a good general
would 've thought o' that. Lucky fur us they didn't.

"All that arternoon o' the twenty-fifth me and others
was detailed to dig holes fur the men to lay in and make
ramparts which we did accordin'. Some o' them rifle
pits are still up thar atop o' Reno Hill, Bud, back o'
prarie dog mounds, the way we dug 'em more'n fifty
years ago. And we drug up bodies o' dead horses and
piled 'em in front o' the pits fur fortifications, wedgin'
blankets and saddles and packin' boxes and mess cups

and sich in between the chinks and thar we lay all the rest o' the twenty-fifth and the twenty-sixth and seventh till Terry and Gibbon got to us the mornin' of the twenty-eighth with the sun blazin' hot and the Indians shootin' up at us from down below and down on us from the hills. Three long days o' hell.

"Soldiers in a fight are purty much like animals, Bud. They ain't s'posed to think, they jist do what they're told to do. Their superior officer does the thinkin' fur 'em. But up thar our superior officer was too skeered to think and his skeer got into our innards too. The Seventh was fightin' men, every last one o' 'em, nat'rally brave, but when their officer was out o' his wits they sensed it the same way a horse senses it when his rider's lost control and they acted accordin'. With a real man to lead us that day I want one of us wouldn't 've gone plungin' down that cliff and charged the Indians and fought 'em like soldiers, maybe licked 'em, too, 'cause Indians ain't ones to stand up agin a face-to-face battle. Wallace tried it with his little bunch o' men. McDougal wanted to. So did Weir and Edgerly and French. All of us 'cept Reno had a feelin' we orter go to Custer but Reno, even arter the Indians'd left us, kept sayin', 'Not yet. Wait awhile,' he said. 'Them Indians'll come back. They got a trap set fur us. Stay whar you are,' he said.

"And so we stayed, like skeered animals in a trap, and shot away our ammunition and the sun beat down on us hot as blazes and our throats was parched fur water. I never did hear how many Indians we killed that day, not very many, though. They buried 'em arterwards in trees and caves in a ravine at the foot o' Reno Hill. You kin still see some o' the skeletons thar, and the beads and trinkets Indians put with their dead. Reno lost three officers, fifty-three men, includin' scouts and sich, most of 'em durin' the retreat up the hill. When the rescue party come to us, on the twenty-eighth, one of 'em—Terry or Gibbon—I think it was Terry, he said to Reno, sharp and quick, 'I see a good many soldiers dead or wounded,' he says, 'but whar are the dead Indians?'

"As I say, the men caught the skeer from the coward Reno and acted accordin'. Dan Neally—he's livin' at Gilt Edge, Montana now—he's been goin' all these years as 'Cracker-box Dan' on account of durin' the fight he kept hid back of a cracker box. And Captain Miles Morland—I've heerd he was buried in Los Angeles a spell back—he was known as 'Aparejo Mickie' 'cause all the time he was layin' behind an aparejo. And then they was young Billy Blake, a private. Fur two days up thar he made out like he was wounded and laid with the wounded so's he wouldn't have to fight, and he want hurt atall. Arter it was over and he come to his senses poor Billy was ashamed o' hisself. He couldn't stand the joshin' he got from the rest o' us and so he got transferred to another company. Now, Billy and Cracker-box Dan and Morland was brave men, nat'ral, good soldiers, but the skirmish they'd been through down below with Reno, plumb out o' his head with skeer yellin' orders they couldn't hear, and the panicky retreat up the hill kinda made 'em crazy fur the time bein'. They was like riderless horses in a fire.

"Bud, all the time I was workin' in the awful heat, draggin' dead horses fur to make breastworks, firin' down at the Indians, I kept wonderin', 'whar was Custer?' And the men that worked with me kept sayin', 'What d'you s'pose happened to Custer?'

"Some of 'em said maybe he'd gone to jine Terry but most of us knowed better than that. We knowed he wouldn't leave us in the lurch 'cause that wasn't his way ever, and along with the heat and the cravin' fur water, constant, was the worry about Custer.

"At fust, whilst we worked, early on the twenty-fifth, we could see a lot o' smoke and dust across on tother ridge. Jist a leetle ways, it was, Bud. About then most o' the Indians left us and went in that direction. If we'd followed 'em—if we'd attacked their rear 'stead o' lettin' 'em bunch up agin Custer—maybe he'd be livin' today. But we didn't. We stayed hid back o' the rifle pits. We heerd some shots fired from over thar. Some one spoke up and laughed and said, 'Reckon Custer's givin' the red devils hell.'

"We kept listenin'. We heerd a volley fired, and then, arter a minute, another. Folks figger now that that was Custer's signal of distress, his last call fur us to come to him. If we'd walked jist a leetle ways, jist up to the next ridge, we could o' seen down onto Custer Hill. But we didn't. Then arter while they want no more shots from over thar and the smoke cleared away and the dust settled.

"Don't know's I kin tell things in reg'lar order, Bud. It's a long time to remember back and even then, what with the firin' and the heat and the torment fur water and our worryin' about Custer and the yellin', shootin', ridin' Indians down below, we was bemuddled. But purty soon Wallace come back up the hill and he was licked. They want many of his men left with him. The rest had been killed down in the brush, tryin' to git through to Custer. But they want to be pitied, those men want. They died like soldiers. I'd ruther be one o' them than to live on, branded a coward.

"Don't git me wrong, Bud. We want all cowards. A lot o' gallantry was showed that day. Some men volunteered to go down right in the face o' Indian fire, to rescue the wounded that was strung here and thar 'long the side o' the cliff. We was all cravin' water. The wounded suffered most. Doctor Porter—he was a good one and a brave fellow—he worked like a beaver, easin' the sufferin' best he could. What with the heat, blood pizen set in quick. I seen him, one time in partic'lar, amputize a fellow's leg. I seen the man lay thar, his face white's a sheet, his lips set tight, not a moan out o' him, nothin' but his eyes tellin' how it hurt. Doctor Porter says, 'My wounded has got to have water! Who'll volunteer to go arter it?'

"Bud, thar was the river jist below us, millions o' gallons of water a-ripplin' and a-sparklin' along, but betwixt us and it was the Indians, shootin' any one that made toward it. A deep ravine led from our hill and men could crawl down through it almost to the river but then there was a short stretch of open space and to dash across it to the water meant death, sure's sartain. Our hankerin' fur a drink got terrible. We sucked raw potatoes. We held pebbles in our mouths. Nothin' helped much. We'd all of us, horses and men, 've sold our souls fur a drink o' that water we could see flowin' along; but the wounded, o' course, was in the worst fix. When Doctor Porter spoke up some men volunteered and crept down the ravine carryin' buckets and kettles and canteens. I started with them. My horse got hit in the flank and I come back, figgerin' I'd jist as soon die of thirst as an Indian bullet. Some of 'em made it. One fellow was hit jist as he stooped over to fill his bucket and the pail was shot away and his leg was shattered. He hung on to another fellow's stirrup and was dragged back up the hill. Arterwards that leg had to be amputized. Most o' them that went down brung back a leetle water, jist enough so' the doctor could trickle it into the mouths of the wounded. Arter that from time to time men kept slippin' down through the ravine to the river, but I didn't try it agin.

"I seen Dandy shot in the neck. Don't recollect who was ridin' him. I seen him fall. He was a purty leetle horse, dark brown. Never could stand to have any other horse ahead o' him. Custer'd got him in '68 and I thought, 'The General'll feel purty bad when I tell him Dandy was killed.'

"I remembered his sayin' jist as we left Fort Lincoln that he'd have to git another horse 'cause Dandy was beginnin' to show his age a bit. He lay thar, jist like he was sleepin' and I thought of all the good times him and Custer'd had gallopin' hell bent fur Sunday across the plains and the tears come to my eyes whilst I stroked his neck. Then he opened his eyes and they was big and soft and sufferin' and he give a leetle nicker.

[168]

I knowed he was beggin' fur water. He was wonderin' why I didn't take keer o' him same's always.

"Wall, the long, hot day dragged on. Seemed like a year to us up thar, us not knowin' whar Custer was, and not knowin' what minute the Indians 'ud charge us from the rear whar they want no cliffs fur pertection. Thinkin' back on it now, Bud, it all seems like a bad dream, seems like it couldn't 've happened. And I git to thinkin', 'maybe it is a dream. Maybe, arter while, I'll wake up, and I won't be old, and I'll be back with the Seventh, tendin' Bleuch and Tuck and Vic and Dandy and Miss Libby'll be thar, and the General'll be around, laughin', jokin', wearin' his big, white hat, same's allus.

"But the bad dream won't never end, I know, till I git the guts to end it.

"All durin' the twenty-fifth and sixth whilst the Indians down below was firin' up at us they was a fellow on a hill overlookin' ours that kept poppin' down at us with a long range buffalo gun. He was a good shot. We couldn't see him but every time his gun popped down dropped one o' our men or a horse or a mule. That Indian did more to pester us than all the bunch down below. Toward the last Captain Ryan got him with a long range gun. Arter the fight I went over to the hill and seen him layin' thar, the buffalo

[169]

gun still in his hand, back o' some boulders he'd piled up fur breastworks.

"Long towards night o' the fust day—the twenty-fifth—the smoke cleared some in the valley and most of the Indians begun dwindlin' away, goin' back to thar village fur a spell o' restin' and mournin' fur their dead, leavin' jist enough warriors around to keep us up thar on the hill. None o' us had eat since leavin' camp with Custer early that day. We chewed on hardtack and raw bacon but the vittals was like hay scratchin' down our dry throats, without any water. All of us was purty much petered out. A lot o' the men jist dropped in their tracks and went to sleep, too tired to keer what happened next. I was one of them detailed to do night guard. I had to guard Reno's tent. He had a keg in thar and he was drinkin' considerable. I couldn't see in but I could hear. Oncst, as I was marchin' past, I heerd him say to another officer that was with him, 'Wall,' he says, 'I wonder whar the Murat of the American army is by this time!'

"And then I heerd them both laugh. I never knowed what 'Murat' meant, but I knowed he was meanin' Custer, and I knowed they was a sneer in his laugh.

"It was dark. I kept on marchin' back and forth in front o' his tent. Here and thar on the ground was splotches whar men was stretched out, sleepin', and they was other dark splotches, bodies of dead horses and dead men. It got awful quiet. Down in the valley whar all day thar'd been fire and smoke, screamin' horses, yellin' Indians it was dark and still. From fur away come the beat o' tomtoms and the wailin' of Indians moanin' fur their dead. No other sound 'cept rustle o' cottonwoods and the swish of the river. Every leetle while I'd stop trompin' back and forth and listen, thinkin' I heerd low voices and crunch o' horses feet, thinkin' maybe it was Custer and his men creepin' up to us through the dark. I kept strainin' my eyes across toward the ridge whar he'd last been seen and seemed like my hull body ached jist to know whar he was. But all night nothin' happened and by'n by mornin' broke."

CHAPTER XII

For a soldier to die bravely is one thing; to die calmly and with
perfect discipline when he knows himself abandoned is quite
another. Custer's men fell company by company where they
stood.

Still on the hills above the Little Big Horn waves an invisible
guidon, the honor guidon of the Seventh saved by the courage of
a regiment which fired its own last proud salute.

Charles Francis Bates, Col. U.S.A.

"THE mornin' of the twenty-sixth broke kinda cloudy
and they was even a few spatters of rain which cheered
us considerable. We all scurried around settin' out
kettles and buckets and stretchin' canvass—anything
that would hold water. Men everywhar was holdin' up
tin cups to ketch raindrops. But purty soon the clouds
rolled away and the sun shone scorchin' hot on us up
thar on that hill, and down in the valley the Indians
was gatherin' full force agin, settin' fire to the grass
so's we couldn't see them plain and guardin' us from
gettin' down to the river fur a drink.

"And this day was purty much like the day afore, us
hidin' behind the breastworks we'd made, poppin' up

[172]

our heads to shoot down at the red, yellin' devils, duckin' agin, swelterin' in the heat, hankerin' fur water, wonderin' whar was Custer, wonderin' when would it all end. We couldn't go on furever without a drink. It was tough on us young, strong fightin' men and the wounded was in an awful fix, but, Bud, it was most pitiful watchin' the horses suffer, them bein' thar agin their will and not understandin' the whyfur o' things. More'n twenty-four hours, now, since most of us had drunk. All day men kept sneakin' down through the coulee then makin' a dash to the river to dip up a leetle water, but what they brung back natural was give to the wounded.

"And all the while we kept sayin' to one another, 'What's happened across the valley and up on tother ridge? Whar's Terry? Whar's Custer? Why don't some one come to our rescue?'

"Not a word from our general since the day afore when he'd sent a messenger to Benteen beggin' him to come quick. Among a few o' the officers—Reno and Benteen and sich—they was some hintin' that maybe Custer'd been defeated and had jined Terry, desertin' us, but they want many troopers thar that believed sich damn lies. Us that had fit with Custer fur years knowed him too well. We knowed that in all the years we'd been with him he'd never once shirked his duty

[173]

nor never oncst thought of danger for hisself. We knowed that he loved the Seventh, Bud, every last man of us. Allus when we needed him thar he allus was. We knowed that and so did every officer up·thar on the hill, so did Reno and Benteen know it too. If he didn't git to us now it was 'cause he couldn't. What with the heat and thirst we begun gittin' kinda woozie in our heads. We kept sayin' continual, 'Wonder what's happened to Custer?' and we kept strainin' to see through the smoke in the valley fur a sight of him comin'.

"Time and agin durin' the twenty-fifth and sixth we come close to mutinizin' and strikin' out, to go to Custer, 'spite o' Reno bein' our superior officer. Some of the officers had conflabs, arguin' and janglin' with Reno, tellin' him Custer'd be needin' fresh men and horses and more ammunition and we orter go. They'd point across the valley all thick with dust and smoke and yellin' Indians to the ridge whar thar was still a lot o' shootin' and yellin'. Them was the Indians on the battle field celebratin' their victory and it was too late to do Custer any good but 'course we didn't know that then.

"Wall, as I kept sayin', they's a lot o' 'if's' in life, Bud. On 'count of 'if's' Custer and his men are dead when they might be livin' but they ain't no use talkin' now. Nothin' kin bring 'em back.

"Sometime durin' the twenty-sixth the smell of dead bodies—horses and mules and men, their flesh rottin' in the heat—got so bad we couldn't stand it. We got orders to take up a new position closer to the river and so we acted accordin', and then it was the same thing over agin, makin' breastworks, diggin' rifle pits in the hard earth with cups and spoons and knives. We fought Indian fashion, jumpin' up, shootin' quick, then duckin' agin. We had to go easy on our ammunition. It want much of a battle. We didn't lose many men and we maybe didn't kill many Indians. The awful part was our bein' cut off so from the hull world, not knowin' what'd happened to the rest, wonderin' jist how long we could stick it out without water. And the enemy down below—they was thousands but what with the dust and smoke we couldn't figger how many—they 'peared to us like a big army. I heerd since they run out of ammunition too. Which is likely the reason why they didn't wipe us clean off that day. As it was we lived by the minute all the long, hot hours o' the twenty-sixth not knowin' what the next minute 'ud have in store fur us.

"Sometime that arternoon Muggins Taylor, the scout, come up the hill to us. How he ever got through I don't know. We all gathered 'round him, anxious fur news. But his fust question was, 'Whar's Custer?'

And when we told him we didn't know he looked kinda dazed. He had a message from Terry addressed to Custer. He told us some Crow scouts'd told Terry's men about a big battle whar a lot o' palefaces had been killed. But whether some o' the men of the Seventh under Custer or some of the Second under Gibbon he couldn't say. (Note 27.)

"I felt some anxious, Bud, when I heerd that, and heavy-hearted, and yet I didn't have no inklin' of what had really happened. I didn't consume that a man like Custer—so full o' strength and youth and laughter—could stop livin'.

"Wall, it all happened more'n fifty years ago, Bud, so I don't know's I can tell the how o' things perxactly but, if I recollect proper, it was the second night whilst I was doin' guard duty that I thought I heerd a sound from the valley down below. It was dark down thar in the brush. I listened. Fust I figgered maybe some Indians was stealin' up on us. Then I heerd voices, talkin' cautious and they was white men's voices. All of a sudden I got excited and tickled in my innards. It was Custer, I thought, and his men creepin' to us. But then one of our sentinels called out, 'Halt! Who goes thar?'

"And then I heerd some one whisper, 'Don't shoot! It's DeRudio.'

"Purty soon they come scramblin' over the edge of the cliff and there was Ton O'Neal and Billy Jackson and Frank Gerard and another fellow by name o' Bob and the scout, George Herendeen, and DeRudio. I'll never forgit the sight of their faces, like sick men, so white and gant. They was nigh tuckered out. Somehow, at the fust, they'd got separated from the rest of Reno's command and fur two days and a night they told us they'd been skulkin' down in the valley, hidin' behind brush, dodgin' bullets, with the Indians so close to 'em time arter time that they could've reached out and touched 'em. And durin' that time they hadn't had nothin' to eat nor drink. They acted plumb tickled to git to us agin and we was tickled to see 'em, too. It was like men comin' back from the dead. Whilst everybody was shakin' hands and talkin', explainin' this and that, I kept thinkin', 'if Muggins Taylor could git through and if DeRudio and his men could, then so can Custer.' I thought like's not him and his men 'ud be poppin' up any minute now.

"I says to Herendeen, 'Seen anything of Custer down thar?'

"I recollect how he looked surprised. 'Custer!' he says. 'Ain't he up here?'

"They'd heerd our firin' up on the hill and figgered we was all together. This was 'long about midnight

[177]

but all the officers was up and a lot o' the men, gathered 'round DeRudio, anxious to hear news of the outside world. Him and his men was most too petered out to talk. Some one volunteered to try gittin' down to the river fur a leetle water and he got it and come back alive and then the cook made hot coffee fur 'em and whilst they drunk it they told us somethin' of what they'd been through. They'd never expected to see any of us agin and some of 'em cried like babies, now that they was safe, bein' played out with skeer and hunger and thirst. Bud, don't know's I'm makin' it plain to you what an awful hell that valley was, all afire, thousands of Indians ridin' through the dust and smoke, shootin' and yellin'. DeRudio said time arter time the fire'd creep up to 'em whar they was hidin' and they'd have to make a dash across open country fur another hidin' place. One of 'em—I think it was DeRudio—had a stallion fur a saddle horse and all through the night it kept nickerin' and they was afeared the Indians'd hear and so they pulled dry grass and stuffed his mouth full to keep him quiet. (Note 28.)

"They told us that whilst they was in hidin' they seen a bunch of men ridin' by, not fur away, and through the dust and smoke they could see they was wearin' uniforms. Fur a minute their hearts jumped into their throats. They thought they was some o' Custer's men. One of 'em had on a buckskin coat and a big white hat and they jumped up and yelled at him thinkin' he was Tom Custer. Then the wind whipped the smoke away a leetle and they seen the men was Indians. That bothered us all considerable. We couldn't figger how the Redskins could o' got hold of the Seventh's uniforms. And still we never guessed the truth.

"Wall, arter that we begun to feel lighter-hearted, what with Muggins Taylor gittin' through and De-Rudio and his men safe and the Indians scatterin' so's we could git down to water occasional. 'Peared like the wust was over. Some of the officers wanted to light out and hunt fur Custer. We could see across the valley onto tother ridge whar a long string of Indians with their travois and horses and dogs was goin' away. But Reno said, no, maybe they was jist settin' a trap fur us. We'd better stay on our hill whar we was fortified. And so we stayed and waited. I carried a bucket of water up fur Dandy who was sufferin' considerable. The bullet wound in his neck was purty bad. I thought he was goin' to die and I dreaded havin' to tell Custer that Dandy was gone. But the drink seemed to help and he nickered grateful-like.

"Sometime the mornin' of the twenty-seventh we could see a lot o' dust stirred up miles away. It come closer. We watched and wondered. It might be the Indians got together to attack us agin but it might be Crook or Terry or Gibbon or Custer. Then, arter while, we seen fur sure it was cavalrymen. Then, Bud, all us up thar on that hill begun to cheer. I can't tell you the feelin' that went over us. We cheered till we was hoarse. The troops kept comin' closer and closer, gallopin' fast. We waved flags and hats and blankets at 'em. We run back and forth like we was crazy. Some of the men broke down and cried, jist 'cause they was so tickled. We never stopped to think it was funny we didn't git no answerin' cheer from those advancin'. They got to the foot of our hill and begun climbin' and we seen it was Terry and Gibbon's men and then we yelled till our throats purty nigh cracked.

"But Terry got to the top and then we seen he want smilin' none. All his men was awful sober. Terry held up his hand and somehow sudden the cheerin' stuck in our throats. He begun to speak. 'Boys!' he says, and he couldn't go on and his voice was husky and tremblin'. Bud, whilst I stood thar, waitin', a sorta funny, cold feelin' went over me, and somehow I knowed what he was goin' to say afore he spoke agin.

" 'Boys,' Terry says, awful slow and quiet, 'we've jist come from Custer's battle field. His entire command's been wiped out.'

"Fur awhile we all jist stood thar, sayin' nothin'. Seemed like we couldn't git the sense of it. Then some one spoke up.

[180]

" 'You mean,' he says, 'Custer's been defeated?'

"Terry says, 'I mean they're dead.'

" 'All of 'em?' some one said. 'Custer and all?'

"Terry nodded. His lips was a-quiverin'. I looked at the others quick, thinkin' maybe I hadn't heerd aright. Some of 'em was sobbin' out loud. Some of 'em looked funny, their faces so white and twisted, the tears tricklin' down their cheeks, makin' white streaks through the powder black and dirt. I walked off a leetle ways and stood alone lookin' off across the valley and I spoke the words to myself. I says, 'Custer is dead. The General is dead.'

"But, Bud, I didn't feel bad, not at fust, not the way you'd expect. I couldn't cry like the rest. I was jist sorta numb all over and awful tired. Like's not I was light-headed from lack o' sleep and sich, 'cause my fust thought was, 'Now I won't have to tell him that maybe Dandy's goin' to die.'

"Then, whilst I stood thar fur a minute, alone, I thought, 'I wished I could 've gone along. I wished I could 've been thar at the last.'

"And I ain't never got over that feelin', Bud.

"I wanted to go right over to the battlefield. It was only two or three miles away. Seemed like if I could see him layin' thar, not smilin' any more, not speakin' to me, then I could believe it was so. I asked the officer

[181]

of the day, could I go over. But he said, no, my duty was thar, on the hill. A lot went over to bury the dead. I stayed on the hill and worked. We didn't talk none whilst we did the things we had to do. We went back and forth, silent, gatherin' together the things we was to take. We packed rations and ammunition on the mules. We piled up the guns we couldn't take—those belongin' to the ones that was dead—and set fire to 'em. We cut up harnesses and saddles. Fixed things so's they wouldn't be no use to the Indians. We made litters to carry the wounded down to the boat. We worked quiet and steady and life was goin' on, same's if Custer want layin' dead over on tother ridge, only another officer was givin' orders now. And whilst I worked funny thoughts went runnin' through my head, same's, 'Wonder what'll become of the hounds now?' Or, 'Wonder can I make Bleuch and Tuck understand?'

"Whilst I chopped up a saddle I thought of Phil Sheridan buried on the Dakota prarie. I set fire to a pile o' guns and remembered how Lulu's pups looked arter the blizzard, smothered in their box, same's though they was jist asleep. I went over and sot down aside Dandy fur a spell o' restin' and I remembered the race we'd planned fur Vic soon's we got back to Fort Lincoln. Then all of a sudden it come to me that I wouldn't never agin hear the General laughin' and jokin'. Seemed like they want no use me goin' on."

CHAPTER XIII

PRESUMABLY no event transpiring in the world's history has attracted more universal interest or stimulated more heated debates than has the battle between Indians and whites fought near the banks of the Little Big Horn in Montana Territory on the morning of June twenty-fifth, 1876. Not because the result of the battle effected any material change in the progress of civilization, not because it stands out as a turning point in historical evolution, but because death shrouded the circumstance in a mystery never to be solved, placing the dramatic seal of finality upon a page which must forever remain unwritten.

On that Sunday morning of late June, five troops of the Seventh Cavalry, numbering some two hundred men, halted their horses for a moment on the high ridge overlooking the Little Big Horn valley, waved broad-rimmed hats in gay farewell, then followed their leader into eternal oblivion.

In that drama two figures, rivals for the interest and sympathy of us all, stand out—Major Reno, who headed the retreat from the Indian attack and George Armstrong Custer, who led his five troops of the Seventh to their death. However much we may desire to study the matter coolly, calmly, without prejudice, we find ourselves, as we pour over volumes of data—all based necessarily upon surmise and theory or upon the shifting testimony of the Indians who survived—alligning ourselves fervidly on one side or the other. Inevitably we become, quite without volition, ardent defenders either of Reno or of Custer. For if one was right the other was wrong. If one performed his duty, bravely and wisely, as a leader of soldiers of the United States army, then the other was a betrayer of his country's trust.

Although death is often the best defender of all, yet Reno may have been vouchsafed an advantage in that he together with many who fought under him survived to vindicate his challenged honor, while the voice of Custer and of those men who followed him up the ridge were effectually silenced by Indian bullets. Reno's advantage at the court of inquiry held in Chicago three years after the Battle of the Little Big Horn may have been further weighted by the fact that Custer, at the time he led his charge and met defeat, was in dire disgrace with the government.

Many writers, attempting to probe the unprobable mystery enveloping Custer's last battle, have accused him of criminally reckless haste in rushing upon the enemy, presumably with the hope of covering himself with glory and thus reinstating himself in the favor of his commanding officers. Such writers, while stressing the disgrace with which he was branded, have been negligent in making clear the reasons for that disgrace. Although they give, and correctly, as one of the many causes which led to Custer's defeat the deplorable graft then rampant in the U. S. army and Indian service department, they quite overlook the fact that it was his bold attacks upon the men who profited by that graft, from the most obscure Indian agent to Belknap himself, which bore fruit in the disfavor with which he, at that time, was regarded. They overlook the fact that other bitter fruits of Custer's meteoric successes—the envy and hatred of some few officers including Reno and Benteen—may have contributed to the final disaster, tempering somewhat their loyal willingness to rally to the support of their leader. That undying antagonism may, too, even though unconsciously, have tinged ever so little the purity of the truth of their statements at the court trial. It is so easy, so human, to adhere to our prejudices and to believe the thing we wish to believe. We have recorded evidence that many witnesses said one thing at the trial when Reno's honor, and Custer's, were weighed in the balance, and quite another thing either before or after the trial.

From time to time Custer has been accused of many offenses. He loitered during the last few days' march from the Rosebud to the Little Big Horn. He pushed his troops too rapidly. He ignored the reports of his scouts concerning the location and number of the hostiles. He erred in dividing his troops into three columns, separating them beyond supporting distances. He failed to abide by his promise to support Reno in the attack upon the Indian village. He was guilty of actual disobedience to Terry's orders.

Let us determine as nearly as may be the justice of those charges. According to Terry's written report to Sheridan dated July second, 1876, it was agreed between him and Custer that the latter was to advance with his troops from the Rosebud to the Little Big Horn at about thirty miles a day. Benteen testified that on the twenty-second the cavalry marched twelve miles; on the twenty-third, thirty-five miles; from five A. M. till eight P. M. on the twenty-fourth, forty-five miles; after night, ten miles further; and then, after resting but not unsaddling, the last twenty-three miles to the battle field. Thus he averaged for the three days from the twenty-second to the twenty-fifth about forty-one miles a day. Obviously he did not loiter on the way. It would rather

[186]

appear that his critics who accuse him of disregarding
Terry's orders and of rushing into the fight so that he
might win all the laurels for himself have some justification for their claims.

But Terry gave Custer no definite written orders as
to his course of procedure. As to what verbal commands he may have issued to Custer we have only the
testimony of Terry who as commander of the entire
force must bear the brunt of the responsibility for the
ill-fated expedition unless such responsibility could be
shoved over to the shoulders of the dead Custer. In
Terry's oft-quoted last letter to Custer he said:

> It is, of course, impossible to give you any *definite* instructions
> in regard to this movement and were it not impossible to do so,
> the Department commander places too much confidence on your
> zeal, energy and ability to wish to hamper your actions when
> nearly in contact with the enemy. He will, however, indicate to
> you his own views of what your action should be, and he desires
> that you conform to them unless you shall see sufficient reason
> for departing from them.

But Terry's letter to Sheridan dated July second, a few
days after Custer's defeat, attempts to convey the idea
that there had been a definite plan and that Custer de-
liberately ignored that plan. Terry said, in part: "The
proposed route was not taken—I do not tell you this

to cast reflection upon Custer—but I feel that our plan must have been successful had it been carried out."

Terry, neither in this letter nor later at the court trial considers that as Custer advanced up the Rosebud and across the Big Horn valley until he was nearly in contact with the enemy a situation arose that prompted him to "see sufficient reason for departing from" Terry's suggestion as to what his action should be. Such a situation, as reported by reliable scouts, being that the enemy was *en masse* in far greater numbers than any previous estimate by Reno or others had reckoned; that they were on the war path; that they were informed of the movements of all divisions of Terry's column; that they, emboldened by their recent victorious battle with Crook (of which, naturally, Custer and Terry knew nothing) were about to attack unless Custer made haste to forestall them. If Custer, confronted by this situation which neither he nor Terry could have foreseen, had followed the latter's suggestions to the letter, making the proposed wide sweep, examining Tullock's creek, waiting until the twenty-sixth for the junction of Terry's and Gibbon's columns, and had the Indians, in the meantime, escaped or attacked either of the latter columns, Custer would have been branded a coward.

Custer's forced marches, then, in view of existing circumstances, would seem to be justified. His attack upon the enemy, without waiting for the arrival of Terry and Gibbon, would seem, in view of existing circumstances, not rash, not headstrong, not greedy, but merely unavoidable. As to actual disobedience, Custer could not disobey orders which were never given, since Terry wisely refrained from "imposing upon him precise orders which might hamper his actions when nearly in contact with the enemy."

Much criticism has been voiced by both Custers friends and his foes because, on the morning of the battle, he divided his column into three divisions, the one under Benteen to scour the hills to the left, another under Reno to advance toward the Indian village in front, while he, Custer, skirted the ridge at the right. In view of all we now know concerning the vast number of Indians, their location, the fact that they were assembled into one huge group ready for battle, Custer's tactics do appear wrong. It was, however, in minutiæ, the identical plan of campaign which Terry had mapped out on a larger scale, he also dividing his forces into three, one under Gibbon, one under himself, and one under Custer, with the hope of surrounding the enemy. Terry wrote to Sheridan, "But I feel that our plan must have been successful had it been carried out." Many officers and men of the Seventh who fought that day under one of the three troop commanders are convinced that Custer's plan, too, would have been successful had it been carried out.

According to Byrne: "Benteen with three troops was ordered by Custer on a wide detour to the south and west (that is, to the left) in quest of Indians. 'A rather senseless order,' Benteen subsequently testified."

But Custer was simply carrying out the plan of Terry whose suggestion, in his last letter of instruction to Custer, was: "He thinks that you should still proceed southward, feeling constantly, however, to your left so as to preclude the possibility of the escape of the Indians to the south or southeast by passing around your left flank."

General E. S. Godfrey, one of the troop commanders of the Seventh, author of *Custer's Last Battle,* says:

The division of the command was not in itself faulty. The same tactics were pursued at the battle of Washita and were successful. There was a surprise attack (at Washita) and there was full co-operation of the separate commands, each commander carrying out his instructions. My studies of the battle of the Little Big Horn leave me little doubt that had Reno made his charge as ordered or made a bold front even, the Hostiles would have been so engaged in the bottom, that Custer's approach from the Northeast would have been such a surprise as to cause a stampede of the village and would have broken the morale of the warriors.

Lieut. Col. W. A. Graham, in his *Story Of The Little Big Horn,* says, rather naïvely, in discussing the matter of the division of the troops:

It is certain, however, that he (Benteen) was not within co-operating distance nor had his orders contemplated cooperation with any other part of the regiment.

Even we laymen, unfamiliar with the science of military tactics, must conclude that Benteen did contemplate cooperation with other parts of the regiment in time of battle since he, with all others of the Seventh, had made the long march from Fort Lincoln in Dakota to the Little Big Horn valley in Montana for the express purpose of attacking the Indians. However, conceding, for the moment, that he did not contemplate cooperation, it still remains a fact that when Kanipe and Martini came to him with urgent messages from Custer he was within hearing distance of the firing on Custer Hill. It still remains a fact that when the message came: "Come on—Be quick—Bring packs!" at a moment when reenforcements and ammunition might have saved the lives of Custer and many of his men, Benteen went to Reno rather than to Custer.

At the court trial and at all other hearings, Reno's strongest defense against the charge of cowardice was based upon the failure of Custer to support him in his proposed attack upon the village. Cooke bore Custer's last order to Reno: "General Custer directs that you take as fast a gait as you deem prudent and charge afterward and you will be supported by the whole outfit."

Reno maintains that Custer broke his promise to support him and that, abandoned, he could not do otherwise than retreat.

Had Reno obeyed Custer's order and attacked the village at the left while Custer, skirting the ridge, attacked from another point, thus dividing the hostile forces, it may be assumed that the Seventh Cavalry, despite the overwhelming number of the hostiles, might have been victorious. The testimony of Sitting Bull, Chief Gall, Rain-in-the-Face and other of the triumphant warriors strengthen that assumption. They have stated that they supposed the entire force of whites to have been assembled at Reno Hill. When the report came to them (while fighting Reno) that reenforcements (Custer's troops) were advancing they were dismayed and were preparing to flee in order to save their women and children when Reno's retreat up the hill left them free to defend the other end of their village.

Daniel A. Kanipe, Ex-Sergeant, C Troop, Seventh Cavalry, says:

Rotting Markers on Reno Hill.

Many Buried in the Grass.

Curley.

Speaking now as a private citizen I do not hesitate to express it as my opinion that if Reno and Benteen had carried out their orders Custer and the five troops would not have met their sad fate. From *Contributions to the Historical Society of Montana.*

We may conclude, then, that Custer, in attacking one end of the village while Reno—presumably—was attacking the other end deemed that he was keeping his promise to the latter to support him.

Among the charges made against Custer was the accusation that he should have known the strength of the force he attacked, that he disregarded the reports of his scouts who warned him of the superior strength of the enemy, that he rushed into the fight with foolhardy bravado.

Custer's—and Terry's—tragically erroneous impressions concerning the strength of the enemy were based, primarily, upon the reports of Reno who, having led a scouting expedition a little way up the Rosebud, concluded that there were about a thousand Indians on the warpath.

In a letter to Mrs. Custer written in camp at the mouth of the Rosebud and dated June twenty-first, 1876, General Custer says:

The scouting party has returned. They saw the trail and deserted camp of a village of three hundred and eight lodges. The trail was about one week old. The scouts report that they could have overtaken the village in one and a half days. I am now going to take up the trail where the scouting party turned back. I fear their failure to follow up the Indians has imperilled our plans by giving the village an intimation of our presence. Think of the valuable time lost! But I feel hopeful of accomplishing great results.

According to General Godfrey, John Burkman and others who were with Custer the last days there was nothing of the rash, impetuous, carefree laughter left in the demeanor of the young general. On the contrary they tell us he seemed unusually grave, thoughtful, even anxious, as though he realized to the full the seriousness of his undertaking. Godfrey tells us:

His manner and tone, usually brusque and aggressive, or some what rasping, was on this occasion conciliating and subdued. There was something akin to an appeal, as if depressed, that made a deep impression on all present.

It was then Wallace remarked: "Godfrey, I believe General Custer is going to be killed."

"Why, Wallace," Godfrey replied, "what makes you think so?"

"Because," said he, "I have never heard Custer talk that way before." (Quoted from *Custer's Last Battle* by Godfrey.)

It is easy now, in view of all the facts that have been gathered, to criticize Custer's faulty impression of the enemy force, but Two Moons told D. J. O'Malley, stepson of Charles White of Montana, a trooper in E Troop, 2nd Cavalry:

Indians fool Custer. Only few Indians show up and shoot. Put up few tepees where Custer can see. Big camp up river where Custer can not see. Custer think only little camp. All soldiers come on. Then lots of Indians show up around soldiers and in little while kill all soldiers.

On the morning of the twenty-fifth, just before starting out on the last few miles of the march, it has been charged that Custer divided his troops, selecting for himself his favorite five, C, E, F, I and L, among them being the famous gray-horse troop. Graham even states: "Custer—withdrew a short distance from the command and with pencil and paper divided the regiment into battalions."

John Burkman denies the truth of this statement. He says that General Custer caused the roll to be called and that just as the various troop commanders responded they were assigned to their positions and that Custer took the five remaining ones. General Godfrey and many others present that morning corroborate John's assertion.

Although a little matter in itself it is significant as indicating the inclination to heap upon the shoulders of a dead man who had unfailingly served his country with courage and judgment all blame for the disaster resulting in the death of five troops of the Seventh Cavalry.

At Major Reno's instigation the court of inquiry was held at Chicago during January of the year 1879, three years after the Custer Battle. It was prompted, at that late date, by many attacks upon his conduct as an officer at the time of the battle. Its result seemed to hinge upon whether he did right in retreating to the hill, ignoring Custer's order to attack the village, and there fortify himself against further onslaught from the enemy. However the numerous charges of cowardice to which he was subjected were based, not so much upon his justification for retreating, but upon the manner of his retreat and his conduct as commanding officer during the three horrible days on the hill, together with his repeated refusal to go to Custer's aid after the Indians had concentrated all their strength against the latter, leaving Reno's troops unhampered.

At the Court of Inquiry every surviving officer of his command except Captain French of M Troop gave their testimony under oath.

General Edgerly stated at the trial that he did not

consider Reno cowardly. But, in a letter to Lieut. Col. Graham, author of *The Story Of The Little Big Horn*, Edgerly said that "though Reno was intensely excited when he reached the hills he soon calmed down and thereafter was perfectly cool though by no means heroic."

We may gather, then, according to General Edgerly, that Reno was not cowardly and he was not heroic.

Lieut. Wallace's testimony at the trial is quoted as follows: "I think Reno did the only possible thing under the circumstances. If we had remained in the timber all would have been killed. It was his duty to take care of his command and to use his best judgment and discretion."

Yet Wallace was one of those who, on the hill, defying the contradictory orders of his excited officer, attempted to lead a company to Custer's aid.

Varnum, in his testimony, expressed it as his opinion that Reno's retreat was justified. He said: "I don't think we had enough men to hold it (the position in the woods on the bottom) and keep the Indians out of it."

In a subsequent statement Varnum admitted: "When I reached the head of the column I said something like: 'This won't do—this won't do! We have got to get into shape.' Or something like that—I don't remember the words. My idea was—*thinking there was no officer at the head of the column*—to take command and see that it was conducted by somebody."

Before the Court Edgerly testified: "Nobody had any idea that Custer was destroyed. The belief was general that he had gone to Terry."

Nevertheless, those present on Reno Hill during the three gruelling days, from the twenty-fifth to the twenty-eighth, state that the following conversation in effect took place between Edgerly and Weir. Hearing the last two distinct volleys ring out from Custer Hill which was hidden from their view by one high ridge, Weir exclaimed: "That's Custer."

Edgerly agreed, saying that they ought to rush to his aid.

Then Weir asked Edgerly if he was willing to take his company D and go. "Yes," said Edgerly, "I am."

Weir asked permission of Reno to go. An argument, heated, according to the testimony of Godfrey and others within hearing ensued between Weir and Reno. Then Weir started off alone except for his orderly. Edgerly, assuming that permission had been granted, followed with his company. When, quoting Elbridge Brooks, Reno shouted: " 'Get back! Get back!' And much against their will the command turned and trotted back to the pits to cower and suffer and fight.

The Court Trial wrung from Godfrey the statement that "There was an impression among the men that Custer had been repulsed and had abandoned them." But in his story, *Custer's Last Battle* he writes:

About five o'clock more by Reno's permission than by his direct command several companies of his battalions moved out in the direction of the firing down in the valley. We were satisfied that Custer was fighting the Indians somewhere and the conviction was expressed that our command "ought to do something or Custer would be after Reno with a sharp stick."

When Godfrey describes his attempt to cover the panicky retreat up the hill lest the whole command be thrown into confusion which would prove disastrous he says: "Lieutenant Hare expressed his intention of staying with me 'Adjutant or no Adjutant.'"

We cannot but wonder why many men—officers of the Seventh Cavalry—said one thing at the trial where Reno's honor—and Custer's—were being weighed in the balance, and exactly the opposite thing either before or after the trial. It is small wonder that we, who must base our judgment upon the conflicting reports of eye witnesses to a tragedy which took place more than fifty years ago, grow somewhat confused.

The Court of Inquiry demanded by Reno after the Hon. Corlett of Wyoming had urged a congressional investigation of the conduct of both Reno and Benteen was composed of three men: Colonel John H. King, Colonel Wm. Royall, and Colonel Wesley Merritt. Their conclusion, after hearing the testimony of witnesses was:

> The conduct of the officers throughout was excellent and while subordinates in some instances did more for the safety of the command by brilliant displays of courage than did Major Reno there was nothing in his conduct which requires animadversion from this court.

The decision of the Court saved Reno from court-martial but it would not protect him from continuous scathing attacks. Whether such attacks were deserved or not, each of us must decide as best we can. Reno had his followers, men sincere and loyal who have handed down to posterity their unwavering faith in their leader. Against Custer there were aligned many who hated him bitterly and that hatred, too, has been undiminished by passing years.

So even today, borne along by the swift current of time, there still echoes the jangle of dissension. Reno was a brave and conscientious officer. Reno was a coward and a deserter. Custer was criminally rash, sacrificing himself and his men on the altar of ambition. Custer was a gallant soldier, betrayed by his troop commanders. The dispute can never be settled. Many have testified in defense of Reno. Those who could have spoken most authoritatively for Custer fell, more than fifty years ago, by Indian bullets on a sunbathed hill near the banks of the Little Big Horn.

The way to that hill is over a well-graveled, much-traveled highway. Upon its crest stands a monument erected in memory of Custer and the men who fought and fell with him. Scattered all about, in threes, in twos, or quite alone are little white stones marking the spots where those men of the Seventh were struck down. Thousands, each summer, visit Custer Hill bathed in Montana sunshine, enveloped in reverent silence, to do homage to heroes.

Just two miles and a half farther west another hill known as "Reno Hill" is also crested, as is altogether meet and just, by a granite monument erected in memory of other men who fell under rain of Indian bullets that bright June morning in 1876. But the hill shows few tracks of visitors' feet. One may still, with knife or spoon, dig a little way down into the rifle pits, even now visible, and unearth bullets which once whizzed their menace about the heads of Reno's men. All about are bleached skeletons of horses undoubtedly the bones of the mounts of the Seventh Cavalry, lying where they fell fifty years ago. Down in the valley and along the steep sides of the cliff whence those gay, dauntless young troopers of the Seventh scrambled toward safety are crudely constructed, rotting wooden markers, many toppled over and buried in the grass, some with the name of him who fell quite obliterated. And the road wending up to Reno Hill is a rough, seldom-traveled trail that leads through a sheep corral and over an unbridged stream.

NOTES

NOTE 1.

Excerpt from letter from General Custer to Mrs. Custer during his expedition with Stanley:

July 19, 1873. Regarding the dogs I find myself more warmly attached to Tuck than to any other I have ever owned. She comes to me almost every evening when I am sitting in my large camp chair, listening to the band or joining with the officers in conversation. First she lays her head on my knee, as if to ask if I am too much engaged to notice her. A pat of encouragement and her forefeet are thrown lightly across my lap. A few minutes in this position and she lifts her hind feet from the ground, and, great overgrown dog that she is, quietly and gently disposes of herself on my lap, and at times will cuddle down and sleep there for an hour at a time. She resembles a well-cared for and half-spoiled child who can never be induced to retire until it has been fondled to sleep in its mother's arms.

NOTE 2.

Excerpt from letter to John Burkman from W. M. Camp who spent years interviewing survivors of the Seventh, gathering data for a history of the Custer Battle:

Sergeant Kanipe has given me a great deal of information for the history and so have a lot of others.—If you can send me a photograph of yourself I shall be glad to have it.—I want to

[205]

compliment you on your memory. I have asked a good many men to give me a list of the men of their troop who were with the pack train, and none of them but you has been able to give me as many as half of them.

Awaiting a reply at your convenience, I am

Yours truly,

W. M. Camp.

John dictated to Mr. O'Donnell a reply to Mr. Camp's letter which reads in part:

You have far too many men as members of "L" Troop at this time as there were only 66 men and out of this number 44 were killed and the rest scattered.—Speaking of photographs, I only have one of the General.—As for a photo of me I do not care to have mine published.—I was pleased to meet Sergeant Kanipe and he has promised to let me know when he starts to Seattle so I can see him at the train as it stops here.

Yours truly,

John Burkman.

By I. D. O'Donnell.

Daniel A. Kanipe, C Troop, was undoubtedly the last man living to see Custer alive. The last words he heard the General say were, "Hold your horses in Boys. There are plenty of them down there for us all." Then Kanipe was sent by Capt. Tom Custer with a message for McDougal: "Go to Capt. McDougal. Tell him to bring pack train straight across the country. If any packs come loose cut them and come on quick. A big

Indian camp. If you see Capt. Benteen tell him to come quick. Big Indian camp."

Further testimony concerning the dependability of John's statements is contained in a letter to Mr. O'Donnell from Rev. Pinckney of Walthill, Nebr., dated July 19, 1916:

Dear Sir: Some 5 yrs. ago an old scout, residing in Billings, and who was Gen'l Custer's personal attendant on his last campaign, was in the hospital at Omaha for treatment. It so happened that I also was a patient there.—About a year ago a certain lecturer made the assertion that Custer was killed by his own men. I had a good deal of confidence in the statements of the old scout above mentioned and would like to know what he would say of this lecturer's assertion.

Yours truly,

H. M. Pinckney.

In reply John, at Mr. O'Donnell's suggestion, dictated a mild denial of the lecturer's assertion, but his first reaction to Rev. Pinckney's letter when it was read to him was characteristically vehement.

"That's a lie," he boomed. "I want with Custer in that last charge but I know same's if I'd been thar that he stood with his men to the last and that when he died it was like a soldier orter die—by enemy bullets. I knowed him so well, Bud, bein's you might say intimate with him fur nine years, nobody can tell me he didn't die like he lived, brave, reckless o' danger fur hisself. Bud, often I try to figger out jist how he musta felt at the last, when he knowed all hope was gone, the bodies of his men scattered all round, him alone up thar on the hill, Sioux in front o' him, Cheyenne cuttin' off retreat back o' him, jist waitin' fur death, maybe prayin' it ud come instant. And it did come instant, one bullet hole through his chest, another through his head. And them bullets was fired by the enemy. They's plenty o' redskins left to swear to that."

NOTE 3.

Excerpt from Curly's statement as given in *The Teepee Book for 1926:*

What I am going to tell is just short.—I was always with Custer's outfit.—We met the camp before ten o'clock in the morning. Just before we go to the camp there was one band went one way and the other band went the other way.—The bugler got killed in the camp. Some of them got killed in the river. They (the Sioux) would not let the soldiers cross the river.—All the soldiers were killed before ten o'clock.—Just before they got all the soldiers killed—my horse was a pretty good runner and he ran off. I was just a young fellow and Custer told me to run off and I did run off.—If I had been older I would have stayed there and got killed. I had to run away.—I went east to the agency where the big pines are and stayed there. After I got off the high hill (where he claims he witnessed the battle) I rode to where the

Hard-Drinking, Loud-Swearing, Warm-Hearted
Calamity Jane.

Photograph by Dr. W. A. Allen.

They Did Not Die in Vain.
Photograph of Custer Hill taken in 1876.

Courtesy of Judge Goddard.

steamboat was. I brought the letter—brought it from the big chief back where they had the war.

(Hamson, author of *Conquest of the Missouri* credits Curley's assertion that he was the sole survivor of the Custer Battle. Dr. Brady, author of *Indian Fights and Fighters,* and Gen. Godfrey join with Rain-in-the-Face, Hairy Moccasins and many others in backing John's charge that Curley's accounts of the last battle were but fabrications.)

Wolf Voice who had been in the fight and was among the prisoners held at Fort Keogh told Mr. O'Malley, step-son of Chas. White of 2nd Cavalry:

Curly could not have been in fight. He must have been far away from Custer when fight began. No one got away. Curly could not have got a blanket from the battle field for the Indians did not have on any blankets when they were fighting. Just breech cloth and moccasins and their war feathers. Curly could not have got horse from battle field. No horses on field. Horses sent back over ridge. Men guarding them all killed. Horses stampeded.

NOTE 4.

In *Boots and Saddles* Mrs. Custer says:

We thought we had made the first step towards savage life when Burkman brought the mother of the one baby of our regiment the dried vertebra of a rattle-snake that he killed, because he had heard that it was the best of anything on which the infant could cut its teeth!

[209]

NOTE 5.

Mrs. Custer also has written of this incident. She says:

They (the officers) never failed to comment when they saw the old defender of his country coming out of the kitchen-tent, his jaws working and his mouth full, while he carried all the food his hands could hold.—At last even Mary began to narrate how he swept everything before him with voracious, convalescing appetite. "Why, Miss Libby," she said to me one day, "I thought I'd try him with a can of raw tomatoes, and set them before him, asking if he was fond of them. And he just drawled out, 'Always was,' and the tomatoes were gone in no time."

NOTE 6.

General E. S. Godfrey in *Custer's Last Battle,* published serially in *The Billings Gazette,* has written:

I have seen articles imputing wholesale drunkenness to both officers and enlisted men, including General Custer who was absolutely abstemious. I do not believe that any officer, except Major Reno, had any liquor in his possession. Major Reno had half a gallon keg that he took with him in the field, but I don't believe any other officer sampled its contents. I saw all the officers early in the morning and again at our halt at the divide and when officers' call was sounded to announce the determination to attack, and I saw no sign of intoxication; all had that serious, thoughtful mien, indicating that they sensed the responsibilities before them.

[210]

Frankly I do not believe Custer's command would have been rescued under Reno's leadership. At no time during the battle was his conduct such as to inspire confidence.—There was a time during the night of the 25th when his authority under certain conditions was to be ignored.

General Custer was not only abstemious himself, he did his utmost to keep his men from drinking. In a letter to Mrs. Custer, dated: Yellowstone River, July 19, 1873, he writes:

I am prouder and prouder of the Seventh, Libbie; not an officer or man of my command has been intoxicated since the expedition left Fort Rice.

NOTE 7.

Mrs. Custer made use of this opportunity to send John a ten dollar gold piece. John had it mounted into a brooch and presented it to Mrs. O'Donnell. It is now among the Custer relics in the Parmly Billings Library.

NOTE 8.

In Mrs. Custer's will she bequeathed such souvenirs of the Seventh's early expeditionary days in the west to Montana with the provision that a suitable memorial building be erected on the Custer Battlefield. The state is at present taking steps to erect such a building.

NOTE 9.

Excerpt of letter from Gen. Custer to Mrs. Custer:

Stockade on the Yellowstone, Sept. 6, 1873.
—I have had the good fortune to kill a fine large buck taller than Dandy.—The photographer who accompanied the scientists hitched up his photograph-wagon and drove over to take a picture of what they call the King of the Forest. All the officers and the photographer insisted that not only the game but the hunter should appear in the picture. So I sat down, dressed as I was in my buckskins, resting one hand on the antlers.—The picture is to form one of a series now being collected on the expedition under the auspices of the Smithsonian Institute.—Often, after marching all day, a light may be seen in my tent long after the entire camp is asleep, and a looker-on might see me, with sleeves rolled to my elbows, busily engaged preparing the head of some animal killed in the chase.—I have just finished heads for two officers,— and one I shall give to the Audubon Club. (It is now in Detroit.)

NOTE 10.

Despite the fact that Custer led many successful expeditions against the Indians he sensed the tragedy of their condition and at heart sympathized with them. He wrote:

If I were an Indian, I often think I would greatly prefer to cast my lot among those of my own people who adhered to the free open plains rather than submit to the confined limits of a reservation there to be recipients of the blessed benefits of civilization with its vices thrown in without stint or measure.

Hunt, in *Last Of The Cavaliers* says:

Before he (Custer) had been long in the West he saw that the Redman was the victim of a vicious circle that was closing in on him and choking out his very life. Forced to their reservations, more often than not they were cheated out of their annuities, their rations and clothing by an unscrupulous agent.

Not less relentlessly than Custer fought the Indians themselves did he fight the insidious system of graft of which they were piteously helpless victims. In the many articles which he contributed to the *Galaxy* and to other current magazines of that time, Custer wrote forcibly and daringly of the political graft which was victimizing the Indians, of how Indian agents stole food and clothing from the reservations and sold to the army, of how army commissaries stole from the army and sold to private citizens. Nor did he hesitate to mention the names of certain dignitaries whom he believed guilty of such fraud, nor to clear Belknap, then Secretary of War and personal friend of the President of the United States, of blame in the matter.

As a consequence George Armstrong Custer, the "Baby General" with his youthful ardor, his utter fearlessness, his ruthless assaults upon swindle and treachery won many friends, but he also incurred many enmities. Almost immediately, says Hunt, a certain element in the officer personnel turned against him. Reno hated him. Benteen, to his dying day, hated Custer. This bitter animosity may have had more than a little to do with the tragic lack of loyal cooperation that proved to be so costly in human lives that Sunday morning of June twenty-fifth, 1876.

During the Civil War, Custer had made for himself a brilliant record but in 1867, at the beginning of his military operations in the West he was courtmartialed, the charge being that he had left the Post without permission. The truth of the matter was that, having led his regiment successfully and brilliantly through a hazardous Indian campaign the young general was homesick to see his bride who was then just ninety miles away. And so, acting with characteristic impulsiveness, neglecting to seek permission of his superior officers in whose favor he deemed himself to be basking, he went to her. Although the captain whose gnawing jealousy had prompted his complaints against Custer was discharged from the army, six months later, for drunkenness, yet the aroma of disgrace hung over the young general. He was deeply hurt by what appeared to him rank injustice.

In March of 1876, just three months before the Seventh Cavalry started out on its fatal expedition into the Little Big Horn country, the clouds of scandal which Custer had stirred into being, lowered over

Washington dimming the brilliance of the administration then in power. Charges of fraud were made against many, including Belknap, intimate friend of President Grant. At the subsequent trial Custer was called to Washington to testify. He stated the truth as he saw it. He asserted that he had refused to accept two thousand sacks of grain for his Post because they were stamped, "U. S. Indian Dept.," and he believed them to have been stolen from the Indian Agency. He stated it as his opinion that Belknap had not only shut his eyes to the fraud which was resulting in the slow starvation of hundreds of Indians corraled within their reservations but had actually profited by it. And he added insult to injury by accusing Grant's brother of accepting money for securing a certain office for a friend. He said, and proved his statement, that large quantities of guns and ammunition were being sold to the Indians. He said, also proving his statement, that Indians in large numbers were constantly leaving the reservation and banding together farther west, notwithstanding the agents' monthly reports that "all wards are present and accounted for," and that the resultant over-supply of food and clothing were sold by those agents. The man whose enemies have accused him, among other nefarious charges, of having waged a cruel and treacherous war upon the Indians, of putting personal ambition high above all other considerations, imperiled his future career in his fight for justice.

Belknap, Secretary of War under a Republican administration, was impeached, chiefly on the testimony of Custer who was a Democrat, and at the urgent request of the bewildered, tormented Grant, who retaliated for the injury done his friend by ordering Sherman to punish the meddlesome young Civil War veteran. Custer, taking into account his brilliant war record and his subsequent and equally brilliant campaign against the Indians, had quite naturally expected to lead the expedition into Montana Territory, but, after the Belknap trial, as he was hurrying westward, he was stopped in Chicago by a telegram from Sherman ending: "And meanwhile let the expedition from Fort Lincoln proceed without him."

No crueler blow could have been conceived. Headstrong, impulsive, honest and honorable Custer had been utterly lacking in finesse and for this lack he must drink, to the last drop, the bitter draught of shame.

After many exchanges of telegrams, after waiting in Chicago through dark days of anxiety and humiliation and despair, he sent his final desperate plea to the President of the United States who had lately been his general:

I appeal to you as a soldier to spare me the humiliation of seeing my regiment march to the front and I not with my men to share their dangers.

This from the man of whom Sheridan, in a letter to Mrs. Custer, had written:

There is scarcely an individual in our service who has contributed more to bring about this desirable result (Lee's surrender) than your very gallant husband.

This from the man who had but recently led his bare-footed, war-weary regiment in their tattered uniforms through the streets of Washington to the tumultuous, hoarse-throated, tearful applause of thousands.

Grant was more soldier than politician. He could not disregard the frantic prayer straight from the tortured heart of another soldier. And so, at the last moment, he relented in so much as to allow Custer to head his beloved Seventh Cavalry in the expedition under Terry.

And so, to the tune of Garry Owen, proudly, under blackest stigma, Custer led his regiment out of Fort Lincoln. He led them across Montana territory and on to the banks of the Little Big Horn. Five troops of that regiment he led across the valley and up the hill to their death. But they did not die in vain, those gallant young soldiers of the Seventh. The awful massacre on Custer Hill led to a merciless probing which resulted in wiping out much of the graft against which Custer had fought.

NOTE 11.

In a letter to Mrs. Custer dated July 15th, 1874, the General said:

As I write the dogs surround me: Cardigan is sleeping on the edge of my bed, Tuck at the head, and Blucher near by. I have killed six antelope at the head of the command—Only think! One fifth of the time expired day before yesterday, and by the time this reaches you one third of our time of separation will have passed!

NOTE 12.

Tuttle was one of Custer's orderlies. He was shot in the forehead and killed by an Indian at the mouth of Buffalo Creek this side Pease Bottom and was buried there on an island.

NOTE 13.

Unfortunately Mrs. Custer's letters to John, all of which were sent in care of Mr. O'Donnell, were undated. To the best of his memory this particular letter was written in 1920. Some years later, in 1931, to be exact, while in New York, he called on Mrs. Custer. So carefully protected was she against intrusion of the curious, the loyal, trophy seekers, ambitious reporters eager for stories, that he despaired of passing the loyal servants who guarded her doors. Long and earnestly he argued with the door man, saying that he was from Montana, that Mrs. Custer would be glad to hear news of the West, that he was an old friend. Eventually he triumphed to the extent that he was permitted to send up his card. After a long, anxious moment of waiting the maid came down to say that Mrs. Custer was not well, that she could not recall any one by the name of O'Donnell, and that she did not wish to be disturbed.

Mr. O'Donnell refused to become disheartened. "Tell Mrs..Custer," he urged, "that I am 'Bud O'Donnell' from Montana. Tell her I am John Burkman's friend."

The name "John Burkman" cast its magic where all else had failed. Promptly the maid returned to lead him up the stairs.

As he stood in the doorway a little, white-haired old lady rose with difficulty from her chair and advanced slowly to meet him. Save for the undaunted glow of youth in the bright eyes there was nothing about this frail, stooped, pain-twisted little figure to remind one of the gay, laughing Miss Libby who, fifty years ago, romped with the hounds and joked with John and dashed across Western plains by the side of her young, handsome, golden-haired soldier husband, sharing with him every anxiety, every hardship, every triumph. She was bent almost double and leaned heavily on the stout cane that tap-tapped across the polished floor. Time and illness were at last taking their toll of her who had boasted to John with a remnant of girlish vanity that in growing old she had not grown stout or crooked either.

But her mind was still alert, clinging to the precious memories of her honeymoon days in the West with their aftermath of stark tragedy. "How was John? Had he been well looked after? Were his last days happy ones? And had he still talked of the General and the hounds and Vic and Dandy? And the West—was there anything remaining of the old, free, wild glamor? Were Montana people evincing interest in the proposed memorial building to be erected on Custer Hill?"

She followed Mr. O'Donnell to the door. "John is gone," she said. "If he were still there I would send my love and ask you to tell him—tell him for me——" there was a flash of youthful zest in the bright, old eyes, "that last month Miss Libby was eighty-nine years old."

NOTE 14.

Quoting Chas. Francis Bates, Col. U.S.A. Retired, from an article in *New York Times,* June 20th, 1926.

In that fight the unbeaten Custer, four members of his family and two hundred troopers of the 7th Cavalry rode boldly to their death while the greater part of the regiment fumbled his plans of battle and failed to respond to his call for reinforcements.—Custer obeyed the letter and spirit of Terry's final letter of advice by hugging the "warm" Indian trail. If he had done otherwise he could not have got back until the 28th of June which would have left Gibbon and Terry with about 350 men to face the Sioux alone.—When Reno with his men galloped toward the upper end of the village there was almost no opposition according to all Indian accounts. His attack caused so much consternation that Sitting Bull took alarm and galloped away forgetting one of his twin children in the melee and never stopping until he was overtaken 14 miles from the battle field. He explained his flight by saying that he had to go into the hills to make medicine to propitiate the evil spirits.

The cause of Sitting Bull's urgent need to make medicine dates back to the famous "Wagon-box Fight." It was the custom among early-day Westerners to use their wagon boxes as corrals, locking wheel into wheel to form a circle in which they placed their horses at night. These wagons, breast high, made of iron, constituted at times a very convenient and effective fort against Indian attack.

In the "Wagon-box Fight" twenty-nine soldiers were attacked by some three thousand Indian warriors who naturally supposed they had the pale faces at their mercy. Yelling and firing they charged thinking that the soldiers, after one volley, would have to stop and re-load. But the pale-face guns spit fire, not once only, but six times. The Indians were puzzled. They could not understand for this was their first experience with magazine guns. It must be that their medicine was not good. They retreated, made medicine, and again charged the wagon-box fort and again each soldier, without pausing to re-load, fired six times. As a result of the battle only two white soldiers were wounded while most of the three thousand Indians were killed. With this tragic event in mind Sitting Bull considered it extremely important that before the Custer Battle his medicine be very good.

NOTE 15.

Quoting from a letter to Mrs. Custer from General Custer:

Mouth of the Rosebud, June 21, 1876.—The scouting party has returned. I feel hopeful of accomplishing great results. General Gibbon's command and General Terry (Gibbon was too ill at the time to lead his command) with the steamer *(Far West)* will proceed up the Big Horn as far as the boat can go. I now have some Crow scouts with me as they are familiar with the country. In their speech they said they had heard that I never abandoned a trail; that when my food gave out I ate mule. That was the kind of man they wanted to fight under; they were willing to eat mule too.

NOTE 16.

The simple, inarticulate soul of old John Burkman held within itself a capacity for devotion and loyalty that was rare and beautiful. When he gave of himself he gave without reservation, without stint or measure. Perhaps only four human beings may justly have claimed the privilege of calling him their friend— General Custer, Miss Libby, and, during the latter years of his life, Bud O'Donnell and Mrs. O'Donnell. When Mrs. O'Donnell died, John assumed, as his indisputable right, a place with the bereaved family, mourning with them, sharing their grief. Their great loss was his loss also.

NOTE 17.

This photograph John presented to the Billings Library together with some letters from Mrs. Custer and a fork and spoon which Custer had used at his last breakfast.

NOTE 18.

Several years later, after John had become a private citizen, when the roots of civilization had sunk deep into the Western plains, after Chief Joseph had met defeat and the Indian tribes were safely corralled on their reservations and the names "Sitting Bull" and "Gall" and "Rain-in-the-Face" no longer struck terror to the hearts of the pioneers, John went in a lumber wagon, one day, to the spot on Canon Creek where the Sturgis Battle had been fought. He had heard that a flood had washed down the canon gouging out of their shallow graves many of the soldiers who had fallen in that battle and he was deeply troubled by the thought of the bodies of his two comrades, the carpenter and the blacksmith, being left unsheltered from sun and wind and snow. One of those two men had been John's bunkie, some forty years ago, at Fort Lincoln, and they had shared all the hazardous joys and sorrows that go to make up the life of a soldier on the plains. They had been young together. Now John, grown old, desired to perform for his comrades the last act of kindness and loyalty possible. He wanted to take them up to their other comrades on Custer Hill. For days he labored with hammer and saw making a wagon box, and then, because the vehicle which was to bear troopers of the Seventh on their last journey to the Little Big Horn must be seemly in appearance, he draped it with the American flag and wished that he might secure somewhere the guidon of the Seventh to add the final touch. His task completed he rode horseback the eighteen miles from Billings to the Horse-Thief Cache, that

[224]

historical spot on Canon Creek where he with others of the Seventh under Sturgis attacked the rear guard of Chief Joseph's command. That was in 1879. He had been young and strong then. Now he was an old man. The long horseback trip had wearied him. And things had changed. They did not look to John as they had looked that exciting day thirty years ago. Calamity Jane's home, a dugout in the Canon Creek bank under cotton wood trees, was still there but it was empty now as were the dugouts of her neighbors, the two famous horse thieves, O'Neil and Fallon. And a flood had ravaged the country, changing its contour, making all seem to the old man dishearteningly unfamiliar. He gazed about. He saw many gruesome relics of the long ago battle, bones a-plenty, an arm or a leg or a head gouged out of shallow graves by the torrent, but he could not find or could not identify the bodies of the two who had marched with him from Yankton to Fort Lincoln and had been his comrades on that last march up to the Little Big Horn. All John's sentimental tenderness vanished. One of his quick, unreasoning fits of fury shook his burly frame. In silent, brooding rage he made the long return trip to Billings from what he was pleased to term his "wild goose chase."

Years later, only a few years ago, others accomplished

what John, for all his loving fealty, had failed to do. Jimmie Yearns, who still lives on Canon Creek and who, as a young lad, helped bury the dead on Custer Hill, was commissioned by the government to remove the bodies of troopers of the Seventh from Sturgis Battlefield and give them fitting burial on Custer Hill. And John, during his last days, was gratified by the knowledge that white marble slabs marked the resting place of his two comrades, the carpenter and the blacksmith.

NOTE 19.

In *A Warrior Who Fought Custer* by Marquis, Wooden Leg says:

I took one scalp. The dead man had a long beard growing from both sides his face and extending several inches below his chin. I skinned one side his face and half the chin so as to keep the long beard yet on the part removed.

(He gave the "scalp" to his mother's mother.)

"Take it," I urged. "It will be good medicine for you."

NOTE 20.

Dr. Marquis, author of *A Warrior Who Fought Custer* has a picture or map drawn by Big Beaver who was fifteen years old at the time of the Custer Battle which shows seven tepees each standing for from three hundred to five hundred lodges. According to Big Beaver, therefore, there must have been about twelve thousand Indians against the nine hundred men of the Seventh, most of whom were banded together in the charge on Custer Hill.

As to old John's bitterly vindictive charges against Reno—a bitterness, however unjustified, born of love and grief—there are some few authors who defend Reno, many who share John's resentment toward the man whose (supposedly) cowardly failure to support his commanding officer caused the death of more than two hundred of the Seventh Cavalry. The court of inquiry held after the Custer Battle acquitted Reno of criminal cowardice and left whatever blame may have been attached to the defeat of the Seventh upon the shoulders of the dead Custer. Some two years later, however, Reno received a dishonorable discharge from the army on the grounds of drunkenness and conduct unseemly in an officer of the U. S. army. It is an undisputable fact that both Reno and Benteen hated Custer. In *The Story of the Little Big Horn* by Lieut. Col. W. A. Graham, U.S.A. even this author who, while endeavoring to present an impartial account of the battle is obviously inclined to defend Reno, has admitted:

Not even death served to change his (Benteen's) attitude; to the day of his own passing he never abated his hatred. But his known character and the habit of his entire life refutes the imputation that—he failed in his duty as an officer and a soldier.

And Graham, refusing to recognize Reno's retreat to the hill as a disorganized and panic-stricken rout, writes:

Reno, startled and disconcerted, ordered the men to dismount and to mount again, and whirling his horse, broke through the timber and so out upon the plain, closely followed by the confused troopers. Here, at a gallop, led by Reno, they started up the valley toward the ford. *Seventeen men were left behind in the woods*, among them DeRudio, Girard, O'Neil, etc.

What to do! Should he (Reno) continue his advance, charge forward into the village, and engulf his whole command in this swirling mass of savages, who, *far from showing any signs of running, were rapidly and confidently attacking front and flank?*

(From *The Story of the Little Big Horn*, Page 39)

But Wooden Leg's account as told by Marquis in *A Warrior Who Fought Custer* is quite different. He says:

Suddenly the hidden soldiers (under Reno) came tearing out on horseback from the woods. I whirled my horse and lashed it into a dash to escape from them. All others of my companions did the same. But soon we discovered they were not following us. *They were running away from us.* They were going as fast as their tired horses could carry them across an open valley space and towards the river.

Graham cites as one of the causes of the disaster the separating of the battalions beyond supporting distance. He says, "Benteen's battalion was at this time miles away to the left and rear, its whereabouts unknown."

But John, who was with the McDougal pack train maintains that while the mules were mired in a mud hole, shortly after the four battalions—Reno's, Custer's, Benteen's and McDougal's—had separated, Benteen also came up to the water hole, so he could not, as Graham states, have gone miles away into the hills. At that time, while Benteen's and McDougal's forces were joined, they heard distinctly, according to John, firing at the front (by Reno's men) and firing from the hills to the right (by Custer's men).

Graham continues:

Not only were all separated by miles of difficult and enemy-infested country but no one of the commanders, Custer, Reno, Benteen, or McDougal knew where either of the others was, or what he was doing.

John, however, insists—and his assertion has been corroborated by many writers and by many survivors of the Seventh—that it was while Benteen and McDougal were loitering at the water hole that messengers, Martini and Kanipe, came to them from Custer, asking for ammunition and urging haste. Daniel A. Kanipe, C Troop, last living man to see Custer alive says:

I received the following message from Capt. Tom Custer: "Go to Capt. McDougal. Tell him to bring pack train straight across

[229]

the country. If any packs come loose cut them and come on quick. A big Indian village. If you meet Capt. Benteen tell him to come quick. A big Indian camp." (From *Contributions to the Historical Society of Montana.*)

John, in his statement to Mr. O'Donnell, says that the pack train was badly strung out and that, instead of hastening to Custer's relief, he with others at the front received orders to wait until the rear caught up. He also declares that, after Martini and Kanipe arrived with messages from Custer, Benteen's men dismounted to water and apparently took their time, and that, when they did continue they—the mounted cavalry—*followed* the slow-moving pack-train.

Graham stresses the "Unfortunate separation" and "fatal ignorance of each other's acts and whereabouts."

In *Custer's Last Battle* by Major E. S. Godfrey, one of Custer's troop commanders, he says:

During a long time after the junction of Reno and Benteen we heard firing down the valley in the direction of Custer's command. The conviction was expressed that "our command ought to do something or Custer would be after Reno with a sharp stick."

Which proves John's contention that they were not so separated as to be "fatally ignorant of each other's acts and whereabouts."

Quoting again from *The Story of the Little Big Horn* by Graham:

Custer's defeat cannot fairly be ascribed to his disregard of Terry's plan of campaign. His disobedience of orders, if such occurred, and his disloyalty to his commander, if that existed, form no proper part of this narration.

General Terry's plan of campaign as given in his last written official order to General Custer is as follows:

It is of course impossible to give you any definite instructions in regard to this movement, and were it not impossible to do so, the Department Commander places too much confidence in your zeal, energy, and ability to wish to impose upon you precise orders, which might hamper your action when nearly in contact with the enemy. (From *Contributions to the Historical Society of Montana.*)

In Lieut. James H. Bradley's Journal, also included in the *Contributions to the Historical Society of Montana,* we find this:

Though it is General Terry's expectation that we will arrive in the neighborhood of the Sioux village about the same time and assist each other in the attack, it is understood that if Custer arrives first he is at liberty to attack at once if he deems prudent.

Varnum, commander of the "Ree" scouts, has voiced his opinion:

As to his (Reno's) exercising the functions of a commanding officer directing the troops, etc. in the presence of great danger, he certainly did that. He was present with the command, giving orders. Certainly there was no sign of cowardice or anything of the sort.

Col. G. O. Shields, author of *The Blanket Indians of the Northwest*, asserts:

These officers (Reno and Benteen) further evinced their utter incompetency by staying and entrenching their forces (On Reno Hill) and awaiting a second attack. . . . Reno and Benteen both admitted after the fight that they had heard heavy firing—and knew Custer was engaged but both hated him bitterly and they said: "Let him get licked. It will take some of the conceit out of him." If Reno and Benteen had been loyal to their leader they could no doubt have saved him and many of his brave men but they were willing to sacrifice him and their comrades in order to vent their own spleen against him.

The *Contributions to the Historical Society of Montana* includes a statement by General Sherman:

Custer's attack on the big Indian village was, under the circumstances and according to well-settled principles of Indian warfare neither rash nor desperate, because, having marched into the zone where the Indians were assembled he could do nothing but attack when he found himself in the presence of the Indians.

General Terry, in his official report, said, "Custer expressed the utmost confidence he had all the force he could need and I *shared his confidence.*"

In his official report General Sheridan said, "Up to the moment of Custer's attack no information was had, public or private, to justify the belief that there were in Sitting Bull's camp more than 500 to 800 warriors."

Wooden Leg, as we have previously stated, estimated

the number at approximately 10,000. Two Moons said about 3000. Wolf Voice said between two and three thousand.

NOTE 21.

The chief cause of the disaster was unquestionably and undeniably the lack of correct information as to the numbers, the organization and the equipment of the Indians. They (the Seventh Cavalry) thought to find a band equipped with ancient muskets and discarded rifles, with primitive spears and bow and arrow. Instead they found a foe far better armed than they themselves, possessing Winchester rifles of the latest pattern and stores of ammunition that seemed inexhaustible. Why were these things not known? The answer lies in the almost criminal policy pursued by the Government during all the period of our Indian wars; a policy that permitted a maladministered Indian Bureau to sow the wind and compelled the army to reap the whirlwind. It is idle now to discuss that policy; it has, happily, passed into history, a black, disgraceful page.

(Quoted from Lieut. Col. Graham's *The Story of the Little Big Horn.*

NOTE 22.

John speaks of the scout, Reynolds, as "Silent Charlie." I believe, however, he was popularly known as "Lonesome Charlie." An article on famous scouts under Custer appearing in the April 11th (1891 issue of the *Billings Times* has this to say of Reynolds:

Perhaps the greatest of all scouts who fought in the Sioux war under Custer and other leaders was "Lonesome Charlie" Reynolds. Reynolds Island in the Yellowstone River is named after him. This man has attained a wide fame along the frontier, quite as wide as that of "Yellowstone Kelly." In the late 60's he drifted to the northwest, where his remarkable gift as a hunter quickly earned him a wide reputation. The phrase "Reynolds' luck" became a familiar one among hunters and trappers. Among the Gros Ventres, Arickarees and Mandan Indian tribes, his prowess was attributed to magic and their superstitious jealousy caused him some narrow escapes from death. He was always cool and absolutely fearless in the face of danger. When he was killed on the Little Big Horn he was 32 years old, a slender, sinewy man, five feet eight inches in height, slightly stooped, with restless gray eyes and a voice as gentle as a woman's. Like "Yellowstone Kelly" he was very chary of speech, seeming even surly on short acquaintance, though such was not the case, for his disposition was cheerful and his generosity such that he would hesitate at no sacrifice for a friend.

Reynolds was shot through the heart in the hot fight that Reno's retreating column had on the river bottom of the Little Big Horn. He had stopped with Dr. Porter of the Seventh Cavalry, who was treating the wounded. Major Hare, who was second lieutenant with the scouts in the fight said later, "I saw him (Reynolds) after his death in the river bottom where he fell. I saw him several times during the fight, and of course was impressed with his remarkable coolness and apparent indifference to the galling fire that was being poured in on us.

NOTE 23.

Mark Kellogg, correspondent for *The New York*

Herald, was killed in the Custer Battle. His body was found on the high ridge where the remaining few of the Seventh had made their last stand close to that of General Custer. Later the *Herald* sent John Cockerill out to the scene of the battle. His story of the fight is rather more sensational than accurate. He wrote:

Not a trooper's life was spared. By Custer's side his brother Tom fell. Then it was that Rain-in-the-Face—ripped open the poor fellow's body and tearing therefrom the reeking heart, made good his savage oath (to eat Tom Custer's heart) with demonaical and exultant cries from the other savages.

After all was over the remains of the brave leader were found undisturbed, but every other body upon that field was hacked and mutilated in the most horrible manner.

Rain-in-the-Face has denied that he cut out the heart of Tom Custer. In a statement made to Dr. Charles Eastman and published in the *Tepee Book* the Indian warrior said:

Many lies have been told of me. Some say that I killed the Chief, and others say that I cut the heart out of his brother, Tom Custer, because he had caused me to be imprisoned. Why, in that battle the excitement was so great that we scarcely recognized our nearest friends! Everything was done like lightning. After the battle, we young men were chasing horses all over the prairie while the old men and women plundered the bodies; and if any mutilating was done, it was by the old men.

All who viewed the battlefield immediately after the fight corroborate the statement of Rain-in-the-Face.

Tom Custer's body was not ripped open nor was his heart taken out. There are many who maintain that the gruesome tales of mutilated bodies have been exaggerated. Mr. William H. White, still living and acting as official guide over the Custer battlefield was one of the F Troop, 2nd Cavalry under Gibbon. He says:

We camped the night of the twenty-fifth on the spot where the village of Crow now stands. We didn't know then of the awful thing that had happened to Custer and his men but as we had marched across the valley we saw many Indians wearing Seventh Cavalry uniforms and mounted on Cavalry horses. The morning of the twenty-sixth we went from camp up the hill and were the first to see the bodies of Custer and his men. Most of them were stripped. A few were hacked or pounded with tomahawk or war club but not mutilated the way folks have said. It looked to us as though the Indians took that way to finish off the wounded.

In the July 6, 1876 issue of the Bismarck, *Dakota Territory Tribune* we read a harrowing account of the mutilated bodies strewn over the Custer Battlefield.

General Custer, who was shot through the head and body, seemed to have been among the last to fall, and around or near him lay the bodies of Col. Tom and Boston, his brothers, Col. Calhoun, his brother-in-law and his nephew young Reed who insisted on accompanying the expedition for pleasure. Col. Cook and the members of the non-commissioned staff all dead—all stripped of their clothing and many of them with bodies horribly

[236]

mutilated. The squaws seemed to have passed over the field and crushed the skulls of the wounded and dying with stones and clubs. The heads of some were severed from their bodies, the privates of some were cut off, while others bore traces of torture, arrows having been shot into their private parts while yet living or other means of torture adopted.—The burial of the dead was sad work but they were all decently interred.

There are a few men still living who claim to have viewed the Custer Battlefield immediately after the fight and who do not agree with the Bismarck reporter as to the horrible mutilating of the bodies. Among these is Charles Wilson, the notorious "Smoky" a negro, who has, for the past forty years, served as United States Marshall on the Crow reservation. The story of his adventurous life, though having no place here, is colorful and interesting in the extreme. Briefly, born of slave parents, he was adopted by a white family when two or there months old.

"I wouldn't," Smoky proclaims dramatically, "know my own mother if she was to stand right in front of me this minute."

He was a boy of fourteen when his white foster father brought him to Montana Territory. Later, having acquired some knowledge of the Crow language, he became interpreter for government agents at the reservation. One June evening there came to the Crows, in that mysteriously rapid manner in which reports do spread among Indian villages, news of a terrible fight which had taken place that day on the Little Big Horn. Smoky with some Crows set forth at once to view the scene of carnage. The Crow reservation was located, at that time, on the Stillwater near the present site of Absarokee, a three day trip from the Little Big Horn. So, according to Smoky, he arrived at the battlefield just three days after the battle, in time to help bury the dead. When asked if he had been able to identify any of the bodies Smoky said that he had seen General Custer many times and recognized him as he lay beside his fallen men. He insists that there were very few bodies of dead horses on the field and that, although the bodies of the soldiers of the Seventh were stripped, few were mutilated. He recalls that beside each shallow grave they piled a little mound of stones. Smoky's own recollection of events has undoubtedly been tinged by stories told around campfires. He is ninety years old. He is interesting and important because he is one of the few remaining links binding us to the past. One event, however, stands out in his memory which, although it has never before been recorded, I think we may credit. He tells us that after the Custer Battle, Sitting Bull, pompous with victory, visioning a future when all pale faces were to be annihilated as Custer's troops of the Seventh had been, came to the Crow villages and talked big war talk, endeavoring to incite the Crows to join the warring tribes. And he recalls how Pretty Eagle called a council meeting of his sub-chiefs and head men to discuss the matter and how Sitting Bull made stirring speeches about the wide buffalo ranges and the glad, free life of the Indian until some of the Crows were ready to go on the war path. And then Smoky recalls that Plenty Coups, a man of twenty-eight, an ambitious young warrior, later to become chief of all the tribes of the northwest, rose and talked gravely to his people. He admonished them that the day of the Indian was past, that their only hope of happiness was in submission to the white man's rule, that instead of hunting buffalo they must be content to push the white man's plow. "Not," Plenty Coups said, "because we think the white man's way is best but because we know he is stronger than we. If we would survive we must become like him."

And the Crows, Smoky says, knew that their young leader had spoken wise words, and Sitting Bull went out of their camp defeated. And even to the day of his death, when eighty-four snows had fallen upon his head, Chief Plenty Coups boasted that he had always been friend of his white brother and that no Crow had ever raised his hand against a paleface.

General Benteen also corroborates the statement of

Rain-in-the-Face, offering as proof the simple fact that Tom Custer's heart was not cut out.

Many writers tell us that the only unmutilated body found on the field was that of Teeman and that he was covered with an Indian blanket as a gesture of gratitude because he had helped Rain-in-the-Face escape after Tom Custer had imprisoned him. But the Indians deny this story also, reminding us that warriors do not take their blankets into battle.

Mr. O'Donnell was with those who assembled at the Custer battle field many years after the battle to hear Two Moons' description of the fight. The old Cheyenne warrior's story was tersely graphic. "Puff!" he said, "and they were all gone."

Mr. O'Malley asked Two Moons, "Two Moons, who killed General Custer?"

The old chief replied: "Who can tell? Plenty Indians. All shoot. Shoot many times. Maybe Sioux man kill him. Maybe Cheyenne. Him killed. All soldiers killed. No can know."

It is true we no can know. We can only surmise. The only survivors of the Custer Battle, Sioux and Cheyenne and Blackfeet, are reluctant to give details concerning the battle in which they triumphed over the invaders of their land, but doubtless they themselves are uncertain as to whose arrow or shot killed the leader of the Seventh. During that brief, tragic hour all was confusion, bodies of the dead, both whites and reds, strewn everywhere, air dense with smoke from the valley below, raucous with the yells of the victors, Sioux circling the hill on fleet ponies, round and round, shooting up at the unmounted, pale-faced, desperate men whose guns would not work and who were hoping, up to the last minute, that their message had reached Benteen and that help would come. In that awful melee, while the Sioux circled closer and closer and the Cheyenne hid beneath the hill to cut off retreat and the few survivors of the Seventh, Tom and "Boss" Custer and Mark Kellogg and young Autie Reed gathered close to General Custer and backed up to the top of the ridge, step by slow step, fighting, hoping, despairing, how could any one be sure which of the whizzing bullets struck any particular man?

Red Horse has said:

Among the soldiers was an officer who rode a horse with four white feet. The Sioux have for a long time fought many brave men of different people, but the Sioux say this officer was the bravest man they had ever fought. I don't know whether this was General Custer or not. I saw this officer in the fight many times but did not see his body.—This officer wore a large-brimmed hat and a deerskin coat. This officer saved the lives of many soldiers by turning his horse and covering the retreat. Sioux say this officer was the bravest man they ever fought.

Many writers, attempting to probe the cloud of mystery that will forever enshroud the hour of battle on the twenty-fifth of June, 1876, have given free rein to their imaginings and have built up colorful stories based upon the fact that Custer's body was not mutilated. Some claim it was his remarkable bravery that won for him this mark of respect from a people who worship courage.

In an article published in *Hearst's International* and reprinted by *The Billings Gazette* Dan R. Conway tells an interesting story of a friendship—a blood-brothership—existing between General Custer and Sitting Bull. According to Conway it was by order of Sitting Bull, in memory of this friendship, that Custer's body was not mutilated. Conway writes:

It was in 1859 that Sitting Bull was sent to Washington. Following a conference there he was taken to West Point. Cadet George Armstrong Custer, a tall, slim lad with frank, handsome face and fair hair, was delegated to escort the Indians through West Point. When they parted he presented Sitting Bull with a complete uniform of the U. S. Cavalry. Custer told the chief he wanted to come out into his country as an officer and renew their friendship. Sitting Bull took him by the hand and called him: "Weh-hunka-wanzi"—Blood Brother. When an Indian declares another man his Weh-hunka-wanzi it brings that man closer to him than his own consanguineous brother.

Conway claims that the truth of the last stand of

Custer was revealed to him by Pakadoshen, Sitting Bull's chief scout.

"I first heard bits of it," Conway tells us, "being whispered around Indian campfires of the Montana prairies when I was a boy."

And this is the story which Conway asserts Pakadoshen told to him:

When all the warriors had gathered Sitting Bull faced his command. He said, "I am Sitting Bull, your chief. Hear me. Tomorrow we fight. We fight Pay-hee-honska (Custer). But I am not happy. A thing has been hurting my heart, and when a man's heart is hurt he cannot fight. (It is true that Sitting Bull did not fight but his failure to appear in the battle is attributed by his own people to lack of valor rather than to remorse.) It is this I want to tell you: kill every bluecoat but Pay-hee-honska. He was once my friend. He is my Weh-hunka-wanzi. Harm him not.

Pakadoshen tells the story of the fight:

We circled round and round them, firing into them and circling closer and closer. Pop-pop-pop-pop—rifles. Whee-hagh-ha—horses make cries like that. Indians whoop—white men shout. Big noise all over the place. We fight hard. Bluecoats falling everywhere. Bugle sound again. Bluecoats get off horses and run up ravines. Other bunch follow Custer on across the river. (He doubtless refers first to the charge on Reno and then to the one on Custer.) We follow into buttes. Find Custer and his men all in line for battle. Ready to fight hard in good fighting place. Buttes all around make it good shield for bluecoats.

There on highest butte we see Custer and his brother (Lieut. Thomas Custer) and six of his big chief officers all in little circle on top this high butte, ready to fight Indians. Custer he shouting loud to his men below. He stand up and shoot and shout; other officers around him squat down and shoot from knees.

Now we had to get Custer. He was fighting like big brave. But we must not kill him for Sitting Bull—We were afraid we would hit Custer. When his officers started to fall he got down behind a dead horse and started to fire at us that way. He had his long hair pushed up under his hat. (We recall John's assertion that Custer had had his hair cut while in the East.) He fought bravely and killed six of our chiefs. Just as we finished all the killing and were going to make the peace sign to Custer we saw him stand up and peer hard all over the battlefield. When he realized he alone was alive he put his gun against his body and pulled the trigger. He was dead right away. Sitting Bull went up to where he lay and stooped down and picked up his pistol. He did not say anything then but when we got to the land of the Red Sun (Canada) he used to be sorry that Custer had done that.

If we accept Pakadoshen's story at all, it must be with more than the proverbial one grain of salt. Sitting Bull, according to Rain-in-the-Face and Crazy Horse, was not in the battle. Some historians have credited the rumor that Custer committed suicide but those who first viewed his body—Gibbon, Benteen, Nolan, Bradley, together with the privates who helped bury the dead—all testify that there were two bullet wounds in his body, one through the temple and one through the left breast, each of which would have caused instant death. These men, some of them Custer's enemies and some his friends, join in ridiculing the statement that their general died by his own hand.

NOTE 24.

A few years before John's death he lead Mr. O'Donnell, step by step, over the trail the Seventh had blazed on the twenty-fourth and twenty-fifth of June, 1876. He showed him their last camping ground about a mile below the present site of Busby, on the ranch now owned by Willis Rowland. (Big Crow, a Cheyenne Indian states that, from a lookout peak, he saw Custer and his men in camp the night before the battle.) John showed Mr. O'Donnell the spot where the troops divided into three battalions, under Custer, Reno and McDougal. He pointed out the place where the mules in the pack train under McDougal became mired in a water hole. He retraced, after fifty years, McDougal's trail up the ridge where he joined Reno and the ravine leading to the river down which men, crazed with thirst, ventured for water. He found the rifle pits, still visible on that lonely, sun-baked hill—pitifully shallow, inadequate shelter against the rain of enemy bullets—which the men had gouged out of the hard earth with spoons and cups. Standing on the ridge overlooking the valley John drew a crude map positioning the troops —in the center of the basin a corral made of wagons, baggage and bodies of dead horses within which the mules and horses were tied. To the right Benteen with Troop H. To the left French with Troop M. In a semi-circle guarding against attack from the rear, Mc-Dougal with Troop B, Godfrey with Troop K, Wier with Troop D, and Wallace with Troop G. Upon reading the various accounts of the battle on Reno Hill we find this map, fruit of the memory of an old, illiterate man, to be surprisingly accurate in every detail. As John, with his friend, stood on the quiet hill overlooking the beautiful valley of the Big Horn with its emerald patches of wheat, its farm houses, its grazing cattle and sheep, visions arose before him of a time when that valley was dense with smoke from the Indians' barrage, hideous with their triumphant war cries and with the moans of dying men and shrieks of wounded horses, when, in the hearts of all, there was one single urge— to kill and kill and kill, and when he, John, young then, and strong, performing the tasks assigned him—digging rifle pits, dragging bodies of dead horses up for fortifications, firing down at the Redskins, hour after hour during four long-drawn out days, felt, beneath mad craving for water and fear of death, a torturing anxiety concerning the fate of the man he loved.

NOTE 25.

It is generally conceded that the only living creature surviving the battle of Custer was the horse, Comanche, belonging to Troop I and supposed to have been ridden by Captain Keogh. The horse was discovered hidden in a ravine, its body bullet ridden. Very tenderly the men dressed its wounds. A soft bed of straw was made at one end of the Far West and together with the wounded troopers from Reno Hill it was borne down the Yellowstone and Missouri Rivers to Fort Lincoln on that trip when *The Far West* under Captain Marsh broke all records for speed—920 miles in fifty-four hours. (According to the Missouri River Commission's Report for 1897) Comanche was never again ridden in battle but he had his place of honor, saddled and bridled, in all subsequent processions doing honor to the memory of Custer and his men. Much has been written of Comanche but in all the voluminous material written about the Custer Battle I have found only one reference, other than John's, to that other survivor of the battle—the yellow dog. In *A Warrior Who Fought Custer* by Marquis, Wooden Leg says:

A dog was following one of the Sioux women among the dead soldiers. I did not see any other dog there neither on that day nor on the day before when the fight was on.

NOTE 26.

As corroboration of John's sweeping statement concerning Reno we have the latter's own admission that he had been drinking the day of June 25th, 1876.

Copied from *The Billings Times:*

General George Armstrong Custer, a fighter of fighters and a soldier of soldiers—from Bull Run to Appamattox his career was meteoric. Second lieutenant at 21, major-general at 24—commander of the Third Cavalry Division which, in six months' time (Civil War) took one hundred and eleven guns, 65 battle flags and more than 10,000 prisoners without losing a flag or a gun—such was Custer's war record. After the war he was appointed lieutenant colonel of the Seventh Cavalry, a regiment which was born with him, lived with him, and a large part of which died with him. Had Reno given him proper support, he might have won. Overcome hopelessly by a red wave of destruction he died as he had lived—a gallant soldier.

Major Marcus A. Reno, whose failure at the Little Big Horn resulted in the tragedy that befell Custer was breveted major in 1863 for gallant conduct at Kelly's Ford, Lieutenant-colonel in 1864 for gallantry at Cedar Creek. He joined the Seventh Cavalry in 1869 as major, having had no Indian service prior to that time.—He was a bitter enemy of Custer and the latter had been begged before starting on that fatal campaign not to entrust the command of any supporting movement to Reno. In 1880 Reno was found guilty by a general courtmartial of conduct unbecoming an officer and a gentleman and was dismissed from the army dishonorably. His sentence was the result of a drunken brawl

[248]

in a billiard hall. Later, having sunk to the gutter, he took his own life. Reno himself told Dr. Arthur Edwards, his faithful friend to the end, that his conduct at the Little Big Horn was the result of drink.

In an article by Mrs. Plassman published in *The Rocky Mountain Husbandman* she quotes from a letter written by Mr. S. R. Graybill, son of Custer's teacher. He writes:

When news of his (Custer's) death reached us I was in the room when the bearer of the tragic news told it to my father, and it was told with this clause: "He did not wait for the rest of the army under General Terry, and, underestimating the strength of the Indians, engaged them."—which statement is now a part of the war record of the Custer massacre. This statement is misleading and untrue and should be struck from the war record.

As the bearer of the news enlarged upon the cause of the tragedy, saying it was the ambition of Custer to procure another crown for his head, my father stopped him and said, "Don't tell such a story as that to me. I knew Armstrong better than to believe any such statement, no matter from whom or where it comes. Armstrong had a nervous temperment and was always looking for some excitement and to do what he did well; but the thought of getting any laurels for himself for any act good or bad was furtherest from his thoughts. If he attacked too large a force in this case and lost I want no one to tell me it was done to gain honor for himself, and I shall not listen to any such comment."

Whatever may be the truth regarding the motives that led Custer to make that fatal charge on the Sioux village it is gratifying to know his childhood friends were loyal to his memory. Certainly no one could have been better informed as to Custer's character up to the time he left home to be enrolled as a student at West Point than the teacher who had watched his development from the very beginning.

We may interpret as a fine and generous gesture the impulse which prompted Custer to give to Reno—his enemy—the lead in the most important engagement of his career. Deeply loyal toward his friends, painfully sensitive to the sting of the arrows of malice, Custer was incapable of harboring resentment toward those who hated him. In a letter dated Sept. 28, 1873, he writes to Mrs. Custer:

When you find I have just sent the 7th Cavalry band to serenade—on his departure you will say to yourself, "He has been too forgiving again." Well, perhaps I have. I often think of the beautiful expression uttered by President Lincoln at the consecration of the Gettysburg monument and feel how nearly it expresses my belief,—"With malice toward none, with charity toward all!" and I hope this will ever be mine to say.

Far more than his characteristic buoyant optimism prompted him to report to his wife in a letter dated Sept. 10th, 1873:

I would be glad to have every one of the officers now with me stationed at my post. My relations with them, personal and official, are extremely agreeable.

[250]

NOTES

It would be well if those writers who love to dwell upon Custer's "harsh disciplinarian measures," his "indifference to the welfare of men and horses" would consider such statements as the following copied from letters written to his wife and presumably for her eyes alone:

Nearly every day we have something nice to send to Lieut. Braden. Only think of him, with his shattered thigh, having to trail over a rough country for three hundred miles! He is transported on a long stretcher pulled and pushed by men on foot. They carry him much more steadily than would horses or mules. The day the command divided I had the band take a position near the route where the rest of the expedition would pass and when he (Braden) approached they struck up *Garry Owen.* He acknowledged the attention as well as he could.

And this:

"What I am going to tell you is for you alone. —— came to me the other day and asked me to arrange that he be stationed at our post next winter. He says he wants to be in a garrison where the duty is strict, and, above all, he desires to prove that he is, and desires to be, a man, and he believes that he could do much better than he has if he serves under me. He says the very atmosphere of his present post seems filled with evil. I have a scheme by which I think I can accomplish his coming and I believe that you will approve."

Mrs. Custer adds a note to this letter from her husband, "We had been extremely anxious about this officer to whom my husband refers, and longed to save him from himself."

NOTE 27.

According to Godfrey, Muggins Taylor reached Reno Hill on the morning of the twenty-seventh, bearing a written message from General Terry to General Custer, dated June twenty-sixth. Terry, in his message, stated that he doubted the report given him by the two Crow scouts concerning the defeat of the column but that he was hastening forward with medical assistance.

Lieutenant Bradley, 7th Infantry, is supposed to have brought the first authentic account of the Custer defeat to the men on Reno Hill. He was with Gibbon whose column discovered the body-strewn battle field. When asked, "Where is Custer?" he replied, "I dont know, but I suppose he's been killed, as we counted 197 dead bodies. I don't suppose any escaped."

(From Godfrey's *Custer's Last Battle* published in *The Billings Gazette*.

NOTE 28.

DeRudio, according to an article written by Brinninstool and published in *Hunter-Trader-Trapper* was with Reno at the beginning of the attack upon the Indian village. As they were fording the river he—DeRudio—became separated from the retreating column when he attempted to secure one of the Seventh's guidons which had been left on the opposite side. Having rescued the colors he was about to remount when his horse, struck by a bullet, ran into the midst of the enemy, leaving DeRudio on foot surrounded by Indians. He managed to escape, unwounded, into a nearby thicket where he found Girard, the interpreter, O'Neil of Company G and the half-breed, Billy Jackson. Later they were joined by another scout, George Herendeen.

At the Reno trial held in Chicago in 1879 and in all subsequent statements DeRudio has loyally upheld Reno, asserting that at no time did the latter show cowardice or conduct himself in a manner unbecoming an officer. DeRudio testified that, according to his opinion, Reno showed judgment and wisdom in retreating rather than attacking the village. He says:

The fire from this numerically-superior force necessitated a retreat which was almost impossible, as we were now surrounded by warriors. When we entered the engagement we were only 112 strong and the fire of the enemy had made havoc in our little band.

George Herendeen took the opposite view. He told Mr. I. D. O'Donnell his testimony at the Reno Court of Inquiry was to the effect that Reno's position, with the high cliff back of him and the steep-sided creek in front, was almost impregnable and that Reno could have held that position, even against a numerically superior force, for an unlimited time, thus dividing the Indian strength and enabling Custer to attack, successfully, the upper end of the village. Herendeen believed and so testified that Reno's retreat was an unnecessary and panicky rout.

We may find some excuse for Reno from the fact that he was not an experienced Indian fighter and did not know or, in that first tense moment, forgot that Indians never advance boldly in a body to attack. As we have stated many surviving Sioux warriors have testified that, had Reno held his grounds, they would have retreated, that, in fact, they were making preparations to flee when Reno's retreat up the hill emboldened them to concentrate upon Custer's forces.

James McLaughlin, in his book, *My Friend, the Indian,* writes:

From what leading Indians in the engagement have told me of the fight, I am of the opinion that if Custer's obvious plan of battle had been carried out,—if Reno had struck the upper end of the Sioux camp when Custer struck the village at the lower end,— there would at least have been no such disaster as that which overtook the leader of the cavalry and the men with him. I am not at all fearful that this flat statement of a conviction acquired from the Indians who participated in the fight, and not from any prejudiced military authority, will embroil me in a dispute. The matter admits of no dispute.

[254]

NOTES

Three days before the battle, in a dispatch dated June 22, 1876, Kellogg, the *New York Herald* correspondent who fell with Custer, gave this estimate of his general:

A man of strong impulses, of great-hearted friendships and enmities, of quick, nervous temperment, undaunted courage, will and determination. A man possessing electric mental capacity and iron frame and constitution; a brave, faithful, gallant soldier —the hardest rider, the greatest pusher, with the most untiring vigilance, overcoming seeming impossibilities and with an ambition to succeed in all things he undertakes; a man to do right as he construes the right, in every case; one respected and beloved by his followers, who would follow him into the "jaws of hell."

McLaughlin writes of Custer:

General Custer was not the dashing, devil-may-care, hard-riding and fast-fighting mounted soldier that the romancers have made him out. He was a careful, painstaking man and officer, devoted to his profession of arms and properly appreciating the tools he had to work with. The dash that was supposed to be his principal characteristic was merely a part of the plan of a man who knows the essentials to success. He was not careless of consequences in any of the matters of life. He was a reserved and somewhat reticent man. He held the admiration of his officers and soldiers, not because he was their idol, one whom they might follow unthinkingly, but because they knew him to be a thorough soldier. He might go into an undertaking when he knew the chances were against him, but he would not do it in a spirit of bravado.

OLD NEUTRIMENT

Excerpt from *Bismarck Tribune*. July third, 1876.

It is the eve of Independence day, the Centennial Fourth, and all the land is ablaze with enthusiasm. Alas, if the tidings of General Custer's terrible disaster could be borne on the wings of the four winds dirges and not anthems would be heard on the streets of Philadelphia, New York, Boston, San Francisco.

A great shadow has fallen on the valley of the Big Horn. The youngest of our generals, the *beau sabreur* of the army of the Potomac, the golden-haired chief whom the Sioux had learned to dread, has fought his last fight.

J'AIME LONDON

100 Culinary destinations
for food lovers.

hardie grant books
MELBOURNE · LONDON

ALAIN DUCASSE

J'AIME LONDON

hardie grant books

INSTITUTION

3

MAYFAIR
ALAIN DUCASSE AT THE DORCHESTER
53 Park Lane – London, W1K 1QA
Tel. : +44-20-7629-8866 – www.alainducasse-dorchester.com

"Exceptional products, precision and skill. Jocelyn Herland interprets my cuisine for Londoners in a modern and refined style. From melt-in-your-mouth cheese puffs to sauté gourmand of lobster, truffled chicken quenelles and homemade pasta, as well as the Cookpot of seasonal vegetables, Jocelyn cooks every dish to perfection, treating each ingredient with the utmost respect. And my head sommelier Vincent Pastorello's clear advice will help you find the perfect wine to accompany each of the dishes. I wanted this taste experience to take place in a unique setting that made the best use of natural materials. The Table Lumière, the showpiece of the restaurant, treats our guests to an extraordinarily sensory experience, masterfully arranged by my restaurant director Nicolas Defrémont." *Alain Ducasse*

WHITEHALL
BERRY BROS & RUDD
3 St. James's Street – London, SW1A 1EG
Tel. : +44-80-0280-2440 – www.bbr.com

The exterior of Britain's most historic wine merchant belies the two acres of labyrinthine cellars that sprawl beneath. Inside the rickety, Mayfair premises, from which the company has traded since the 17th century, you can explore not just the world of fine wine, but Britain's history. Relics on display include: a letter from the Titanic (the merchant lost six cases when it sank) and the original scales used to weigh its customers for 150 years. The family company has held a royal warrant since the reign of King George III, but it's anything but archaic – having been the first wine merchant to open an online shop in 1994. Nothing beats an actual visit where the knowledgeable staff will find whatever wine you're after – be it a £13 Picpoul or a £13,000 Romanée Conti.

HOXTON
BREAKFAST CLUB (THE)
2–4 Rufus Street – London, N1 6PE
Tel. : +44-20-7729-5252 – www.thebreakfastclubcafes.com

Children of the 1980s find a happy haven in this Hoxton outpost of the American-diner-meets-British-greasy-spoon cafe. Having started in Soho and expanded all over London, the people behind this quirky mini-group have stayed true to what originally made them such a hit – big, bolstering breakfasts and lunches eaten inside a fun, kinetic cocoon of kitsch memorabilia. This East End site is bigger than the others, but is still packed with 1980s treasures that woo retro junkies, like a Mickey Mouse statuette and an archaic TV. That woo retro-junkies. Living up to its name, breakfast is still the main draw; try the wicked breakfast burrito of chorizo, scrambled egg, guacamole, Cheddar and spicy pepper sauce.

CONNAUGHT (THE)

Carlos Place – London, W1K 2AL
Tel. : +44-20-7499-7070 – www.the-connaught.co.uk

Amidst all its elegance and refinement, a brilliantly bacchanalian spirit pervades this iconic Mayfair hotel, thanks to its distinguished food and drink offerings. Its two bars, The Connaught and The Coburg, are deluxe drinking dens with impressive selections of vintages, limited-edition champagnes and world-famous cocktails served in smart, elegant surroundings. French two-star Michelin chef Hélène Darroze has a gastronomic restaurant in the hotel, and is also responsible for the breakfast, lunch and tapas menu at The Coburg. At The Connaught, the martini, made with crispy Gancia Dry vermouth from Italy, is so famous it warrants its own trolley.

FORTNUM & MASON

181 Piccadilly – London, W1A 1ER
Tel. : +44-845-300-1707 – www.fortnumandmason.com

Strong links to the East India Company when it was just a grocer in the 1700s ensured this quintessentially British department store's trailblazing access to rare, quality teas and spices. To this day, the Piccadilly stalwart is the go-to place for everything from artisan British produce, like Herefordshire Ragstone goat's cheese and hand-raised pork pies made with outdoor-bred Lincolnshire pork, to its weird and wonderful preserves, like unripe hedgerow blackberries in cider vinegar or 'fig cheese', and its homemade biscuits, chocolates, macarons and sumptuous hampers. The Diamond Jubilee Tea Salon is one of the best places in the capital to take afternoon tea.

GALVIN AT WINDOWS

Hilton Hotel, 22 Park Lane – London, W1K 1BE
Tel. : +44-20-7208-4021 – www.galvinatwindows.com

Chef patron Chris Galvin's Michelin- starred restaurant in Mayfair is still a cut above. Up on the 28th floor of the Park Lane Hilton, with dramatic views overlooking Buckingham Palace and the City, visitors are beckoned into a glamorous art-deco setting, where they can unwind in 1930s-style window seats with delicious bar snacks, house champagne or a carefully crafted cocktail. In the dining room, head chef Joo Won's seasonal, globally inflected dishes divert from the superb views in flavour-packed ensembles. In terms of service, front-of-house aficionado Fred Sirieix and his team make you feel like royalty, even if you're only taking advantage of the exceptionally well-priced set menus.

HARRY'S BAR

26 South Audley Street – London W1K 2PD
Tel. : +44-20-7408-0844 – www.harrysbar.co.uk

Members or guests at this Mayfair institution get a secret glimpse into London's glamorous past every time they ring the doorbell. This place has been going since 1979, and still attracts the old-school crowd, but to call it a 'bar' is a bit misleading. While you can enjoy crumbling chunks of 24-month-aged Parmigiana Reggiano, Sicilian bread and Bellinis at the shiny marble bar, this place is as much about the dining room, which hangs with glittering chandeliers and the works of Peter Arno and other *New Yorker* artists. Impeccable, authentic northern Italian food is the offering here, and the Piedmont beef carpaccio with garden pea sauce is a favourite.

LA PETITE MAISON

53–54 Brook's Mews – London, W1K 4EG
Tel. : +44-20-7495-4774 – lpmlondon.co.uk

'When I went to the restaurant in Nice, the dish which won me over was the warm prawns in olive oil. It's so simple – just prawns, olive oil, lemon juice and basil – but it's awesome, and I knew I could build a menu around that,' says chef patron Raphael Duntoye, who brought the light, olive oil-bathed cuisine of Côte d'Azur to Mayfair when he opened the London cousin of the legendary Nice restaurant in 2007. Previously head chef at Zuma and alumni of Pierre Koffmann, Duntoye has crafted a restaurant that rings with Riviera bonhomie in the midst of Mayfair – its tables laid with lemons, ripe tomatoes and bottles of olive oil. Finely sliced octopus, set with its own gelatine, is drizzled with garlicky lemon oil, and melts on the tongue; slivers of marinated scallop are studded with jewels of cranberry and given crunchy depth by toasted flaked almonds. 'I want you to have the first bite and not be able to wait to have the second bite, and to share various plates. This is how food should be. It should be fun. It should be like a journey.'

LA POULE AU POT

231 Ebury Street – London, SW1W 8UT
Tel. : +44-20-7730-7763 – www.pouleaupot.co.uk

Unashamedly eccentric, with its stage-set interior of plastic grapes, wicker baskets and candelabras, this Belgravia bistro is a rare time warp on a restaurant landscape defined by re-invention. Having remained almost unchanged since it opened in the 1960s, it's the kind of place you'll find couples who first came here 40 years ago reliving the romance alongside French expats looking for a taste of home. And, boy, do they find it in the proudly French-only written menus, the buttery, garlic-laden escargots and heady, fish-stock-rich soupe de poisson. The three-course table d'hôte lunch menu is incredible value; though choosing between the Toulouse sausage and steak frites is not an easy decision for any Francophile to make.

LE GAVROCHE

43 Upper Brook Street – London W1K 7QR
Tel. : +44-20-7408-0881 / +44-20-7499-1826
www.le-gavroche.co.uk

Heston Blumenthal has compared the impact of the Roux brothers on British gastronomy to that of The Beatles on pop music, and the epoch-defining influence the French brothers would have on UK dining all started with the launch of Le Gavroche in 1967. Fast-forward almost half a century, and the Mayfair restaurant is still a beacon of fine dining in the capital, with Michel Roux Jr having taken over the restaurant from his father Albert in 1991. This is a place for special-occasion meals, and the signature cheese soufflé – a mixture of Gruyère and Cheddar, swimming in a rich bath of cream – sums this place up: generous, delicious and exquisitely indulgent.

NOTTING HILL
LEDBURY (THE)

127 Ledbury Road – London, W11 2AQ
Tel. : +44 20 7792 9090 – **www.theledbury.com**

Far from the madding-central-London-chef-crowd, on a serene street in leafiest Notting Hill, Australian-born chef Brett Graham has been quietly turning out some of London's most exceptional and exciting fine dining fare since 2005. Having previously worked under one of the capital's most cherished and respected chefs – Philip Howard at The Square – Graham's gone on to achieve the elusive accolade also held by his former mentor in the form of two glittering Michelin stars. He has a way with British ingredients that delights visually, intellectually and culinarily; while rooted in the classics, his food harnesses a refreshing lightness and modernity. Inside The Ledbury's simple, sophisticated dining room it's the food, not the 'concept' or decor, that does the talking – along with the amenable and knowledgeable staff. A dish of deeply savoury grilled onion broth with subtle buffalo milk curds and Saint-Nectaire and truffle toast is sublime, balanced and somehow nostalgic – French onion soup and cheese on toast lurking on the peripheries of its conception. Berkshire muntjac deer comes moist, rare and tender on a bed of ruby-red beetroot, endive, radicchio and cherry blossoms, with two pearls of buttery bone marrow on top.

MAYFAIR
PROMENADE AT THE DORCHESTER (THE)

53 Park Lane – London, W1K 1QA
Tel. : +44-20-7629-8888
www.thedorchester.com/afternoon-tea

At the Dorchester, afternoon tea is still what this most elegant of English rituals should be: an unapologetically lavish, deliciously tradition-steeped three-course affair. Fine china and white linen are a given. Champagne is optional – though bubbles suit the mood of such a grand setting, amidst soaring marble pillars and towering palms in 'The Promenade' lobby of this legendary Mayfair hotel. Settle into the sumptuous, pristinely upholstered furniture and prepare to be beguiled by this gracious service, which begins with carefully filled crustless sandwiches, accompanied by your tea of choice – be it smokey Lapsang Souchon or fragrant Earl Grey. Warm scones made to a recipe unchanged for over half a century follow. Slather on the strawberry jam and Devonshire clotted cream, but save room for the pièce de resistance – the pastry platter: an immaculately crafted parade of delightful treats including white chocolate and praline pyramids, mini raspberry macaroons, perfect pineapple financiers and a creamy apple and macadamia delice.

QUO VADIS
26–29 Dean Street – London, W1D 3LL
Tel. : +44 20 7437 9585 – **www.quovadissoho.co.uk**

When Jeremy Lee – darling of the London food scene, feted for his unfussy British cooking at the Blueprint Café – took over the kitchen of Quo Vadis, the grande dame of Soho dining, in 2012, it made a lot of sense. 'I'd been coming from day one to this iconic London restaurant,' says Lee. Working with lauded brother restaurateurs Sam and Eddie Hart, Lee has put his simple, seasonal stamp on the food and feel of the restaurant. 'We wanted to create a friendly, cheery place for people to come and have gorgeous moments. In terms of food, we do as little to it as possible, so the produce can speak for itself. And we bake everything ourselves in the bakery downstairs. Our mantra is: "if we can't make it, we don't sell it".'

ST. JOHN
26 St. John Street – London, EC1M 4AY
Tel. : +44-20-7251-0848 – **www.stjohngroup.uk.com**

'Mother Nature writes brilliant menus in this country, with its short, exciting seasons. Whether it's asparagus or gull's eggs, there are these wonderful things that come for a moment, and we just follow nature's pointers,' says Fergus Henderson, co-founder of St. John, messiah of nose-to-tail cooking, and one of the most influential chef-restaurateurs London's ever seen. He trained as an architect, but his attention was soon taken up with cooking pot au feu and cassoulet for his fellow students, and he then became an architect of a different kind, opening St. John in Clerkenwell in 1994. With its stark white walls and gutsy plates of roasted bone marrow and parsley salad, it's become fabled as an egalitarian eating place, where you can come for a pint of beer and decent rarebit, or for grouse and a bottle of claret. The acclaimed St. John Bread and Wine in Spitalfields followed in 2003. 'I have a no-crutch theory,' Henderson says. 'There's no brass or marble, no velvet or artwork. We've removed all those things so the decoration and entertainment of the restaurant comes through the eater. It should be all about the glugging of wine and the cutting of cheese, the crack of a whole crab, the sucking of bones – that's the music of the restaurant.'

RIVER CAFE (THE)
Thames Wharf, Rainville Road – London, W6 9HA
Tel. : +44-20-7386-4200 – **www.rivercafe.co.uk**

Down by the river, inside a long, light room, well-heeled Londoners come together to eat Italian food that's been setting standards for its quality and unapologetic simplicity for over 25 years. Most settle in at one of the tables and feast for hours on sublime plates of artichoke with explosively creamy burrata, glossy spaghetti vongole and wood-oven roasted Dover sole that is soft, sweet and sharpened with capers, lemon and parsley. During service the room fills with the buzz of laughter, cutlery, plates, glasses and chat. It's the hum of happiness: something the late Rose Gray and Ruth Rogers, who still works the pass, brought to London in spades in 1987, when they set up their kitchen that would go on to train the likes of Jamie Oliver and Hugh Fearnley Whittingstall.

PICCADILLY

WOLSELEY (THE)

160 Piccadilly – London, W1J 9EB

Tel. : +44- 20-7499-6996 – **www.thewolseley.com**

Breakfasting at Chris Corbin and Jeremy King's grand European 'Cafe' in Mayfair has become a legendary dining ritual that counts celebrities, influencers and culinary movers and shakers among its denizens. There's just something about the soaring vaulted ceilings, black and white marble floor and tables of fresh pastries that sets this former automotive showroom and bank apart. Accessible glamour is the modus operandi, and the surprisingly egalitarian brasserie menu offers everything from a humble but perfectly crispy bacon roll, to the famous omelette Arnold Bennett: an opulent confluence of smoked haddock, cream and hollandaise. It will keep you going until supper, when you might just find yourself back there to get cosy with a very good wiener schnitzel...

KNIGHTSBRIDGE

ZUMA

5 Raphael Street – London, SW7 1DL

Tel. : +44 20 7584 1010 – **www.zumarestaurant.com/
zuma-landing/london/en/welcome**

Over a decade since it opened its doors, chef Rainer Becker and businessman Arjun Waney's original restaurant collaboration in Knightsbridge – which has since expanded to as far afield as Miami and Bangkok – is still one of London's hottest culinary tickets. Having spent six years ensconced in the Tokyo food scene, working at the Park Hyatt hotel and acquiring an intimate knowledge of Japanese dining rituals and methods, Becker created something unique when he opened this relaxed, upscale playground for hungry, urbane Londoners. This is where media darlings, business suits, Japanese food junkies and restaurant obsessives looking for a slice of Tokyo pie come to feast; and the food doesn't disappoint, with clean, punchy flavours in stalwarts like the sliced sea bass with yuzu, truffle oil and salmon roe, or the spicy beef tenderloin with sesame, red chilli and sweet soy. Loosely based on izakaya – Japan's more informal dining experience – the restaurant has a cool, relaxed vibe that's enhanced by its sleek, natural design, with earth-tone granite, Japanese rice-paper panels and imported Indonesian wooden tables.

ALBION

2–4 Boundary Street – London E2 7DD
Tel. : +44-20-7729-1051 – www.albioncaff.co.uk

Terence Conran and Peter Prescott's stylish, airy cafe-cum-bakery and deli prides itself on the Britishness of its setting, ingredients and recipes. Located in the former Victorian warehouse which also houses their Boundary boutique hotel in Shoreditch, it's a cool, clean, all-day dining space in which to enjoy everything from a sausage sandwich or oysters and Bloody Marys – to hearty heritage dishes like rabbit stew. If you're just passing through the neighbourhood, it's worth popping in to pick up a loaf of sourdough from the award-winning bakery or to try one of the baked products created by the in-house pastry chefs.

BARBECOA

20 New Change Passage – London, EC4M 9AG
Tel. : +44-20-3005-8555 – www.barbecoa.com

London's love affair with barbecue stepped up a notch when golden boy Jamie Oliver opened his firepit fantasy restaurant in 2010. Floor-to-ceiling windows overlooking St Paul's Cathedral add a certain drama to this industrial-chic inferno, where kitchens celebrate the various forms of traditional, fire-based cooking methods: sporting a Texas pit smoker, tandoors, robata grills and wood-fired ovens. Before being expertly flame-licked, the meat here is hand-picked by the restaurant's butchers to ensure quality, while beef is dry-aged in-house for anything up to 70 days. Prosecco cocktails like the 'Death in The Afternoon', made with Pernod, absinthe and lemon, ensure it's not a purely butch affair.

BALTHAZAR

4–6 Russell Street – London, WC2B 5HZ
Tel. : +44-20-3301-1155 – www.balthazarlondon.com

Keith McNally has been many things in his life – a scene-defining restaurateur in New York being the most obvious (though he's also acted in, and directed films) – but he was born a Londoner, and in 2013 he returned to bring his Big Apple baby home. Balthazar – his Parisian-style brasserie behemoth – landed spectacularly, and suitably theatrically, in Covent Garden, opening in a grand room with leather banquettes, enormous mirrors and whirring ceiling fans that make it seem as ancient as its antique fixtures suggest. It's every bit as glamorous as its New York cousin, and in the kinetic 170-seat dining room, plates of French brasserie fare with a slight New York accent are devoured by dine-hard devotees. At the 26-foot pewter bar, cocktails are mixed just as you like them and might precede a curly endive salad, dressed lusciously with bacon–shallot vinaigrette and a soft poached egg sprawling its silky yolk over the top. Main courses might mean brasserie stalwarts like lapin à la moutarde with spaetzle, or more modern interpretations like the umami-rich duck shepherd's pie.

FITZROVIA

BUBBLEDOGS – KITCHEN TABLE

70 Charlotte Street – London, W1T 4QG
Tel. : +44-20-7637-7770 – www.bubbledogs.co.uk

'I wanted to talk and show people how, why and what we're doing. I just wanted to cook for a few people, with the best possible ingredients – to interact with the guests and have fun with what I'm cooking,' says James Knappett, the Thomas Keller alumni behind London's hottest chef's-table restaurant. The 19-seat, tasting-menu-only gastro-diner can be found behind a heavy leather curtain at the back of Bubbledogs, a lively gourmet hot-dog joint with rare grower champagnes chosen by Sandia Chang, Knappett's wife and business partner. 'The food revolves around the ingredient. We start with the ingredients and work forwards from there.' This could mean a sparklingly fresh sliver of mackerel with bright dots of intensely lemony lemon purée, or a simple bowl of home-made tagliatelle, lush with butter and flakes of summer truffle. 'It's uncomplicated. I don't like to cloud flavours – if you're having pork, you will taste pork.'

VAUXHALL

BRUNSWICK HOUSE CAFÉ

30 Wandsworth Road – London, SW8 2LG
Tel. : +44-20-7720-2926 – www.brunswickhouse.co

'Brunswick House started as a ten-seat espresso and sandwich bar. Between my brother Frank and I, we had a cool £2000 saved up from tips, with which we leased a coffee machine, and struck a deal with Lassco, the London architectural salvage institution who had bought and restored this beautiful 18th-century mansion house in Vauxhall. We agreed we'd rent the floor space and they'd keep the walls and ceilings from which to hang antique panelling, and chandeliers. It was our simple goal to combine focused seasonal cooking with a culture of old-fashioned hospitality appropriate to such a fabulous setting. The restaurant has slowly expanded over the last three years, and now comfortably seats 80.' *Jackson Boxer*

MAYFAIR

BURGER AND LOBSTER

29 Clarges street – London, W1J 7EF
Tel. : +44-20-7409-1699
www.burgerandlobster.com

Surf or turf – the choice is yours. Although, there's nothing stopping you from ordering all of the menu items on offer at this vibey, original Mayfair outpost of the Burger and Lobster mini-group. After all, there are only three options, and they each cost just £20. Pick from a juicy, sweet steamed Canadian lobster that has the option to be finished on a charcoal grill with butter sauce; a moist, 10-ounce ground-beef patty sandwiched between a home-made sesame bun; or a soft, sumptuous brioche encasing mayonnaise-swathed lobster meat, topped with a fresh claw. This place has made an art out of simplicity, serving each item with golden, crunchy fries and a salad.

CAMDEN
CARAVAN

11–13 Exmouth Market – London, EC1R 4QD
Tel. : +44 20 7833 8115 – www.caravanonexmouth.co.uk

There are few things that could kick-start any food-lover's weekend more pleasurably than brunch at this thriving, breezy Antipodean restaurant, bar and coffee roastery in culinarily cool Exmouth Market. Thick slices of grilled coconut bread topped with lemon curd-flavoured cream cheese and – depending on the season – the ripest, sweetest strawberries or rhubarb is one way to soak up the brilliance of this globe-trotting menu. During the week, attentions turn to the fusion-focused sharing-plates menu, where you might find an expertly seared onglet with miso, green beans and peanut dressing to soak up your martini made with Sipsmith gin, earl grey, lemon and egg white.

FITZROVIA
DABBOUS

39 Whitfield Street – London, W1T 2SF
Tel. : +44-20-7323-1544 – www.dabbous.co.uk

'The primary objective was to still be open after year one,' says Ollie Dabbous, the young chef behind one of London's most fervently received, scene-shifting restaurants. 'We had no money when we opened, but we always envisaged offering a good night out, as opposed to just dinner. I wanted it to be stripped-back fine dining without the fuss, and to have a sociable bar aligned with the restaurant. We also wanted somewhere devoid of any ceremony or self-importance, where people would feel immediately at ease.' Dabbous' creative, natural cuisine – dishes such as iced sorrel with peas and mint, or mixed alliums in a chilled pine broth – elevates ordinary ingredients into something very special.

BETHNAL GREEN
COLUMBIA ROAD FLOWER MARKET

Columbia Road – London, E2 7RG
Tel. : +44-20-7613-0876
www.columbiaroad.info/flowermarket

Hipsters, tourists and locals collide at this East End street market every Sunday between 8am and 3pm, to lose themselves in the jungle of lilies, daffodils, roses, chrysanthemums and other cut flowers and foliage. Originally a Saturday food market set up in 1869, it moved to Sundays to accommodate its Jewish traders, and became a hub for Covent Garden and Spitalfields traders to sell their leftover cut-flower stock. These days the market is surrounded by over 60 independent shops and art galleries, as well as artisan eateries like miniature bakery Lily Vanilli, where you'll find creative, daringly decorated cakes strewn with chocolate shards and edible flowers.

SOHO
DEAN STREET TOWNHOUSE

69–71 Dean Street – London, W1D 3SE
Tel. : +44-20-7434-1775 – www.deanstreettownhouse.com

Though a hip all-day hangout and boutique hotel, this place comes alive for breakfast, lunch and dinner, sucking in the workers and characters of Soho with its speakeasy-style cocktails and unfussy British food. As you might expect from the minds behind media-darling member's club Soho House, there's an easy, undulating cool to the place – from the hanging Tracey Emins to the prohibition-styled bar staff, who mix creative, quenching tinctures like celery gimlets from behind their beards. Food celebrates seasonal native produce and British culinary heritage, appealing to both the comfort eater and bon viveur in dishes like the homely mince and buttered potatoes and the sea trout with buttered peas, lettuce and lovage.

NOTTING HILL
ELECTRIC DINER
191 Portobello Road – London, W11 2ED
Tel. : +44-20-7908-9696 – **www.electricdiner.com**

Brendan Sodikoff, the chef behind Chicago's feted Au Cheval French–American diner, is one of a clutch of US chefs to cotton on to London's love of his country's pimped-up junk food and bring it over for our enjoyment. Along with the minds behind Soho House, he opened this cool, exposed-brick, red leather banquette-clad all-day hangout in 2013, adjacent to the famous Electric Cinema in deepest Notting Hill. Like Au Cheval, the menu is French–American, featuring creations like his famous bologna sandwich and the lush bone marrow with beef-cheek marmalade, but those looking for something a little more saintly will find solace in cleaner dishes like sea bass with capers and lemon.

PECKHAM
FRANK'S CAFÉ
10th Floor, Peckham Multi-story carpark,
95A Rye Lane – London, SE15 4ST
www.frankscafe.org.uk

Every summer, at the top of a bleakly urban multistorey car park in deepest Peckham, one of London's coolest, most unusual bars pops up, courtesy of Frank Boxer – brother to Brunswick House's Jackson and grandson of famous food writer Arabella. With its red tarpaulin roof covers, wooden benches and makeshift bar slamming out short, sippable cocktails, there's a scintillatingly rough and ready, Berlin-meets-Ibiza-in-the-early-years energy to this place. Food scenesters and the art crowd, drawn to the kitchen's simple, seasonal plates of sardines and harissa, grilled sweetcorn with smoked paprika or wonderfully rustic hummus with toasted sourdough.

SPITALFIELDS
GALVIN LA CHAPELLE & CAFÉ A VIN
35 Spital Square – London, E1 6DY
Tel. : +44-20-7299-0400 – **www.galvinrestaurants.com/
section.php/61/1/galvin_la_chapelle**

'It was the site really; it was this building that made us want to open another restaurant,' says Jeff Galvin, who, along with brother Chris, fell in love with the Grade II-listed chapel of a former girls' school in Spitalfields. 'It even looked beautiful derelict, with no roof. It was a challenge – in a building with so much history you want to do it justice.' The Francophile chef brothers have since won a Michelin star for the grand, sumptuous fine-dining restaurant La Chapelle, where you can eat their signature Bresse pigeon tagine, rich with aubergine purée and harissa sauce. They have also gained wide acclaim for the attached Café a Vin, which showcases natural wines and simple, delicious French fare like the crave-inducing tarte flambée.

SPITALFIELDS
HAWKSMOOR
157a Commercial Street – London, E1 6BJ
Tel. : +44-20-7426-4850
thehawksmoor.com

It's true that there were steakhouses in London before Hawksmoor, but none of them quite captured the capital's frenzied inner carnivore quite like this meaty restaurant group. The founders insist that, affectionately reared rare-breed longhorn cattle from North Yorkshire is the tastiest in the world, and the capital has absolutely agreed with them. Properly aged, flame grilled and offered up in its various cuts – bone-in prime rib, porterhouse, T-bone – by weight and according to availability, the steak here is unparalleled. Pour over the bone-marrow gravy and dunk in your triple-cooked chips, while you sink a palate-provoking 'Full-fat Old Fashioned', made with butter-infused bourbon. Then go for a run.

BRIXTON
HONEST BURGERS 🍴

Unit 12, Brixton Village – London, SW9 8PR
Tel. : +44-20-7733-7963 – **www.honestburgers.co.uk**

The burgers created at the original, miniature Honest Burgers site in Brixton Village covered market created such a frenzy amidst the capital's carnivores, and such a long queue, that the owners took pity and opened another site in Soho, and then Camden. Forget American burgers though, these patties are proud to be British, and are made with meat sourced from the excellent Ginger Pig butcher and rare-breed farmer, whose pigs, cattle and sheep are reared on the North Yorkshire Moors. All burgers come in a glazed bun with rosemary-tossed home-made fries, and specials include creative, produce-driven delights like the beef and black pudding burger with apple tempura, tarragon and caper mayonnaise, and baby leaf lettuce.

SHOREDITCH
LES TROIS GARÇONS 🍴

1 Club Row – London, E1 6JX
Tel. : +44-20-7613-1924 – **www.lestroisgarcons.com**

A good decade before Shoreditch would become a swarming ground for art, fashion and food-scenesters, Hassan Abdullah, Michel Lasserre and Stefan Karlson – three successful interior designers – had the foresight to buy this glorious building on the Bethnal Green Road and make it their home. In 2000, these 'trois garçons' opened the ground floor up as one of London's most memorable and eccentric dining rooms, while keeping the upstairs for their living quarters and the cellar stocked with fine wine. A meal here is taken in the company of a veritable Noah's Ark of antique taxidermy, including Boris the bulldog (a Victorian-era fighting dog donned in a pair of fairy wings) and George the giraffe (who was one of the first of his species at London Zoo), plus a rare blue Murano chandelier from the 1920s. A visual feast indeed, but also a culinary one, as chef Michael Chan melds classic French haute cuisine with Asian and New World accents to produce memorable, harmonious dishes like crayfish and sweetbread spring roll with black sesame-dressed bean sprouts. Front-of-house guru Fabien Babanini is a wine enthusiast who loves nothing more than exploring regions and grapes with you as you eat, making for a beautifully bacchanalian experience.

MARYLEBONE
LA FROMAGERIE 🧀

2–6 Moxon Street – London, W1U 4EW
Tel. : +44-20-7935-0341 – **www.lafromagerie.co.uk**

Patricia Michelson's quest to bring brilliant farmhouse cheeses to the capital started on a whim after she returned from a Méribel ski trip. She eventually opened her first shop in Highbury in 1992 and Marylebone in 2002. Both shops now house on-site maturing cellars, where cheeses are delivered direct from artisan producers and matured by in-house affinage (specialist cheese maturers), as well as impressive, wonderfully pungent walk-in cheese rooms, delis and cafes. Cheeses span goat's, buffalo, sheep and cow's milk, and include creations like the lovely soft Portuguese sheep's milk cheese Azeitão, which is made with artichoke thistle rennet and has a sharp, sweet earthiness to it.

MARYLEBONE
MONOCLE CAFÉ

18 Chiltern Street – London, W1U 7QA
Tel. : +44-20-7725-4388
www.monocle.com/about/contacts/london-cafe

In 2013, international affairs and design-bible *Monocle* followed its Tokyo cafe opening with one in London, near to its headquarters, on Chiltern Street in Marylebone. To create their 'dream cafe', the team behind the magazine led by publisher and *Wallpaper** founder Tyler Brûlé, called on their multiple industry-leading connections, resulting in a unique and modish coffee shop. As you'd expect from a global design journal, the interior is captivating, if somewhat understated – a sleek confluence of clean lines and beautiful natural materials like red oak, which has been used to create bold Japanese-style screens. Coffee is roasted daily, and comes courtesy of the New Zealand–Australian team Allpress Espresso, while food is fresh and hearty cafe fare: wholesome Bircher mueslis, seasonal salads and cheese toasties. The cakes here are even worth putting down a copy of *Monocle* for; created by former Le Gavroche pastry chef Masayuki Hara's Lanka bakery, they include fresh macarons, green tea roll cake and strawberry gateau.

SOHO
PITT CUE CO.
1 Newburgh – London, W1F 7RB
www.pittcue.co.uk

What started as a food truck on the South Bank, delighting with its seriously smoking southern American-inspired barbecue, moved into a tiny, 24-cover premises in Soho a year after it began peddling its slow-cooked brisket, pulled pork and proper home-made baked beans. Led by a crack team, including lauded head chef Tom Adams and bourbon expert Jamie Berger, this basement barbecue joint has a bar upstairs where you wait (there are no reservations) in the good company of picklebacks – bourbon shots chased by pickle juice. When your table is ready, descend into the cosy dining room and fill your belly with smoky, meaty treats from the ever-changing menu. Watch out for the 'burnt ends mash': potato purée mixed with the smoky, charred ends of the brisket.

SHOREDITCH
PIZZA EAST
56 Shoreditch High Street – London, E1 6JJ
Tel. : +44-20-7729-1888 – www.pizzaeast.com

Eating pizza in London got a whole lot sexier when the brains behind the Soho House group launched this flagship site in the ground floor of Shoreditch's sprawling Tea building. Inside, a dimly lit industrial-chic interior is the setting for friends to come together over wood-fired pizzas. Melding classic Neapolitan simplicity with more progressive ideas, pizzas span everything from the classic margherita to the more elaborate pork belly with tomato, mozzarella and mushroom, or the veal meatballs with prosciutto and cream. This is very much a modern pizzeria that makes a point of using carefully sourced, seasonal ingredients, and there's a take-away counter where guests can pick-up cavolo nero, radicchio and fennel bulbs for their own kitchen.

POLPO

41 Beak Street – London, W1F 9SB
Tel. : +44-20-7734-4479 – www.polpo.co.uk

This was the first solo restaurant from Russell Norman – the man credited with starting a 'fun dining' revolution in London just as recession took hold – and it's still one of the capital's coolest places to eat. Tucked away in Soho, and based on Norman's interpretation of the booze-soaked bàcari of Venice, it's a place to come with friends and lovers to share the small, addictive plates of Venetian food. Slurp on Campari house cocktails while you nibble arancini, other cicheti dishes and the famous pizzetta bianca, then get stuck into main dishes like the linguine vongole, calf's liver with onion and sage, and fennel, almond and curly endive salad.

ROKA

37 Charlotte Street – London, W1T 1RR
Tel. : +44-20-7580-6464 – www.rokarestaurant.com

Tell any food-loving Londoner you've got a table at Roka and there'll be a flicker of jealous rage across their face and then a wide, dreamy-eyed smile as they recall the last time they ate there. Inspired by six years of cooking in Tokyo, chef Rainer Becker, along with restaurateur Arjun Waney, took the informal Japanese dining concept of izakaya and brought it to London with the hit launch of Zuma in Knightsbridge in 2002. Roka in 2004, with an emphasis on robatayaki – dishes from the robata grill. Sit at the wooden counter, sip a shóchu cocktail and watch the chefs at work while you hoover up the beautiful poached king crab leg with avocado, gems of punchy tosazu jelly and wasabi roe.

ROCHELLE CANTEEN

Rochelle School, Arnold Circus – London, E2 7ES
Tel. : 020 7729 5677 – www.arnoldandhenderson.com

Ring the bell to be let into this hidden feasting spot, set in a converted school bike shed on Shoreditch's Arnold Circus in the Boundary Estate – London's first, and arguably most handsome, council housing development, which is now home to bijou shops and eateries. Margot Henderson (wife of Fergus) can be found serving up confident, unapologetically rustic breakfast, lunch and dinner dishes from the open kitchen during the week. A slow-braised cuttlefish sings of the Mediterranean and comforts the palate: rich and unctuous with sweet fennel and melting tomatoes. Sliced sirloin is ruby red and served on dripping fried bread with creamy, cutting horseradish. Cabbage comes a vital bright green, crunchy and slathered in butter.

SCOTT'S

20 Mount Street – London, W1K 2HE
Tel. : +44-20-7495-7309 – www.scotts-restaurant.com

First an oyster warehouse founded in 1851, and then a restaurant in its current Mayfair location since 1968, Scott's has long been a haunt of the rich and influential, and it's still got it. Famed for its seafood, and for being the place Ian Fleming discovered the dry martini 'shaken, not stirred', this is a proper grown-up London restaurant. It's a place best reserved for blow-outs, but it's open all day, so you can just slink in for a quick bite at the twinkly oyster bar, if that's how you do things. In the summer, there are few things better than spending a few hours mining a lobster – alone or in good company – with a bottomless carafe of white Burgundy.

SOHO
SPUNTINO

61 Rupert Street – London, W1D 7PW
Tel. : +44-20-7734-4479 – **www.spuntino.co.uk**

When the queue subsides and you bag your seat at the shining zinc counter of this diner-cum-dive bar in the heart of Soho's porn district, one of the tattooed staff will plant down a perfectly battered enamel cup of freshly popped popcorn. Then it's a case of choosing your poison. Try the 'Cynar Gin Fizz' – a lively, quenching blend of gin, lemon juice, Prosecco and Cynar – before you settle into the menu. Small plates are a signature of restaurateur Russell Norman and the food is Italian with a strong New York accent. Pimped-up junk food like the rich, runny truffled egg toast, beef and marrow sliders and stuffed fried olives are crave-inducing, but it would be a shame not to try some of head chef Rachel O Sullivan's more demure dishes, like quail with romesco or the puntarelle, fennel and anchovy salad.

BETHNAL GREEN
VIAJANTE & THE CORNER ROOM

Town Hall Hotel, Patriot Square – London, E2 9NF
Tel. : +44 20 7871 0461 – **www.viajante.co.uk**

'Viajante means traveller, and I wanted it to be reflective of my experiences and of my story. It's about tastes, textures and flavours from all over the world, which will evoke memories of your own childhood or places you've been. There's a lot of creativity and starving artists around here in Bethnal Green, and we're very much reflective of that. Viajante does this through the relaxed service, the creative thinking in the kitchen and the wine offer; it's informal, fun, eclectic and modern. But having a restaurant where the entry-level menu is £70, I know a lot of my friends won't be able to come very often, so we offer a similar cuisine at a more affordable price at The Corner Room. It's rooted in the same philosophy.' *Nuno Mendes*

HACKNEY
VIOLET

47 Wilton Way – London, E8 3ED
Tel. : +44-20-7275-8360 – **www.violetcakes.com**

'It's the artisanal – it's about making something by hand in the best possible way, with the best possible ingredients, because it tastes better, and because it's just nice. It's nice to have this connection with people along the way – to build relationships with the people that give you your organic eggs or your milk. When I first opened the bakery, people wouldn't deliver all the way out to where I am on Wilton Way in Hackney, but now there are so many different businesses it makes sense for suppliers to do so, which is great for everyone. The name comes from my childhood obsession with these delicious-smelling flowers. The violet is a flower you can't cultivate: if you try, it loses its scent, and that speaks to the whole thing too.' *Claire Ptak*

CAMDEN
YORK & ALBANY

127–129 Parkway – London, NW1 7PS
Tel. : +44-20-7388-3344
www.gordonramsay.com/yorkandalbany

We all know Gordon Ramsay isn't one to do things by halves, and this ambitious venture in Regent's Park shows us why his restaurant portfolio is still holding steady on the fickle London scene. At once a bar, gastronomic restaurant, boutique hotel, gourmet deli and wood-fired-pizza takeaway counter, this elegant Georgian townhouse is a cordial place to find yourself if you're in need of any kind of refreshment. In the restaurant, long-time Ramsay protégé and head chef Kim Woodward has created a harmonious menu of seasonal, proudly British dishes; you'll find lamb sweetbreads flirting with bedfellows mint and broad bean in the summer, or whole, roasted plaice cosying up to white asparagus, monk's beard and a melting pat of shallot and herb butter.

BARRAFINA
54 Frith Street – London, W1D 4SL
Tel. : 0207 813 8010 – www.barrafina.co.uk

At midday on the dot, a queue starts forming outside this small but serious no-reservations Soho tapas joint, as Londoners clamour for one of the 23 coveted stools around the kitchen-facing counter. Once you're in, you can order a chilled glass of aged, single vineyard Pastrana Manzanilla and breathe a sigh of relief, because you're in for one of the best meals London offers. Watch as the chefs pluck wanton-looking scallops from their shells to sear on the plancha, or dress tender, meaty octopus with capers, olive oil and chives. But when your plates arrive, close your eyes for a second, let the Jamón Señorio de Montanera melt on your tongue, and savour every clean, brilliantly composed mouthful.

BOCCA DI LUPO

12 Archer Street – London, W1D 7BB
Tel. : +44 20 7734 2223 – boccadilupo.com

The seasonal menu of Jacob Kenedy's sleek small-plates features ever-changing versions of raw and cured alongside fried and grilled ingredients, plus home-made breads, pastas and sausages. A fennel salad is piqued by deep, savoury mullet bottarga, fried sage leaves are stuffed with melting anchovy and the classic Tuscan salad panzanella is served with crispy grilled quail, while tagliatelle comes simply dressed with butter, girolles and parmesan. Over the road, sister-venture Gelupo serves up some of the city's best gelato and sorbet, all made by Italian chefs on the premises. Try the fresh mint and chocolate chip or the intense, refreshing blood-orange sorbet.

BRIXTON
BRIXTON VILLAGE & MARKET ROW
Atlantic Road – London, SW9 8PS
www.brixtonmarket.net

These two historic covered markets in Brixton were almost knocked down for development a few years ago, but thankfully the space was opened up to small businesses at cheap rents, and a whole host of small, idiosyncratic food start-ups launched. What's brilliant is that all this operates alongside the wet fishmongers, butchers and grocery shops, and cool kids rub along with locals buying their weekly shop. You can eat your way around the world here – slurping Beijing noodles from Mama Lan, scoffing Neapolitan pizza from Franco Manca or eating cross-Caribbean fare from Fish, Wings & Tings – but don't neglect to investigate some of the resident traders too: Nour Cash & Carry is an Aladdin's cave of diverse ingredients, and Market Row Wines sells some fabulous bottles from small growers.

MARYLEBONE
DININGS
22 Harcourt Street – London, W1H 4HH
Tel. : +44 20 7723 0666 – www.dinings.co.uk

Getting a seat at this tiny townhouse Japanese in Marylebone can be tricky, and – at just 28 covers – it needs to turn tables, but once you taste the flavours coming out of the former Nobu chef Masaki Sugisaki's kitchen, you'll understand why Londoners are clamouring to get in. The food is Japanese tapas: small sharing dishes that combine Japanese and modern European cuisine to exceptional effect. Tiny bites of home-made potato crisps, topped with silky Scottish salmon and chilli miso or fatty toro tuna and wasabi mayo, are just a hint of what's to come on the extensive menu. Don't miss the sparkling sea bass ceviche with fresh truffle and ponzu jelly, and watch out for seasonal specials, like the tempura asparagus with miso.

SHOREDITCH
DISHOOM

7 Boundary Street – London, E2 7JE
Tel. : +44-20-7420-9324 – **www.dishoom.com/SHOREDITCH**

The eccentric, eclectic spirit of Mumbai's crumbling Irani eateries is alive and well in this corner of Shoreditch, thanks to Kavi and Shamil Thakrar, the cousins who brought their take on the Indian city's Zoroastrian cafes to London. While its spectacular interior is a visual love letter to the fading art deco grandeur of the originals, chef Naved Nasir's menus celebrate the broader cuisine of Mumbai – from its irresistible street snacks and the famous dishes of Chowpatty Beach to the Parsi specialities of the cafes. Vada pau, a souped-up version of the ubiquitous Mumbai chip butty, is a must-try: spiced, deep-fried potato patties topped with crispy batter and green chutney inside a soft white bread roll.

SOHO
FERNANDEZ & WELLS

43 Lexington Street – London, W1F 9AL
Tel. : +44-20-7287-1546 – **www.fernandezandwells. com**

There are few places you can absorb the hungry, lively buzz of lunchtime Soho more acutely than in Fernandez & Wells' original food and wine bar on Lexington Street. Here, amidst the hanging hams, the rather lovely oak counter becomes a mound of ciabatta-based sandwiches, filled with well-combined, carefully sourced ingredients that tell of this small cafe group's farmers'-market ethos. Favourites include the grilled chorizo with roasted red pepper, rocket and olive oil or the made-to-order 36-month-cured jamón Ibérico de bellota with tomato. Finish off your lunch with a Portuguese custard tart and single-estate-bean espresso from its Beak Street cafe just around the corner.

BERMONDSEY
GARRISON (THE)

99–101 Bermondsey Street – London, SE1 3XB
Tel. : +44-20-7089-9355 – **www.thegarrison.co.uk**

Bermondsey's transformation from industrial backwater to uber-cool gourmet heartland (see also Maltby Street Market, Zucca and José) has developed along with this much-loved pub/restaurant, which opened in 2003. The venue's exposed brick and whitewashed wood-clad walls give an airy ambience, while its vintage treasures and curiosities – including a taxidermied antelope – lend a wry eccentricity. Food is modern British, so you can expect plates of pork-cheek fritters with butternut squash purée and salsa verde for lunch, or pan-roasted sea bass with red chicory, runner beans and red-wine sauce for dinner. Brunches have always been a strength here – you can break fast with a generous plate of smoked haddock kedgeree and an organic, fair-trade, London-roasted coffee.

STOKE NEWINGTON
HANSEN & LYDERSEN

3–5 Shelford Place – London, N16 9HS
www.hansen-lydersen.com

This smokehouse in Stoke Newington has a backstory that takes in four generations of Norwegian craft. Ole Hansen uses the old brick chimney of a former printing works as a kiln, following a smoking method developed by his great-grandfather, Lyder-Nilsen Lydersen – a fishmonger and salmon fisherman, whose smoked salmon was famous in and around the Varanger fjord. Sourced directly from the northern Norwegian Arctic, the salmon is traditionally hand-filleted, hand-salted, hung and cold smoked in the kiln for a minimum of 10 hours using a delicate blend of juniper and beechwood. The result is an intense, memorable artisan product that's won countless plaudits, and is supplied to some top London restaurants including NOPI and Sake No Hana.

JOSÉ

104 Bermondsey Street – London, SE1 3UB
www.josepizarro.com/restaurants/jose

'When I first came up with José – a proper tapas bar inspired by the Boqueria in Barcelona – I never imagined it would be such a success. I was thinking 25 for lunch, 40 for dinner. We do 1,400 a week, and we only have 17 stools,' says José Pizarro, the Spanish chef who's been elevating Spanish cuisine in the capital through his cooking for over a decade. His two eponymous restaurants José and Pizarro in Bermondsey have been full since opening, wooing diners with the wonders of unusual Ibérico pork cuts, battered fried lamb's brains and – much to his delight – sherry. 'My customers are young people – it's not the granny drink anymore. People say that they come to my restaurants and feel like they are in Spain, and that's the nicest thing anyone can say to me.'

KOYA

49 Frith Street – London, W1D 4SG
Tel. : +44 20 7434 4463 – www.koya.co.uk

This cosy Soho spot looks unassuming, but with Japanese-born Junya Yamasaki behind the stove, it's turning out some of London's most compelling, fare. This place is revered for its foot-rolled Sanuki udon noodles and traditional hot and cold udon dishes, and also for Yamasaki's creative specials, which apply a minimal Japanese approach to seasonal and local British produce. These are where the chef's fine art background – he studied for an MA in Paris before launching into cooking – shines through. Depending on the season, you could find a venison miso and ramson udon, or grilled, nuka-fermented sardines with pickled rhubarb; and the cold udon with hot dashi, pork and miso is a year-round winner.

KERB

Kings Boulevard – London, N1C 4AH
www.kerbfood.com

'KERB King's Cross is the ultimate lunchtime street-food hub in London. It's in this incongruous place – like a little oasis, existing behind the crazy transport nucleus that is Kings Cross and St Pancras on a pedestrianised, tree-lined boulevard. There's a great community of traders that vary daily, and each one is chosen because they have something amazing to offer the city. People find out about what's happening through Twitter or the website, and it's a real smorgasbord. There's everything from Japanese gyoza to Nashville buttermilk-fried chicken tacos; ox-heart burgers; or amazing handmade ice cream with salted caramel doughnuts.'

Petra Barran

L'ANIMA

1 Snowden Street, Broadgate West
London, EC2A 2DQ
Tel. : +44-20-7422-7000 – www.lanima.co.uk

'The idea for L'Anima was to put Southern Italian cooking on the map. When we first opened in May 2008, people said "Why do we need another Italian in London?", but I believed in the cooking of the South. The food of Calabria is spicy, and people didn't associate spicy with Italian cooking, so in that sense L'Anima brought the City a new wave of smells and tastes from Italy. We showed off our spices and our Moorish influence, and used ingredients like couscous and 'nduja', which is everywhere now. I grew up with this kind of food and, after working in very high-end restaurants all over the world, I decided to go back to making the food I want to eat.'

Francesco Mazzei

FITZROVIA

LIMA

31 Rathbone Place – London, W1T 1JH
Tel. : +44 203 002 2640 – **www.limalondon.com**

The magic of Peruvian gastronomy – with all its globally influenced twists and turns of flavour and texture – has reached London's food scene, thanks to lauded chef Virgilio Martinez. His restaurant Central, in Lima, now features on the 'World's 50 Best list', and this London cousin in Fitzrovia is turning out some of the capital's most vital and relevant food. Sit in the jewel box of a dining room and have your palate perked by unusual ingredients that speak of Peru's incredible biodiversity, artfully combined with prime indigenous British produce through the prism of Martinez's clean, contemporary cooking style. Try the signature ceviche of sea bream with tangy Tiger's milk (the citrussy marinade that cures the seafood), ají limo pepper, red onion and cancha corn.

STOKE NEWINGTON

MANGAL II

4 Stoke Newington Road – London, N16 8BH
Tel. : +44-20-7254-7888 – **www.mangal2.com**

The charcoal grill has latterly become the must-have toy for London's more modish kitchens, but long before the 'Josper' or the 'Big Green Egg' hit high-end chefs' wish lists, this Turkish Ocakbasi (fire pit) restaurant in Dalston was rocking the hot coals. Ali Dirik was a chef in Istanbul before he came to London in the 1980s, and this place has garnered a reputation as the best Turkish in the capital. Meze dishes like silky, savoury stuffed aubergines are a delight, and the onions cooked with pomegranate juice, spices and parsley wouldn't look out of place on one of the capital's trendier gourmet menus. But it's the smoke-spilling grills that will captivate your eyes, nostrils and palate when you visit.

BERMONDSEY

MALTBY STREET MARKET

Maltby Street – London, SE1 3PA

What started as an unofficial, esoteric offshoot of Borough Market has grown into a fully fledged food oasis – you'll now find coffee roasters, craft brewers, artisan bakers and biodynamic-vegetable purveyors. This is the place to come for pastrami-packed reuben sandwiches at Monty's Deli, specialist imported Greek oils from Maltby & Greek, and small-grower natural wines and seasonal plates at 40 Maltby Street. Sip a smooth, site-roasted Monmouth Coffee, or a flavourful IPA from The Kernal Brewery, as you hunt down the perfect courgette flower from Tayshaw greengrocer. And make sure you carry a napkin – you'll need it to wipe the custard off your chin after one of the St. John Bakery's renowned doughnuts.

NOTTING HILL

MAZI

12–14 Hillgate Street – London, W8 7SR
Tel. : +44-20-7229-3794 – **www.mazi.co.uk**

A thoroughly modern Greek restaurant is not an easy thing to find in London, but the young, bright brains behind Mazi in Notting Hill have managed to create just that. Mazi's version of taramasalata is a captivatingly light mousse of fish roe, mixed with delicious imported olive oil and breadcrumbs, topped with intense strands of lemon confit. Spanakopita is deconstructed to a savoury millefeuille, with spinach and feta melding against crisp wafers of filo pastry; and lamb comes as saddle and cutlet with a perky, crispy tzatziki spring roll. Like much of the produce, the wine list is proudly 100 per cent Greek.

MILDREDS

45 Lexington Street – London, W1F 9AN
Tel. : +44-20-7494-1634 – www.mildreds.co.uk

When best friends Diane Thomas and Jane Muir moved to London from Bristol to open Soho's only vegetarian restaurant in 1988, the word on the street was that it wouldn't last six months. But their 'hip' rather than 'hippy' approach to meat-free food struck a chord with the capital, and, though Thomas has sadly passed away, her legacy lives on at this buzzy restaurant. The daily-changing burger is a must-order; based on what comes in fresh each day (this could mean carrots and courgettes one day or beetroot and black beans the next). It is seasoned with different herbs and spices, served on an organic sourdough bun and topped with rocket and home-made basil mayo.

MIN JIANG

Royal Garden Hotel, 2–24 Kensington High
Street – London, W8 4PT
Tel. : +44-20-7361-1988 – www.minjiang.co.uk

The tenth-floor views, dainty dim sum and sexy, sleek vibe of this upscale Chinese spot are all very well, but make no mistake: you come here for the now-famous Beijing duck. Served in two preparations, it comes first as crispy duck skin served with granulated sugar for dipping. This is accompanied by the shredded meat with a succession of home-made pancakes, coming with sweet plum sauce with shredded leek and cucumber, then with garlic paste with pickled radish and tangy Tientsin cabbage. Next, you choose one of four different preparations of the remaining duck – fried noodles with sliced duck or spicy minced duck with lettuce wrap are highly recommended, but you should see for yourself ...

MORO

34–36 Exmouth Market – London, EC1R 4QE
Tel. : 020 7833 8336 – www.moro.co.uk

The previously overlooked offerings of the southern Mediterranean and its Moorish cuisine were given the dining platform they deserved when chef spouses Sam and Sam Clark unveiled their restaurant in Exmouth Market back in the late nineties. It's since gone on to become one of London's most influential and important dining rooms, loved for its laid-back, buzzy ambience, heartfelt open kitchen and flavour-packed plates. It has spawned various cookbooks, a little sister tapas bar and deli Morito next door and has trained up chefs like Bocca di Lupo's Jacob Kenedy. The menu changes weekly, but you could find wood-roasted chicken with slow-cooked flat beans, dukkah and seasoned yoghurt, or charcoal-grilled lamb with mechouia and harissa.

OPERA TAVERN

23 Catherine Street – London, WC2B 5JS
Tel. : +44-20-7836-3680 – www.operatavern.co.uk

While the pig-trotter beer taps and plates of five-year-aged jamón Ibérico de bellota give the game away, it's not just the cured stuff that's worth sniffing out in this tapas restaurant. After chef director Ben Tish spent time in Spain observing the way swine is prepared there, he introduced London to such previously little-known cuts as 'secreto', the tender bit from the back of the belly, and 'presa', a shoulder cut with a sublime meat-to-fat ratio. Vegetables and fish are by no means also-rans though, and the courgette flowers stuffed with fluffy goat's cheese and drizzled with honey are a must-order.

ISLINGTON
OTTOLENGHI

287 Upper Street – London, N1 2TZ
Tel. : **+44-20-7288-1454 – www.ottolenghi.co.uk/
locations/islington/**

Few can claim to have shaped London's palate in the way that Yotam Ottolenghi has. Before the Israeli-born chef brought his brand of vegetable-led, Middle Eastern-meets-Mediterranean-meets-Asian cuisine to the capital, words like 'tahini', 'za'atar' and 'harissa' were not a regular part of the culinary vernacular. Queue for one of the best takeaways you can get in the capital, or go and sit at one of the bright white tables and feast on rainbows of flavour: a perky slaw of rhubarb, cabbage, celery, apple and radicchio with cranberries and hazelnuts, or roasted cauliflower with cardamom yoghurt and pickled red onion.

WESTMINSTER
QUILON

41 Buckingham Gate – London, SW1E 6AF
Tel. : **+44-20-7821-1899 – www.quilon.co.uk**

'When we opened in 1999, we wanted to represent food from the south-west coast of India – the cuisine of Kerala, Goa, Bangalore – as this coastal food was very different from what was generally seen as Indian food in this country,' says Sriram Aylur, the chef behind Westminster's Quilon: the only south-coast Indian restaurant to hold a Michelin star. Inside the stylish dining room diners taste a mixture of dishes that meld southern coastal flavours and spicing with non-traditional ingredients, to stunning effect. Aylur enhances prime proteins like black cod, which is subtly spiced and baked, and venison fillet, which is tossed with onion, tomato, ginger and spices and cooked alongside coconut slivers.

SHOREDITCH
STORY DELI
123 Bethnal Green Road – London, E2 7DG
Tel. : **+44-79-1819-7352 – www.storydeli.com**

Another exponent of Shoreditch's increasingly grown-up food scene, this pizza 'hut' on the Bethnal Green Road likes its walls whitewashed and its produce 100% certified organic. Inside, it's bright, light and breezy, with long communal wooden tables and restored crates to perch on, and the wood-fired pizzas come thin, crispy and topped with a fresh-from-the-farm selection of happily married toppings. At £17 a pop, this is some of the capital's dearest dressed-up dough, but it's also some of its best. Try the 'Fico': a confluence of goat's cheese, fig and olive tapenade, fresh red onion, capers and thyme along with parma ham on a heap of fresh salad leaves.

WHITECHAPEL
TAYYABS
83–89 Fieldgate Street – London, E1 1JU
Tel. : **+44-20-7247-9543 / +44-20-7247-6400 /
+44-20-7247-8521 – www.tayyabs.co.uk**

You don't go to Tayyabs, a Pakistani cheap eat in deepest Whitechapel, for its charming service or chic decor. You go there for the tandoor – and the marinated grills and freshly baked naans the chefs fire out with it. Go in groups to try everything on the menu; book in advance to avoid queueing for hours; and try to sit upstairs, as you practically need a torch to read the menu downstairs. The lamb chops are the star here: they come sizzling, covered in a punchy marinade that will have you sucking the bones. You may not have room for dessert, but you should forget your fullness for a minute and order one of the cool, creamy house-made kulfi – pistachio and mango are the best.

UMU

14–16 Bruton Place – London, W1J 6LX

Tel. : +44-20-7499-8881 – **www.umurestaurant.com**

When Yoshinori Ishii joined the upscale Japanese kaiseki restaurant in 2010 as head chef, he began a progressive overhaul that would result in today's daily-changing, market-led menu of freshly supplied, seasonal bristish fish. Impressed by the UK's wealth of fresh fish and seafood, he travelled to the coast to teach fisherman the traditional Japanese 'ikejime' preservation technique, to ensure the quality of the fish. The result is a menu that melds exquisite Japanese technique with sparklingly fresh native produce. Guests can enjoy wild Welsh eel, which is steamed and then chargrilled and smoked, and Cornish mackerel, which features in the beautiful chef's sashimi selection, along with translucent slivers of turbot and tiny purple shiso flowers.

UYEN LUU'S SUPPER CLUB

London, E8 3PA

www.leluu.com/p/menus.html

Saigon-born, long-time Hackney resident Uyen Luu is a creative power house, counting writing, fashion, film-making and cooking among her many talents. Since 2009 she's been running her supper club from her flat – transforming its intimate, softly lit ground floor into London's coolest, most contemporary Vietnamese restaurant every Friday night. After a day of cooking and prep, she dons kitten heels, turns on her ample charm and plays hostess, furnishing mesmerised guests with perfectly crisp pork belly and angel's hair vermicelli while, upstairs, her mother turns out bowls of steaming, fragrant pho or big platters of tongue-tinglingly hot shredded chicken salad with daikon and banana blossom, ready to be scooped into prawn crackers and savoured.

YAUATCHA

15–17 Broadwick Street – London, W1F 0DL

Tel. : +44-20-7494-8888 – **www.yauatcha.com/soho**

Since it opened in 2004, people have flocked to this modern Chinese restaurant-cum-teahouse in the depths of Soho for many things: the rare blue tea selection, imported from Taiwan and Fujian; the best lychee martini you'll ever taste; and the perfect patisserie. In the most part, however, they come for the dim sum. The heritage dish of Shanghai siew long bun – a soup-filled dumpling usually made with pork broth – is updated with the addition of fragrant king crab, and the roasted duck and pumpkin pastry puff with pine nuts is fashioned into a beautiful miniature pumpkin. The char sui pork buns are the daintiest you'll find anywhere, and the soft prawn and bean curd cheung fun rice noodle's crisp layer of bean curd adds structure before you reach the sweet prawn filling.

ZUCCA

184 Bermondsey Street – London, SE1 3TQ

Tel. : +44-20-7378-6809 – **www.zuccalondon.com**

'The food of Italy always struck a chord with me so much more than any other cuisine, and I wanted to create a modern Italian in London,' says Sam Harris, chef patron of this stylish, affordable restaurant. None of us grew up in Italy – it's our own interpretation of Italian food.' As such, Harris and his team make about 6–8 kg pasta every day and five or six or 6 types of breads twice a day, creating daily-changing menus. You might find curling octopus tentacles that have been carefully braised for five hours before being grilled and served on a silky sweet stew of aubergine, pepper and olive oil, then seasoned with mint oil and capers; or yellow polenta slick with basajo cheese and spinach.

BRITISH 31 TERROIR

SOUTHWARK
ANCHOR & HOPE (THE)

36 The Cut – London, SE1 8LP
Tel. : +44-20 7928 9898

The gutsy, unapologetic British bistro cooking at this no-reservations gastropub in Waterloo has rooted it firmly in London food legend. Spawned from the alumnus of St. John and celebrated kitchen-pub The Eagle, and itself spawning Great Queen Street in the West End, this place has been turning out affordable, seasonal plates of well-combined, simply cooked ingredients for over a decade. Attention is paid to unusual cuts – you might find a slow-braised lamb neck with dauphinois potatoes, or braised pigs cheeks alongside fennel, chorizo and mashed potato; and, while there are European inflections, dishes like potted shrimp and snail and bacon salad sing the British national anthem as you gobble them up.

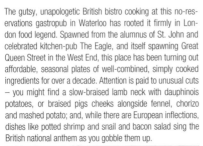

BETHNAL GREEN
BRAWN

49 Columbia Road – London, E2 7RG
Tel. : 0207 729 5692 – **www.brawn.co**

Provenance is the thing at this stripped-back restaurant on Columbia Road, the second venture from Oli Barker and chef Ed Wilson – the guys behind celebrated food and wine bar Terroirs in Covent Garden. Interesting, 'natural' wines, made by small producers fond of biodynamic methods and organic viniculture, draw the capital's hippest oenophiles, while its sharing plates of carefully sourced produce, cooked with Wilson's instinctive, no-nonsense approach, bait the greedy. His Scotch eggs are made with ultra-addictive with 'nduja, the spicy, soft Calabrian sausage, while boudin noir has actual chunks of yielding pork running through it, and comes from the award-winning French producer Christian Parra.

HACKNEY
BROADWAY MARKET

Broadway Market – London, E8 4PH
www.broadwaymarket.co.uk

Jellied eels were first sold at this Victorian East End market in 1900, but these days its offering is a little more exotic. Alongside sharply dressed Hackney locals shopping for their fruit and veg, food obsessives swarm every Saturday for street food like the perky Vietnamese pork baguettes from Banh Mi 11, or chocolate wafer sandwich cookies from the Chez Panisse-trained baker Claire Ptak at Violet Cakes bakery stall. Permanent sites and boutique restaurants along this stretch also buzz with folk stocking up on fresh fish at sustainable fishmonger Fin & Flounder (whose seafood shack in nearby Netil Market is well worth a look), grabbing some single-origin coffee from Climpson & Sons or kicking back with some charcuterie at L'eau à la Bouche deli.

STOCKWELL
CANTON ARMS

177 South Lambeth Road – London, SW8 1XP
Tel. : +44-20-7582-8710 – **www.cantonarms.com**

Australian-born chef-patron Trish Hilferty lived in the Stockwell area for 20 years before she took over this south London boozer in 2010 and began turning her generous, French-inflected, modern British plates out of its kitchen. 'But, far from gutting, refitting and gentrifying the pub and its dining room, Hilferty and her team have retained its original character, as well as many of its regulars – even if they now find themselves and their pints sharing the bar with government workers or younger locals sipping natural wine. Hilferty is proud of her suppliers and likes to push rare-breed meats on the daily-changing menu, with 7-hour-braised salt-marsh lamb shoulder rarely leaving her repertoire. 'It's food I like to eat – I like great big cuts – and, of course, it has to be very, very seasonal.'

CHELSEA
CHELSEA FISHMONGER (THE)
10 Cale Street – London, SW3 3QU
Tel. : +44-20-7589-9432
www.thechelseafishmonger.co.uk

It's hard to believe that this thriving, white-tiled wet fishmonger in the heart of Chelsea started as a tiny stall in Surrey, but that's how Rex Goldsmith – the fish fanatic behind this place – originally set up shop. After building up a reputation supplying local restaurants with his immaculately fresh, well-sourced sea swag, business boomed, and in 2004 he took over the legendary Chelsea Fishery on Cale Street. The shop itself has 100 years of fish-trade heritage, but Goldsmith carried out a complete refit and now runs it with care for sourcing seasonal and sustainable fish and shellfish – all of which is still hand-picked from the markets in Newlyn, in Cornwall, and Billingsgate.

NOTTING HILL
COW (THE)
89 Westbourne Park Road – London, W2 5QH
Tel. : 020 7221 0021 – **www.thecowlondon.co.uk**

Tom Conran's Notting Hill Irish pub serves up big, indulgent platters of British seafood and some of the best Guinness in town. 'Eat heartily and give the house a good name' is the gastropub's mantra, and that's easy to do, either downstairs at the bar – picking your way through a whole cracked crab, whelks, winkles and Irish rock oysters with a glass of black velvet (Guinness and champagne) – or upstairs in the quirky dining room. Head chef Martin Hurrell's seasonal British menu makes for generous portions, which might include devilled lamb's kidneys on toast or smoked eel with mash, bacon and horseradish.

SHOREDITCH
CLOVE CLUB (THE)
Shoreditch Town Hall, 380 Old Street
London, EC1V 9LT
Tel. : +44 20 7729 6496 – **www.thecloveclub.com**

Here, hip young things mingle with the dining cognoscenti for plates of chef Isaac McHale's proudly home-made rare-breed British charcuterie and cocktails in the bar, or in the stark dining room for full-blown tasting menus flaunting pristine British produce rendered through McHale's creative cooking style. His food often features unusual ingredients or parts of ingredients, like garlic scapes (the tops of the garlic plant), which come with the roasted Lincolnshire chicken and English peas. He's also one for doing progressive riffs on classic dishes – so a trout meunière might be updated using Irish pollan with green tomatoes, brown butter, elderflower vinegar sauce and dill.

HACKNEY
E5 BAKEHOUSE
Arch 395, Mentmore Terrace – London, E8 3PH
Tel. : +44-20-8525-2890 – **www.e5bakehouse.com**

Looking for a change of direction from his career in renewable energy, Ben Mackinnon enrolled in a five-day course in the essentials of sourdough at The School of Artisan Food and Wine and came back a convert to the lure of natural, slow-fermentation bakery. Setting up as a nomadic baker, using a neighbourhood oven to bake his loaves, he honed his craft, eventually building his own wood-burning oven out of reclaimed materials in a derelict railway arch in Hackney; and so the E5 Bakehouse was born. Food often takes in global influences, in plates like aubergine and coconut curry with Rajasthani mango pickle. There are also two in-house pastry chefs, so sweet treats, like chocolate and salted caramel tart, are as tempting as the savoury slow foods.

EAGLE (THE)

159 Farringdon Road – London, EC1R 3AL
Tel. : +44-20-7837-1353

This place is largely considered to be London's first proper gastropub. It opened in 1991 in Clerkenwell at a time when the area was not known as the thriving drinking and dining neighbourhood it is now. Inside the charmingly sparse, bedraggled bistro interior, blackboards are chalked with the rotational menu. You could find a lunch of whole mackerel from the charcoal grill served with spinach, or the trademark Portuguese steak sandwich, which is served in a white roll with its cook marinade with a red-wine reduction. Dinner is even heartier – so perhaps roasted lamb, stuffed with couscous, dates, coriander and spiced onion, or pasta with a thick, yielding beef ragú.

FIN & FLOUNDER

71 Broadway Market – London, E8 4PH
Tel. : +44-20-7998-4929 – www.finandflounder.com

At this wet fishmonger on Broadway Market, mounds of crushed ice shimmer with perfect specimens of local, seasonal fish from around the UK's coastline. Clams and squid vie for your attention next to whole crabs and glittering bass. The friendly staff are keen to share their knowledge and will talk you through how exactly to cook your cod's cheeks, while they fillet you a fresh mackerel or clean you some bream. Following the lead of the MSC (Marine Stewardship Council) in using sustainable approaches to provide its plentiful sea bounty, the shop has everything else you might need to conjure a fishy feast – from fresh herbs and spices to a wine selection chosen to compliment the seafood on offer.

ELLIOT'S

12 Stoney Street, Borough Market
London, SE1 9AD
Tel. : +44-20-7403-7436 – www.elliotscafe.com

This is the sort of restaurant you'd imagine might grow out of its surroundings in Borough Market: an organic dining microcosm which, like the market itself, relies on networks of trusted suppliers and exceptional produce to define it. Sourcing and seasonality are central here, underpinning every element of the menu, from the 40-day-aged Galloway rib-eye to the wild garlic on the garlic bread in spring, or the luscious floral honey that accompanies the goat curd on brioche – immediately transporting you to some pastoral summer meadow. If you go at lunchtime you'll also be privy to the cheese-burger, which is dreamy with melted Comte, beer braised onions and coarsely minced beef from the Ginger Pig. Exposed brickwork and simple wooden tables make for a low-key setting in which to enjoy harmonious plates like the mussels, clams, leeks and spicy 'nduja, or the Middle White pork with cabbage, pear and chervil salad. Like the culinary offering, wines are all natural, coming from small, organic or biodynamic vineyards, and the coffee is from the capital's renowned Square Mile Roasters.

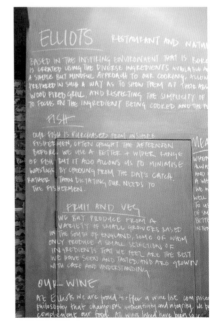

SOHO
FRENCH HOUSE (THE)
49 Dean Street – London, W1D 5BG
Tel. : +44-20-7437-2477 – www.frenchhousesoho.com

This legendary Dean Street drinking den opened in 1910 and has long been a favourite among Soho's bohemians, artists and food influencers – pouring its half pints (the only measure for beer here) for everyone from Lucian Freud to Dylan Thomas. A fine choice of champagnes and French wines keep the oenophiles coming back, and its tiny upstairs kitchen has a reputation for launching chefs: having been the place that first introduced London to the cooking talents of Fergus and Margot Henderson, and later Florence Knight. These days its two floors are all about the drinking and conversation, with a no-music, television or phone policy and simple plates of charcuterie, salad and soup until 4pm.

HACKNEY
GINGER PIG (THE)
8–10 Moxton Street – London, W1U 4EW
Tel. : +44-20-8986-6911 – www.thegingerpig.
co.uk

London's most respected rare-breed farmer-cum-butcher began trading its high-welfare meat products at Borough Market in the 1990s. It now has shops across London, as well as supplying some of the capital's top chefs. This East London butcher opened in 2008, and is a meat fiend's dream, stocking nose-to-tail cuts of lovingly grown, rare-breed animals – from grass-fed longhorn cattle to Tamworth and Old Spot pigs and blackface sheep. This shop doubles as a deli downstairs, so make sure you snaffle out one of its legendary sausage rolls while you stock up on pies, pâtés and preserves.

HAGGERSTON
HACKNEY CITY FARM
1A Goldsmiths Row – London, E2 8QA
Tel. : +44-20-7729-6381
hackneycityfarm.co.uk

Goats, pigs, forest gardens and beehives might not be the first thing you'd expect to find in inner-city Hackney, but this urban–pastoral dichotomy has been delighting visitors with its rural rituals for over 20 years. As well as being a fun day trip, with the chance to get up close and personal with some furry farmyard animals, the city farm offers a wide selection of courses, which cover everything you might need to know about self-sufficiency, from edible-mushroom cultivation to keeping chickens, building your own wood stove and growing vines for city wine-making. An award-winning cafe with agriturismo menus of ingredients sourced from Kent farms and salad leaves grown, and picked by Hackney's Growing Communities, keeps visitors well nourished.

NOTTING HILL
HEREFORD ROAD
3 Hereford Road – London, W2 4AB
Tel. : +44-20-7727-1144 – www.herefordroad.org

'It always seemed a shame to me that there were never many British restaurants here in London. The perversity was that young people learning to cook were learning French and Italian things. So my aim with Hereford Road was to have a neighbourhood restaurant that did accessible, reasonably affordable British food, using local, seasonal produce, and the whole of the animal. There was a challenge there, in that we needed to get away from the school-dinners, meat-and-two-veg associations, and we've had to be inventive. So rather than chunking up an oxtail, as is usual, I cook it whole, braising it in a rich stock with baby carrots for a long time.

SOHO
HIX SOHO
66–70 Brewer Street – London, W1F 9UP
Tel. : +44-20-7292-3518 – **www.hixsoho.co.uk**

'When I first walked into the building I had a vision of what it was going to be immediately,' says chef restaurateur Mark Hix of his eponymous Soho sensation. 'I could see that there would be a bar downstairs and a restaurant on the ground floor. I wanted a mix of fish and shellfish, with a heavy sense of meatiness, with cocktails that reflected the British menu.' The resulting daily-changing menu might include pan-fried Torbay cod with surf clams and water celery or Roast Pock Stones Estate grouse with bread sauce and elderberry jelly, while downstairs at the apothecary-style bar, oysters are sloshed alongside seasonal British cocktails like the Hix Fizz.

KENSINGTON
LAUNCESTON PLACE
1A Launceston Place – London, W8 5RL
Tel. : +44-20-7937-6912
www.launcestonplace-restaurant.co.uk

'I don't do surprises – the surprise should be the quality of what you eat,' says classically trained, Yorkshire-born head chef Tim Allen, who won Launceston Place its first Michelin star in 2012. At this sophisticated Kensington spot, prime British vegetables, meat and fish are treated with the utmost respect, being cooked with assured French technique and assembled into picture-perfect plates with simple, stunning elegance. The innovative vegetarian salad has become a hero dish, flaunting myriad vegetables at the peak of their freshness, each cooked sublimely and in a different way – perhaps you'll find pickled carrots or salt-baked root vegetables – combined with ice lettuce.

COVENT GARDEN
NEAL'S YARD DAIRY
17 Shorts Gardens – London, WC2H 9AT
Tel. : +44-20-7240-5700 – **www.nealsyarddairy.co.uk**

'When does tradition begin? It's a sort of nebulous term because every "tradition" has begun somewhere,' says Jason Hinds of Neal's Yard, the dairy and cheese monger that has been championing British cheesemaking for the past few decades through both its wholesaling and its shops in Covent Garden and Borough Market. As well as supplying well-known 'territorial' British cheeses like Colston Bassett Stilton – to which Alain Ducasse at the Dorchester has dedicated an entire trolley – it stocks unusual cheeses, made by what he calls a 'new wave' of British cheesemakers, like the raw, almost meaty, Cumbrian sheep's milk St James. 'There are people who are creating new and original cheese, and there's this pioneering spirit, which is exciting to be around.

FITZROVIA
NEWMAN STREET TAVERN
48 Newman Street – London, W1T 1QQ
Tel. : +44-20-3667-1445 – **www.newmanstreettavern.co.uk**

Chef Peter Weeden is so scrupulous about his suppliers and so passionate about British produce – wild and otherwise – that given half the chance he'll tell you how exactly how the dayboats he uses jig-lure the squid on his menu, or why their position on Cornwall's Helford River is so special. Weeden leads a kitchen with an emphasis on tradition, so the chefs are up with the lark to bake bread, and ageing, butchery and fishmongery are all done on site. Sit on the bustling ground floor of this former pub in Fitzrovia and slurp Colchester rock oysters and natives from the raw bar, or head upstairs to the dining room proper for the à la carte menu, which might feature Middle White pork, beer and onions, or hot cockles and clams with pickled ramson.

PIMLICO
PIMLICO ROAD FARMERS' MARKET
Orange Square – London, SW1W 8UT
www.lfm.org.uk/markets/pimlico-road

Perhaps the most Parisian of London's farmers' markets, this gentle confluence of British food producers gathers every Saturday in this most bourgeois part of town, just on the borders of Sloane Square, Belgravia and Pimlico. Set in the picturesque Orange Square, which is notable for its statue of Mozart (who composed his first symphony nearby in 1764), it's a prime place for lazy-weekend mooching and munching, and for stocking up on gourmet treasures. You'll find: fragrant honey and honeycomb from The London Honey Company; sensational seasonal oysters from Essex's Richard Haward; ripe, organic fruits from Chegworth Valley farm; and wonderfully sharp and nutty 'Lincolnshire Poacher'.

CAMDEN
PRUFROCK COFFEE
23–25 Leather Lane – London, EC1N 7TE
Tel. : +44 207 242 0467 – **www.prufrockcoffee.com**

Coffee geeks converge at this award-winning coffee bar on Clerkenwell's oh-so-hip Leather Lane for much more than a frothy cappuccino. One of the founders of a new wave of coffee houses with an emphasis on the science behind the perfect cup, the company's manifesto is to 'approach your coffee like a cook'. Highly trained baristas weigh out ingredients, regulate temperatures and use all the latest coffee kit, like Chemex, AeroPresses and syphons, alongside ground-breaking brew methods to create some of London's most delicious coffee. Prufrock also runs a coffee school, which trains professional baristas and enthusiasts in everything from making the perfect espresso to latte art.

HANOVER SQUARE
POLLEN STREET SOCIAL
10 Pollen Street – London, W1S 1NQ
Tel. : +44-20-7290-7600
www.pollenstreetsocial.com

'In 2011, when we launched, we were in the middle of a really bad recession and flexibility was the key idea. In the past, haute cuisine has been all about tasting menus and doing things a certain way, and I felt London was ready for a restaurant where you could still have the standard of cuisine you'd expect in a high-class restaurant but in a setting where you could do what you wanted. So if you wanted to have two starters and a glass of wine you could, or if you wanted three desserts and a pint of beer you could do that. It was always about celebrating British produce, and modern ways of thinking about food, but in a cool, young and happening environment, and not some stuffy old dining room.' *Jason Atherton*

CAMDEN
QUALITY CHOP HOUSE
92–94 Farringdon Road – London, EC1R 3EA
Tel. : 020 7278 1452 – **www.thequalitychophouse.com**

In the business of serving food since 1869, this place was originally designed as a social eating house for the masses to mingle over plates of bread and wine. Nowadays small, focused plates in the wine bar-cum-shop might include a perfect bouillabaisse of mussels and razor clams, or Middle White pork, sliced paper thin with marinated anchovies and luxuriantly dressed baby gem. In the dining room it's a set menu, which could begin with simple radishes or melting confit garlic with toasted sourdough and crescendo with Galloway beef with broad beans and Jersey Royal potatoes. Wines span small, interesting producers, like the sulphur-free Languedoc red from Jean-François Coutelou.

ROCK & SOLE PLAICE

47 Endell Street – London, WC2H 9AJ
Tel. : +44-20-7836-3785

The great British tradition of fish and chips is thriving in Covent Garden, and it has been since 1871, when a chip shop was first established on this site. The current owners took over in the 1980s and were taught the original frying methods by two old ladies – former employees who'd had the shop in their family for three generations and were keen to preserve its good reputation. And their legacy lives on: queues for takeaway form on a daily basis, but eat in the restaurant you get the benefit of warm service and cosy, casual decor. Choose between rock, sole, halibut, haddock, skate, cod and plaice, slather on the complimentary ketchup and tartar sauce and prepare for the simplest of pleasures.

RULES

35 Maiden Lane – London, WC2E 7LB
Tel. : +44-20-7836-5314 – www.rules.co.uk

In the heart of a thriving theatreland, London's oldest restaurant is still going strong. Owned by just three families throughout its 200-year history, Rules is about heritage and tradition taken with a generous helping of fun. A collision of antlers, fixed to the entrance as you walk in, tells of the restaurant's love affair with game, which it sources from its very own estate in the High Pennines. The walls hang with artwork indicative of its cultural significance – having long been a culinary 'green room' for literary, theatre and film figures – and the menus sing with traditional British dishes like steak and kidney suet pudding (with optional oysters). Make sure you make time for a pre- or post-prandial gimlet.

SHED (THE)

122 Palace Gardens Terrace – London, W8 4RT
Tel. : +44-20-7229-4024 – www.theshed-restaurant.com

As food-scene buzzwords go, it doesn't get much more 'family-run' or 'farm-to-plate' than this little restaurant in Notting Hill. But far from courting cliché, this place provides a raucous romp into country-style hospitality. Owner brothers the Gladwins have multiple talents they lend to this operation: Richard provides his restaurant management, Oliver, his modern British cooking, and Greg, his farming, which he does from Nutbourne, in the family home of West Sussex, while the other two are based on-site in London. Inside, a pastoral–dining mash-up – including a tractor-bonnet bar, wagon wheels and reclaimed-barrel tables – lend a merry, welcoming setting, while Richard's menus sing like a dawn chorus with British terroir flavours and ingredients. This could mean crab and samphire fritters with chive mayonnaise, followed by fennel-cured pollack with pickled cucumber, radish and lemon, or deep-fried slow-cooked lamb 'chips' with parsley, lemon and harissa. Wines are well selected and interesting, and even include the family's own Sussex Reserve, which is made on the banks of the river Arun.

DALSTON
WHITE RABBIT
15–16 Bradbury Street – London, N16 8JN
Tel. : +44-20-7522-7896 – **www.whiterabbitdalston.com**

Dalston's food scene is still in its embryonic stages, but leading the way is this sceneish side-street eatery, where young maverick chef Danny Rogers is tantalising taste buds from his tumbledown kitchen, complete with makeshift wood oven and indoor barbecue. On reclaimed crates flung with faux-fur throws, as tea lights twinkle and a modish playlist hums, stylish young things sip cocktails from jam jars and fawn over small plates of Rogers' flavour-packed, internationally-inflected food. This could mean an explosively creamy burrata flecked with fennel pollen and lemon rind and slooshed with grassy extra-virgin olive oil, or soft charred aubergine with jewels of pomegranate, ash and thick, sour yoghurt. Unusual cuts are a penchant of the chef, who keeps the menu affordable to his young, local crowd with dishes like lamb belly with miso baba ganoush, spring onion and radish, or pork neck with pickled peach, chicory and almonds. The drinks list is short, accessible and relevant, and features a very slurpable Picpoul de Pinet.

SOHO
WRIGHT BROTHERS
13 Kingly Street – London, W1B 5PW
Tel. : +44-20-7434-3611 – **thewrightbrothers.co.uk**

When it launched back in 2002 in Borough Market, this oyster wholesaler and now-restaurant group was supplying some of London's top restaurants with French oysters. Over the years though, it's become synonymous with championing and popularising home-grown British oysters from both its own farm on the Helford River in Cornwall and all over the UK, shifting 4 tonnes of the sought-after molluscs a week. A visit to its stylish Soho site reveals a spectacular journey into British tidal terroir, with, depending on the season, a selection of Cornish natives, Dorset rocks, Northumberland Lindisfarne oysters and fresh dayboat fish and shellfish from sustainable stocks.

41

LEGEND

Bakery

Brewery

Butcher

Cake and
Pastry Shop

Cheese
Shop

Coffee

Department
Store

Fishmonger

Flower
market

Hotel / Bar

Hotel /
Tea Room

Market

Restaurant

Restaurant /
Bar

Restaurant /
Catering

Restaurant /
Coffee

Restaurant /
Coffee /
Food Store

Restaurant /
Farm

Restaurant /
Private Bar

Street
Food

Wine
merchant

Workshop /
Smokehouse
(fish)

© Editions Alain Ducasse 2014 / © Hardie Grant Books 2014 / Legal Deposit 1st quarter 2014 /
Photos Pierre Monetta / Graphic Design Soins Graphiques